PREVENTION'S
Low-Fat, Low-Cost Cookbook

. . . .

Over 220 Delicious Recipes
Plus Twenty $2 Dinners!

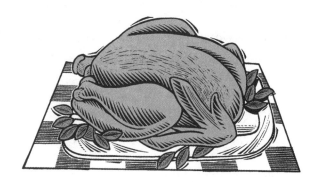

Edited by Sharon Sanders,
PREVENTION
Magazine Health Books

Rodale Press, Inc.
Emmaus, Pennsylvania

Front Cover: Pork Tenderloin with Mustard Marinade (page 21),
Scalloped Herbed Potatoes (page 22), and Southwestern Confetti
Corn (page 23).
Cover Photography: Tad Ware & Company, Inc.

Library of Congress Cataloging-in-Publication Data

Prevention's low-fat, low-cost cookbook : over 220 delicious recipes!
    / edited by Sharon Sanders.
        p.   cm.
    Includes index.
    ISBN 0–87596–396–X hardcover
    ISBN 0–87596–397–8 paperback
    1. Low-fat diet—Recipes. I. Sanders, Sharon. II. Prevention
Magazine Health Books.
    RM237.7.P7385   1997
    641.5′638—dc21   97-3674

Distributed in the book trade by St. Martin's Press

2 4 6 8 10 9 7 5 3 1 hardcover
2 4 6 8 10 9 7 5 3 1 paperback

OUR PURPOSE

*"We inspire and enable people to improve
their lives and the world around them."*
RODALE ✿ BOOKS

Prevention's Low-Fat, Low-Cost Cookbook
Editorial Staff

Editor: Sharon Sanders
Managing Editor: Jean Rogers
Writing and Recipe Development: Mary Carroll
Associate Art Director: Faith Hague
Book and Cover Designer: Tad Ware & Company, Inc.
Design Coordinator: Darlene Schneck
Book Layout: Tad Ware & Company, Inc.
Illustrator: Cindy Wrobel
Photographer: Tad Ware Photography
Food Stylist: Robin Krause
Nutritional Consultant: Linda Yoakam, M.S., R.D.
Manufacturing Coordinator: Melinda B. Rizzo

Rodale Health and Fitness Books

Vice-President and Editorial Director: Debora T. Yost
Design and Production Director: Michael Ward
Research Manager: Ann Gossy Yermish
Copy Manager: Lisa D. Andruscavage
Studio Manager: Stefano Carbini
Book Manufacturing Director: Helen Clogston

In all Rodale Press cookbooks, our mission is to provide delicious and nutritious low-fat recipes. Our recipes also meet the standards of the Rodale Test Kitchen for dependability, ease, practicality and, most of all, great taste. To give us your comments, call 1-800-848-4735.

Contents

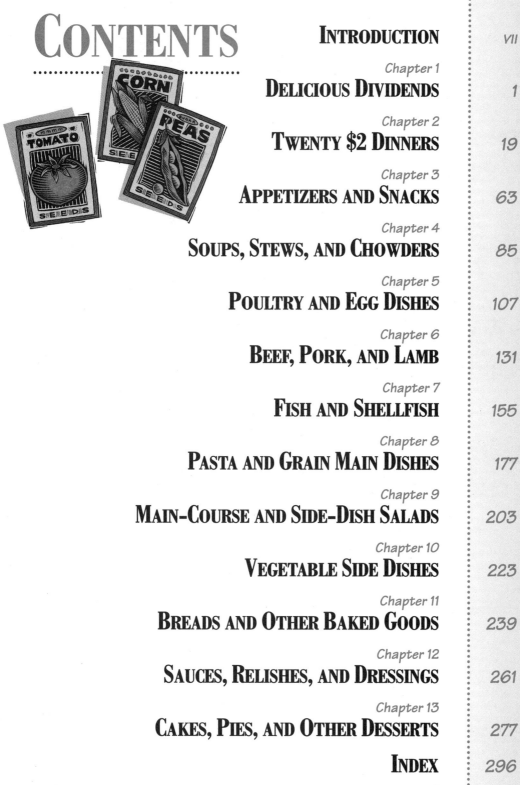

INTRODUCTION

A fresh spirit of self-reliance is blowing across America. Individuals are taking more control of their lives with gardens and do-it-yourself home-improvement projects. The I-can-do-it-better philosophy has even breezed into the kitchen.

No longer willing to pay inflated prices for highly processed convenience foods (that are all too frequently loaded with unhealthy saturated fat and sodium), millions of consumers are sending a message to food manufacturers: We're not going to buy it anymore.

What savvy shoppers are buying is the highest quality nutritious food at the lowest possible price. Consider some of the findings of a study by Mark Clements Research conducted for *Parade* magazine.

- 96% of all female respondents said that they buy less expensive private-label products
- 65% of Americans regularly or sometimes shop at warehouse clubs, and the majority of club customers are adults in upper-income brackets
- 57% of adults cite saturated fat as the nutritional element of most concern to them

You may have pondered how you can eat more healthfully without spending a fortune on specialty ingredients. Maybe you're confused or unsure about how to start. This book will show you how to plan, shop for, and cook satisfying, healthful meals that cost far less than you might imagine.

Our featured chapter of twenty $2 dinners will have you smiling all the way to the bank. And many of the recipes throughout the book cost just pennies per serving.

Each recipe includes the price per serving and the nutritional analysis—so you can monitor your monetary budget and your fat budget at a glance. And with dozens of special tips scattered throughout the book, you'll discover a treasure trove of economical, healthy cooking ideas.

With recipes as delicious as these, it's easy to be penny-wise and pound-wise.

Sharon Sanders

Sharon Sanders
***Prevention* Magazine Health Books**

CHAPTER 1

DELICIOUS DIVIDENDS

Sad to say, we've gotten used to plunking down $100 or more at the supermarket checkout each week. We don't need to read daily newspaper headlines to know that everything from beef to butter costs more than it did last month. As economists predict little reduction in what we pay in the checkout lane, we wonder how we can continue to afford flavorful, wholesome meals.

What's the secret our grandmothers knew? How can we merge their old-fashioned thrift and scratch cooking with our modern, fast-paced lives?

All it takes is a new look at your menu planning, shopping habits, and recipes. We'll help you rediscover time-honored ways to prepare applause-worthy meals at home—for family meals or entertaining—and bank the delicious, health-giving rewards.

You'll learn how to serve savings from the kitchen every day with dishes like Pork Chops with Herbed Apple Dressing, Mediterranean Baked Fish, Chicken Lasagna, and Italian Meatball Sandwiches. These delectable dishes won't pad your waistline or your arteries, but they'll surely fatten your bank account.

First, we'll show you how to just say no to high food prices by getting back to basics—avoiding highly processed foods and costly convenience items. Just this simple step can makes your meals healthier and drastically reduce your grocery bills. Experts say it's easy, if you (1) shop the sales, (2) plan your weekly menus around what's cheap and in season, and (3) stockpile staples you use regularly.

Next, we'll show you how to build your meals more simply and healthfully around a variety of nutritious grains, legumes, vegetables, and fruits—flavored by small amounts of lean meats, seafoods, unsaturated oils and low-fat cheeses. Your meals will naturally taste better and be low in cost and fat. Eating foods with minimal processing saves you money. You're paying only for the food itself, not added seasonings, preparation, or precooking.

The big bonus in this book is found in chapter 2. You'll find 20 classic menus you can mix and match, all for under $2 a serving, including side dishes. For less than the price of lunch at McDonald's or a cup of cappuccino, you can enjoy a meal like Asian Beef and Vegetable Stir-Fry, Rice with Scallions, and Pineapple Cabbage Slaw. Complete dinners like this can cost you upward of $4.95 per person even at a family restaurant, but we'll show you how to create them in your own kitchen and bank the savings.

With the recipes in this chapter, you can prepare literally dozens of money-saving, great-tasting dinners. And each menu includes nutritional data and the cost of each course in the meal, so you can plan meals, adjust for special health concerns, and budget—all at the same time.

Prices are based on the lowest seasonal, bulk, and sale prices in Minneapolis supermarkets, including homemade yogurt, stock, and other items on hand in the low-cost kitchen. Prices in your area may vary.

The more than 220 recipes in this book are designed for people who want great value, great nutrition, and great taste on their table every night. They will prove to you that you can eat better for less. This book gives you a real road map to become healthier and thriftier.

WHAT CONVENIENCE REALLY COSTS YOU

TOP LOW-FAT STAPLES TO MAKE AT HOME

	Made at home	Purchased
Apple juice (1 gallon)	79¢ (from frozen concentrate)	$2.96 (frozen juice pack)
Bean soup (1 quart)	89¢	$3.50 (from soup mix)
Bread crumbs (1 cup)	25¢	89¢
Carrot sticks (1 pound)	40¢	$3.18
Chicken stock (1 cup)	11¢	23¢
Chocolate syrup (4 ounces)	11¢	23¢
Garlic, minced (1 teaspoon)	1¢	15¢
Lettuce salad mix (1 pound)	69¢	$2.50
Low-fat salad dressing (1 pint)	$1	$2.39
Muffins (2 medium bran)	14¢	$1.90
Orange juice (1 gallon)	79¢ (from frozen concentrate)	$3.29 (fresh)
Spaghetti sauce (1 cup)	15¢	42¢
Yogurt (1 quart)	68¢	$3.20

The High Price of High Fat

Let's talk about the high price of high fat. High-fat eating not only drains your pocketbook but can also drain your most precious resource—your health. When you build your menus around high-fat meats, oils, and dairy products, you pay a hefty price in both arenas, according to thrift expert Amy Dacyczyn, author of *The Tightwad Gazette* books. *Dateline NBC* challenged Dacyczyn to cut a family's grocery bill by 40 percent. When the family cut back on processed foods, the children all lost weight. Dacyczyn knew it was because they were making foods from scratch and the added fat in their diet was visible for the first time in many years.

As you cut back on high-fat ingredients, such as premium meats and convenience foods, you automatically save money and dramatically reduce the fat in your diet, says Dacyczyn. And as the high fat goes down, so does your risk for the hidden costs of catastrophic illnesses, such as heart disease, diabetes, some cancers, and obesity, which are solidly linked to eating too high on the hog, cow, or sheep—foods that are high in saturated fat and processed with added fat.

But we're not talking bleak sacrifice here, adds Dacyczyn. You don't need to deprive yourself of flavor to eat healthier or low-cost if you follow the example of many of the world's cultures. An Indian curry that uses lamb as a flavor booster rather than the star attraction on the dinner plate costs you less than $1 a serving compared with $3 or more for a 4-ounce portion of beef tenderloin. Asian stir-fries typically cost less than 50 cents per serving and use only 6 to 8 ounces of fish or chicken to serve four. Smaller portions of lean protein, flanked with plenty of hearty grains, legumes, and vegetables, give you a meal that will also delight your family with a variety of flavors.

Certain high-quality foods give you more flavor than their cheaper counterparts, so many thrifty cooks include small amounts of real Parmesan cheese, olive oil, balsamic vinegar, and seasonal fresh herbs in their recipes. For example, freshly grated Parmesan is so flavorful that you can use a tablespoon (for about 25 cents) instead of the ¼ cup you'd need of pregrated bulk cheese. Intensely flavored olive oil and dark sesame oil add excitement to many dishes in this book. A tiny amount of stone-ground, honey, or Dijon mustard jazzes up sauces, marinades, and salad dressings and allows you to reduce the amount of oil.

You might not expect to find a convenience product like no-stick spray in the low-cost kitchen, but such a small amount is needed that it saves fat grams, money, and time over oiling baking pans.

Whole eggs, which the American Heart Association lauds as a good part of a healthy eating plan, are much less expensive than liquid egg substitute, even if you're using only the egg white in some recipes. Extra yolks can be cooked and used as pet food.

Nutritionists recommend planning each meal around the base of the USDA Food Guide Pyramid, where the ingredients are naturally economical and the nutritional payback is the highest. The Food Guide Pyramid illustrates current scientific views on nutritious eating and suggests how Americans can modify their meal planning to cut the risk of chronic disease.

The base of the pyramid holds foods lowest in fat and highest in fiber: whole grains, legumes, vegetables, and fruits. (Think fiber-rich oatmeal instead of fat-rich granola, ripe berries in season instead of sugary candy bars.) It only makes sense that these foods are also the building blocks of health that may help prevent chronic illnesses.

At the top of the pyramid are the least desirable choices. As we rethink the dinner plate to cut cost, we naturally avoid more expensive, fat-rich, or sugary foods at the top of the pyramid, like oils, other fats, and sweets. And we naturally build in five servings a day of the fruits and vegetables that are rich in vitamins and other nutrients.

Thrift and good nutrition go hand in hand. They both guard our well-being and quality of life for years to come.

10 BEST BULK BUYS FOR REAL SAVINGS

Our experts recommend these all-time winners in bulk buying for great savings.

* Cabbage
* Carrots
* Extra-lean ground beef
* Flour
* Onions
* Potatoes in 10-, 20-, or 50-pound bags
* Rice and other grains
* Sugar
* Sweet potatoes
* Whole chickens

Smart Shopping for Low-Cost Eating

If you are like most Americans, food accounts for a big chunk of your weekly budget. The average family of four spends at least $125 a week on groceries, according to thrift expert Jonni McCoy, author of *Miserly Moms: Living on One Income in a Two-Income Economy*. But by using smart planning and shopping techniques, and by rearranging her understanding of what makes a satisfying meal, McCoy was able to cut her family's weekly food spending to $40. Imagine banking over $300 a month in grocery savings alone, without a moment's deprivation!

Your first step toward this kind of real dividend in your food budget is to understand the psychology of supermarkets. Supermarkets are selling machines. Everything is designed to sell you more convenience, more variety, and often more of what you don't need. Food companies spend a lot of money in research and advertising to learn what will tempt you. So if you're thinking about breezing into your favorite store and walking out with substantial savings—without any advance planning—think again, says McCoy.

Marketing experts know that most people shop after work or on Saturday morning—when they're in a hurry, hungry, and tired. These are the worst times to shop because they're the best times for impulse buying. Everything in a supermarket is oriented toward impulse. Staples like potatoes, flour, and dried beans are placed far away from the entrance, so you have to pass plenty of cake mixes, TV dinners, and other high-profit items to get there. Even shelf position is designed to lure the unwary shopper, with more expensive brands at eye level where you'll see them first.

How do the experts strategize their shopping trips to avoid marketing traps? How do smart shoppers like McCoy and Dacyczyn regularly save $50 to $125 a week on their grocery bills—without selling themselves short on nutrition or taste?

Dacyczyn follows three basic rules: (1) take stock before you shop, (2) build a price book, and (3) shop only the sales.

Take Stock Before You Shop

Stocking up is a tried-and-true method of saving money. Dacyczyn slowly builds a supply of staples at home, so her weekly or monthly shopping trips focus on replenishing fresh produce, not essentials like meat, flour, or spices. "Look for staples on sale all year long

EQUIVALENTS CHART

If you buy fruits and vegetables in bulk, use this chart to determine how much you'll need in each recipe.

3 medium apples = 3 cups sliced apples
1 medium banana = ⅔ cup sliced bananas
1 pound beets = 2 cups sliced beets
1 pound broccoli = 4½ cups chopped broccoli
1 pound cabbage = 4 cups chopped cabbage
4 small carrots = 1½ cups shredded carrots
1 small head cauliflower = 4½ cups chopped cauliflower
1 stalk celery = ½ cup chopped celery
1 medium ear corn = ½ cup corn kernels
1 bunch scallions = ⅔ cup chopped scallions
1 medium lemon = 3 tablespoons lemon juice
1 small onion = ⅓ cup chopped onions
1 medium orange = ⅓ cup orange juice
1 medium sweet red pepper = ½ cup chopped sweet red peppers
2 medium red potatoes = 1½ cups diced potatoes
3 medium tomatoes = 2½ cups sliced tomatoes
3 medium zucchini = ⅔ cup sliced zucchini

and purchase them at the lowest possible price," says Dacyczyn.

Stockpile large quantities—as much as you can reasonably afford. Go in with other families in your neighborhood or at work to buy case lots and save even more—most stores give at least 10 percent off each case. Eat what's in season. In the summer, Dacyczyn gets her best produce buys from local farmstands—and grows what she can in her own garden. Fresh fruit and vegetables appear regularly on her menus. In winter, frozen vegetables supply more nutrients for the money than imported produce grown in warmer climates. You can often buy fruits and vegetables in bulk at farmers' markets and freeze them for winter meals. McCoy looks for zucchini—often as low as 10 cents a pound at summer's end—to slice and freeze in meal-size bags for winter use.

Most meats can also be stockpiled on sale. A good resource is a meat-packing company, says McCoy. Call ahead and ask if you can get a discount, then pool resources with other families. For greatest savings, buy chicken whole. Skin and bone your own chicken at home and save up to $1 a pound. Make a big pot of chicken stock with the bones. For more information about skinning and boning poultry, see page 114.

Co-ops and health food stores also offer reduced prices for case lots, so you can stock up on foods you eat regularly, like grains, beans, or anything that stores well. Be sure to use your bargains in a timely fashion or share bulk buys with like-minded friends.

As your stockpile of sale items diminishes, be flexible. Try new dinner recipes that feature other items, says Dacyczyn. When her family uses up all the fresh tomatoes from that year, she'll

KITCHEN EQUIPMENT VALUES

Most experts recommend investing in good quality cookware and knives, a one-time buy that can be very economical in the long run. Good cookware makes your daily time in the kitchen a pleasure instead of a frustration. You look forward to cooking as a relaxing activity.

* *Knives*. High-carbon stainless-steel knives are long-lasting and easy to sharpen—and a better value than the cheap knives that "never need sharpening" (all knives eventually do). Most large department stores regularly run sales on popular brands.

* *Pots and pans*. Look for pots and pans with a stainless-steel exterior and aluminum core—a mix of metals that will provide you with even, easy cooking for years. Heavier pans are usually better constructed and resist warping. No-stick surfaces are a must for low-fat cooking. The best pans have the no-stick surface bonded directly onto stainless steel, which has the hardest surface and holds the bond best. If you buy individual pots and pans, rather than sets, you'll get what you really need instead of cluttering up your cabinets. Cookware experts recommend owning at least a 10" no-stick skillet, an 8-quart stockpot, a 2-quart (medium) saucepan, and a 4-quart (large) saucepan.

Some experts recommend buying your cookware with a credit card that offers double the warranty, so you're protected longer. But pay the bill right away so finance charges don't inflate the price.

switch to canned or frozen rather than purchasing out of season. This also speeds up supermarket visits, because it eliminates the type of shopping where you buy one of everything. "Most shoppers feel they need fresh lettuce and tomatoes all year round," said Dacyczyn, "but buying tomatoes shipped from Mexico in wintertime doesn't give you a good value, either in nutrition or price." Valuable nutrients are lost during shipping and storage. In addition, you pay dearly for out-of-season convenience. Be willing to substitute. Look at the nutritional economy as well as the price. Brighten winter salads with fresh orange slices, shredded carrots, or chopped red cabbage, said our experts.

Learn your own shopping patterns, says Michele Urvater, author and television host of *Feeding Your Family on $99 a Week*. Urvater recommends keeping a record for a week of what you cook, how you shop, and what it costs. Once you know which items you buy regularly, what you spend, and how much you really use of each ingredient, you can watch the sales to stock up on family favorites.

Build a Price Book

Starting a price book is Dacyczyn's number-two strategy for smart shopping. Each staple you regularly buy rates a full page in this pocket-sized spiral notebook. When Dacyczyn shops, she writes down the cheapest price for that item and which store is offering that price—so she knows the best place to get everything from milk to macaroni.

Either collect prices while you're shopping or jot them down later from store receipts, says Dacyczyn. This especially helps when visiting a warehouse store, where familiar items are sold in unfamiliar sizes, or natural foods stores, where grains, beans, and spices are in self-serve bulk bins. It's a small strategy, but it can fine-tune anyone's shopping system and dramatically cut down on both cost and shopping time each week.

Shop Only the Sales

All our experts scan the sale flyers each week from several supermarkets looking for the best deals. "Never shop at just one store," says McCoy. Stores compete in an area, often offering tempting prices on different items. You might find beans on sale for rock-bottom prices at one and flour at another, so it's worth visiting the two stores to stock up. When the price of one of your staples, like whole-wheat flour or oatmeal, hits an acceptable low, just inventory your current supply and decide how much to buy.

At the store, McCoy recommends looking at the unit price of

each sale item to determine its real value. Unit prices are listed on small markers tacked to the supermarket shelves (usually not on the item itself). The unit price gives you the price per pound—or other amount—per brand. Sometimes, surprisingly, a smaller size is a better value. For example, we found that 8-ounce cans of tuna often cost less per ounce than their 12-ounce counterparts.

When two perishable items, like apples and oranges, are both on sale and you're trying to determine if one is a better buy that week, Dacyczyn recommends asking yourself, "How many real servings will I get out of this item?" Always stay flexible to the better bargain. A head of broccoli might be cheaper than a head of cauliflower, but if you get fewer servings, the actual portion cost is higher. "Don't approach your shopping with the attitude that you want broccoli this week. Consider instead the cost of broccoli per portion versus cabbage or sweet potatoes," says Dacyczyn. Compare the actual cost per serving with other produce alternatives, particularly when seasonal pricing is in effect.

Careful shoppers also look at the nutritional value of each item. Carrots and sweet potatoes are five-star bargains in terms of cost and nutrition due to their high vitamin A content, says Dacyczyn. One head of cabbage gives enormous value for the price, both

TOP 7 SUPERMARKET SURVIVAL STRATEGIES

Use our experts' guerrilla tactics for getting in and out of the grocery store with your budget intact.

* Shop during a store's off-hours (call the manager to find out when it's quietest).

* Shop from the sale flyers, look for in-store specials, and avoid impulse buys.

* Make a price book and keep it up to date.

* Compare prices by portion—how many servings you get from an item—for the real cost.

* Look into joining your supermarket's preferred customer program—the more you buy, the more you save.

* Leave the kids at home.

* Snack before you shop—you buy more when you're hungry.

nutritionally (for its possible cancer-preventing properties) and in number of servings, while leaf lettuce ranks very low. Eyeball the item and ask yourself if it will feed your family and will there be leftovers?

Warehouse Stores and Buying Clubs

Our experts gave mixed reviews of warehouse and buying clubs. Warehouse stores offer a bare-bones atmosphere and buy in large quantities, but they don't take coupons, offer generics, or have loss leaders like traditional supermarkets, says Dacyczyn. And it's often difficult to compare prices when you're overwhelmed by the very large sizes. Always use your price book with warehouse clubs and take along your calculator to figure unit pricing. Don't sign up for membership (which usually costs about $25) until you are sure you'll save enough to warrant it. If you aren't going to spend around $500 a year, you're better off getting a one-day pass each time you need it and paying the five percent surcharge.

Careful price shopping can make warehouse stores a valuable part of your overall shopping system. You can stop in once a month for a few carefully priced items. Don't assume you'll save on items that regularly go on sale in your supermarket, warns McCoy. Warehouse stores rarely beat out supermarket sale prices on weekly grocery items.

Generic Brands: Name Those Savings!

Supermarkets often offer select staples in generic or store-brand packaging, which can be real bargains if you shop carefully. For example, some major-brand cereals cost as much as $4.78 a pound while the generic duplicate comes in as low as $1.32 a pound. Many store brands are identical to nationally advertised brands, says Urvater. Some items are even packed at the same plant!

We asked our experts which generic items are safe bets and which suffer in quality. They recommend the following foods:
- Baking powder and baking soda
- Cooking oils
- Cornstarch
- Dried herbs and spices
- Honey and molasses
- Powdered milk
- Raisins, dates, and other dried fruits
- Salt
- Vinegars
- White sugar and brown sugar

Cornering the Market with Coupons

Susan Samtur is the author of *Refundle Bundle,* a coupon and rebate savings newsletter. Using coupons, she saves enormous amounts of money on each shopping trip. One week, she purchased over $145 worth of groceries for less than $5.50 at her local supermarket.

Samtur says there are two rules for successful coupon savings: (1) purchase an item only when the product is already on sale, and (2) always use a coupon to increase the sale savings. Even when savings are less dramatic than $139.50 in one shopping trip, Samtur says she routinely saves a minimum of 50 percent on her grocery bill. Not a bad bargain.

You can pick up coupons from a variety of places: newspaper inserts, magazines, supermarket flyers, in-store shelf dispensers, the backs of product labels, and the coupon bin at the front of many supermarkets. Always pick out the best bargains for cost, nutrition, and how much you actually eat that food. Avoid the coupons for higher-priced luxury items or prepared convenience foods you wouldn't ordinarily buy. Watch the unit price as you use the coupon—again, sometimes the coupon gives you a better buy on a smaller size, says Samtur. Organize your coupons carefully and keep track of expiration dates. Always compare equivalent generic brands to your coupon special—sometimes a generic of similar quality is even cheaper.

Samtur recommends scouting out a store in your area that offers double or triple coupons on a regular basis and watching for sales from that store. If the sale is exceptional, buy a second newspaper and return to the store with a second set of coupons. Supermarkets will often honor sales flyers from other stores, Samtur says, especially if you live in a large metropolitan area where couponing is a common practice. If a store is out of a special, always ask the manager for a "rain check" so you can get the discount price when the product is restocked.

"Always ask yourself if the coupon will bring the item down to a low enough price to make it better than other shopping strategies you use," Dacyczyn adds. A coupon for $1 off a box of high-priced cereal may not save you anything if other breakfast options are cheaper and more nutritionally sound.

Menu Planning

Once you've fine-tuned a shopping strategy, the next step is learning how to build menus around the bargains you bring home. Although you need to stay more flexible with menu planning to take advantage of sales and in-store specials, you can't treat low-cost cooking like a lucky accident, say the experts.

Don't expect to come home from work and put together a great meal without some basic planning. You'll more likely dial out for Domino's. Instead, set aside 10 or 15 minutes each week to structure your menus around what you have in your pantry stockpile. Then add on recipes you can make from foods on sale that week in your local supermarket. Planning keeps you out of the traditional money trap of running out for take-out when you're tired after a long day at work. Having an inspiring selection of ingredients on hand means sitting down to a great low-cost dinner every night.

Planning also helps you know where to shop, because you know exactly what staples and perishable foods you need to buy. You can design your shopping trip around the day of the week that offers the best selection, triple couponing, and sales. And you'll know when to visit warehouse stores or buying clubs to replenish your kitchen stock with bulk buys.

Dacyczyn focuses each menu around these bulk buys. For example, essential foods she stockpiles (whole chicken, beans and grains, long-storing vegetables like potatoes) can become a soup, casserole, or salad and function as the center of the evening's menu. She rounds out the meal with bread and fresh fruit in season or an easy dessert created from whatever foods are on sale that week.

Strive for nutritional and cost balance in your menus. If you have quiche that costs $1 a serving one night, serve a Mexican rice-and-beans dish that costs 25 cents a serving the next. For best protein values, focus most of your meals on whole grains and beans, says McCoy. She believes grains and beans are a good financial alternative to meats and are tops nutritionally because they give you more fiber, vitamins, and minerals and less fat per serving. Tofu, for example, is an excellent protein and costs about 75 cents a pound. It's hard to find a lean meat that beats that price, McCoy says. The recipes in this book allow you to explore a wide range of grain-and-bean-based ethnic meals—often the best cuisines for economical eating using ingredients that are easy to find in your local supermarket.

Dacyczyn recommends looking over your weekly meal plans in advance and noting which foods have to be soaked (dried beans) or thawed (cooked chicken). If you have a Crock-Pot meal planned, have the ingredients ready to assemble in the morning before you

Makes 4 quarts

Per 1 cup
Calories 70
Total fat 0.3 g.
Saturated fat 0.2 g.
Cholesterol 4 mg.
Sodium 103 mg.
Fiber 0 g.

Cost per serving

17¢

MAKING YOUR OWN YOGURT

Making your own yogurt takes 10 minutes of hands-on time, and each quart saves you almost $2.50 over store-bought. Use clean quart jars to make and store the yogurt. Provide a constant temperature by wrapping the jars in an old down jacket or quilt or by setting them on a heating pad (the kind used for backaches) and wrapping them in a blanket. We use noninstant powdered milk because it is much less expensive than instant.

3¾   quarts lukewarm water (about 100°F)
  1   cup plain low-fat yogurt, made without stabilizers
  4   cups noninstant powdered skim milk

❋ If using a heating pad, set the temperature to medium and place it in a draft-free corner of the kitchen counter. Cover the pad with a towel.

❋ Pour the water into four 1-quart glass jars and let them stand for 2 minutes, or until the jars are warm. Pour the water from one of the jars into a blender. Add ¼ cup of the yogurt and 1 cup of the powdered milk; puree. Pour back into the jar. Repeat with the remaining water, yogurt, and powdered milk until all four jars are filled. Cap the jars.

❋ Place the jars on the heating pad. Cover with additional towels. Let the yogurt stand for 3 to 4 hours, or until completely set. Refrigerate.

leave for work. Thawing foods in advance makes meal preparation less rushed.

Each week, set aside time to browse through the recipes in this book and choose three to five favorite dinner entrées that make use of what you have in the pantry, what's ripe in the garden, or what needs to be used up from the freezer. If tomatoes are bursting on the vine, you might make a pan of lasagna and a skillet beef-noodle dinner, plus a vegetable soup. All three save you time during the week if you make enough to have leftovers for lunches. McCoy bakes and freezes double and triple batches of muffins and quick breads—great snacks or low-cost alternatives to purchased breakfast cereals.

Remember to always build your menus around what's plentiful in your pantry or what's on sale at the supermarket, farmers' market, co-op, or warehouse store, says Dacyczyn. "Stick-to-your-list thinking doesn't work with frugal shopping, since it doesn't allow you to take advantage of unadvertised deals," she says. Planning around what's plentiful lets you clean out leftovers from a crowded freezer or use up a perishable you'd forgotten you had.

Timely Tips for Quantity Cooking

You probably guard your time as carefully as you do your money. Cooking in quantity saves you plenty of both, plus it gives you an array of ready ingredients in your refrigerator or freezer for rushed evenings or unexpected company. Here's the basic approach: Why cook two small pots of rice when you can cook a big one with the same time and effort? Quantity cooking allows you to stock your refrigerator and freezer with staples like cooked beans, grains, pasta, soups, stews, casseroles, and sauces. Dinner becomes an extraordinarily easy affair.

Leftovers are a welcome part of the low-cost kitchen, something to be planned creatively rather than endured. You automatically cook extra quantities of your favorite casserole or spaghetti sauce, knowing that you'll get three or four meals out of one cooking session. Planned leftovers are like brand-new meals—with none of the work.

Each time you cook something, ask yourself if you can make extra for next week or next month. Doubling up on cooking time cuts your work in half. When you are working on household chores or relaxing with a good book, it's easy to have a pot of soup simmering on the stove or a pan of muffins baking in the oven. Then admire your fully stocked refrigerator and freezer, and realize how rich you feel having all this delicious food on hand.

Setting Up the Low-Cost Kitchen

Your pantry, refrigerator, and freezer become your best friends when you cook the low-cost way. Since thrifty cooks buy in bulk and store as much as possible, careful organizing is a must to get full value from shopping bargains.

Cindy Van Gelder, author of the newsletter *Keep Your Cash*, found storage a challenge at first. Inundated with leftovers when cooking for herself after a divorce, Van Gelder was forced to realistically assess what she ate, how much she ate, and how much variety she liked in her meals. Then she began to organize her kitchen to stockpile these foods more efficiently.

Van Gelder's favorite recipes often called for chicken, but when she cooked it in advance and froze it in large containers, the meat clumped together. She ended up thawing more than she could easily use up at one time, and extra chicken went to waste. After experimenting, Van Gelder learned to freeze the shredded meat in a single layer on a baking sheet before transferring it to freezer bags. This simple storage technique saves her money. It makes cooking easier, too. She just pulls out what she needs for each stir-fry, pot pie, soup, or casserole.

Our experts recommend dividing both the refrigerator and the freezer into storage sections by type of food. Use clear storage containers so you can separate at a glance the chicken soup from the spaghetti sauce. Always label and date your freezer items, so you'll use up perishables like meat and fish before they're past their prime. It's not thrifty to buy chicken on sale for 29 cents a pound then forget to use it, Dacyczyn says. She also uses her freezer to store excess garden produce and bulk grains such as oatmeal, whole-wheat flour, and rice. Meats purchased in bulk or family packs should be repackaged into smaller portions according to what your family uses. Remove the meat from the supermarket trays and wrap in aluminum foil or heavy plastic wrap to prevent freezer burn.

Make good use of your refrigerator's crisper drawer: it's specially designed to provide a humid environment that helps vegetables and fruits last longer. Keep all produce out of the light, which speeds up ripening. Remove the greens from radishes, carrots, beets, and other root vegetables before storing them, since the greens age much faster and can spoil other vegetables. (Eat the edible greens as soon as possible.) Poke a few breather holes into plastic bags used to store produce and line the crisper drawer with newspaper to absorb excess moisture. Store potatoes, garlic, onions, and hard-shelled squash outside of the refrigerator in a cool, dark place with plenty of air circulation. A wire basket is a good choice. Store the onions and potatoes away from each other, because the potatoes spoil faster if they're kept together.

For pantry storage, use clear plastic or glass jars, which are easy to find in thrift stores or at yard sales. Store bulk buys of whole grains and beans in a cool, dark location, marked with the purchase date. To maintain freshness, rotate your pantry stock regularly just like a supermarket does. When you buy more, place the oldest item at the front of the shelf so you'll use it up first.

Good storage prolongs the life of fresh, wholesome food. It means having a clear sense of what is on hand so you always get the quality you paid for.

Eating Economically on the Run

Rushed schedules and frantic days on the run benefit from low-cost eating if you stock up on foods to take along.

If you are always rushed for breakfast, follow McCoy's advice and fill your freezer with homemade muffins, quick breads, and other low-fat, low-cost breakfast foods. Always cook extra with leftovers in mind. Small containers of chili, soup, or casseroles can be reheated in the office microwave for a quick, thrifty lunch at your desk.

To avoid the afternoon slump (and the overpriced, high-fat items in the office vending machine), pack along fresh fruit, cut-up vegetables, leftover spreads, and low-fat crackers—snacks that make sense health-wise and penny-wise.

Remember that changing what we eat—and how we approach eating—is a long-term process, so start by trying something new each week. Set aside a weekend afternoon to start a price book. Begin comparing what you pay for homemade versus what convenience really costs you.

In the following chapters, you'll find the tools you need— a collection of delicious, money-saving recipes you'll really use and love, plus tips and techniques to help you begin cutting costs. Start today, for rich rewards you'll reap for many years.

CHAPTER 2

TWENTY $2 DINNERS

Food prices continue to climb. Since we can't stop eating, the affordable solution is to eat better for less! You can become more self-reliant and take advantage of economical, great-tasting, nutritious food. The menus in this chapter will point you on the road to a cooking style that will pay you back twofold—with good health and cash to spare. Save deliciously with these 20 great dinners—all at less than $2 per serving.

As you take this first step to giving your food budget a makeover, you'll take home big dividends. Food accounts for a major chunk of our weekly budget, and money experts say that trimming food costs is the quickest way to dramatically save dollars. Most people spend twice what they need to on their groceries, says Amy Dacyczyn, author of *The Tightwad Gazette* books. All it takes to eat better for less is shopping know-how and good-tasting, economical menus.

Imagine cutting your food costs from the staggering national average of $500 a month for a family of four to an astonishing low of $250 or less—that's a savings of $3,000 a year! You can do it easily, with the recipes in this chapter.

As you take a big chunk out of your food expenses, you'll also improve your nutritional intake. Replacing high-fat packaged convenience foods with the best bargains on lean meats, poultry, vegetables, fruits, whole grains, and legumes means healthier choices. Cooking low-cost meals puts you in control of your family's nutrition. You can personally monitor fat, calories, and sodium intake. You become more self-reliant as you save.

You can serve a satisfying meal of Pork Tenderloin with Mustard Marinade, Scalloped Herbed Potatoes, and Southwestern Confetti Corn—a meal that could easily cost you $10 or $15 a person in a restaurant—for only $1.92 a person. Or Szechuan Chicken and Vegetables with Jasmine Rice and Poached Pineapple Rings for just 76 cents a person. Or even an Italian favorite—Meatballs in Herbed Tomato Sauce over Spaghetti with an Orange and Spinach Salad. Five dollars a person? Nope, just 78 cents! You'll love the great taste and good health, but it'll be the super savings that will keep you making these menus again and again—and smiling all the way to the bank.

We want to eat well, but we also want to get the most nutrition and flavor for our buck. So put yourself in control of your health and your wallet. Just say no to high food prices and enjoy these enticing dinners in the bargain.

Autumn Harvest

Pork tenderloin is lean, and there's no waste—you use it all. Shop your warehouse store for great bargains. The mustard marinade enriches the lean cut. Creamy scalloped potatoes and a colorful corn stir-fry round out the meal.

- Pork Tenderloin with Mustard Marinade
- Scalloped Herbed Potatoes
- Southwestern Confetti Corn

Makes 4 servings

Per serving
Calories 481
Total fat 10 g.
Saturated fat 3.7 g.
Cholesterol 75 mg.
Sodium 914 mg.
Fiber 3.3 g.

Cost per serving

$1.91

Pork Tenderloin with Mustard Marinade

3 tablespoons stone-ground mustard
2 tablespoons frozen apple juice concentrate
1 tablespoon balsamic vinegar
1 teaspoon minced garlic
1 teaspoon ground black pepper
½ teaspoon salt
1 pound pork tenderloin, trimmed of fat

- In a shallow nonmetal dish, combine the mustard, apple juice concentrate, vinegar, garlic, pepper, and salt; stir well. Add the pork, turning to coat. Cover and refrigerate for 2 hours, basting frequently.

- Preheat the grill or broiler. Pour the marinade into a small saucepan, reserving 2 tablespoons. Grill or broil the tenderloin 6″ from the heat for 18 to 20 minutes, or until the tenderloin is no longer pink in the center, basting twice with the reserved marinade. Let the tenderloin rest on a cutting board for 5 minutes, then cut it into ½″ slices.

- Meanwhile, set the saucepan over medium-high heat; bring the marinade to a boil. Boil for 2 minutes, stirring occasionally. Drizzle over the pork slices.

Makes 4 servings

Per serving
Calories 169
Total fat 4.8 g.
Saturated fat 1.5 g.
Cholesterol 65 mg.
Sodium 334 mg.
Fiber 0.3 g.

Cost per serving

$1.50

SCALLOPED HERBED POTATOES

Per serving
Calories 212
Total fat 4 g.
Saturated fat 2 g.
Cholesterol 10 mg.
Sodium 443 mg.
Fiber 0.4 g.

Cost per serving

21¢

  1 teaspoon chopped fresh thyme
  1 teaspoon chopped fresh rosemary
 ½ teaspoon salt
 ⅛ teaspoon ground nutmeg
1¼ pounds red potatoes, thinly sliced
 ½ cup minced onions
  2 teaspoons reduced-calorie butter or margarine
  1 tablespoon all-purpose flour
  2 cups 1% low-fat milk
  2 tablespoons grated Parmesan cheese
  2 tablespoons shredded extra-sharp low-fat Cheddar cheese

❀ Preheat the oven to 400°F. Coat a 9″ round no-stick cake pan with no-stick spray. In a small bowl, combine the thyme, rosemary, salt, and nutmeg.

❀ Layer the potatoes and onions in the pan, sprinkling each layer with the herb mixture.

❀ In a saucepan over medium heat, melt the butter or margarine. Add the flour; cook and stir for 2 minutes (the mixture will be dry). Gradually add the milk; increase the heat to medium-high. Cook, whisking constantly, for 3 to 5 minutes, or until the sauce thickens slightly. Pour the sauce over the potatoes.

❀ Bake for 40 to 45 minutes, or until the potatoes are very tender. Sprinkle the Parmesan and Cheddar over the potatoes; bake for 10 to 12 minutes more, or until golden brown. Cut into wedges; garnish with the rosemary sprigs.

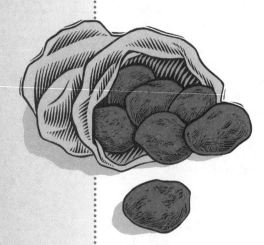

SOUTHWESTERN CONFETTI CORN

Makes 4 servings

Per serving
Calories 100
Total fat 1.3 g.
Saturated fat 0.2 g.
Cholesterol 0 mg.
Sodium 137 mg.
Fiber 2.6 g.

Cost per serving

20¢

2 large ears corn
2 tablespoons dry sherry or defatted chicken stock
½ teaspoon olive oil
¼ cup minced onions
2 cloves garlic, minced
¼ teaspoon ground cumin
1 sweet red pepper, minced
2 tablespoons minced fresh cilantro or parsley
¼ teaspoon salt
¼ teaspoon ground black pepper

❋ With a sharp knife, cut the corn kernels from the cobs; set aside.

❋ In a 10″ no-stick skillet, heat the sherry or chicken stock and oil over medium-high heat. Add the onions, garlic, and cumin. Cook and stir for 3 minutes, or until the onions are soft but not browned. Add the red peppers and corn; cook and stir for 5 minutes, or until the peppers are soft. Add the cilantro or parsley. Remove the skillet from the heat. Add the salt and pepper.

MENUS MADE EASY

Caterers recommend these tips for stress-free menu planning:

❋ Choose a maximum of three dishes per meal, including bread and sides. Make sure only one of the three needs last-minute preparation or assembly.

❋ Vary the colors and textures of the different dishes. For example, if you're serving pasta with a white creamy sauce, choose sides that are bright green or red and have some crunch.

❋ If you're stumped for side dish ideas, round out the meal with a big salad and a loaf of warmed whole-grain bread.

A Fast Wok

Chinese take-out can take you for more than $4 per person. Just as satisfying but only $1.30 a serving, this menu of marinated beef stir-fry and pineapple-spiked slaw will spirit you away on a short trip to exotic ports.

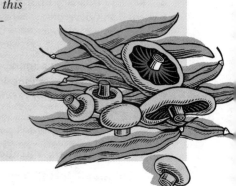

* Asian Beef and Vegetable Stir-Fry
* Pineapple Cabbage Slaw
* Rice with Scallions

Makes 4 servings

Per serving
Calories 514
Total fat 8.8 g.
Saturated fat 2.8 g.
Cholesterol 61 mg.
Sodium 668 mg.
Fiber 5.2 g.

Cost per serving

$1.30

Asian Beef and Vegetable Stir-Fry

Makes 4 servings

Per serving
Calories 219
Total fat 7.9 g.
Saturated fat 2.6 g.
Cholesterol 60 mg.
Sodium 390 mg.
Fiber 1.5 g.

Cost per serving

87¢

 1 pound lean chuck roast, trimmed of fat and cubed
 2 tablespoons minced onions
 2 tablespoons minced garlic
 2 tablespoons grated fresh ginger
 2 tablespoons reduced-sodium soy sauce
 1 teaspoon cornstarch
 1 teaspoon ground coriander
 ½ teaspoon ground cumin
 ½ teaspoon ground red pepper
 2 tablespoons white wine or defatted chicken stock
 1 teaspoon dark sesame oil
 1 cup cauliflower florets
 1 cup julienned carrots
 ½ cup julienned celery
 2 scallions, julienned
 1 tablespoon water

❋ Slice the beef into thin strips. In a shallow nonmetal dish, combine the beef, onions, garlic, ginger, soy sauce, cornstarch, coriander, cumin, and red pepper; toss to combine. Cover and refrigerate for 4 hours, stirring occasionally.

- In a wok or 10″ no-stick skillet, heat the wine or chicken stock and oil over medium-high heat. Strain the beef from the marinade, reserving the marinade. Add the beef to the pan; cook and stir for 2 minutes. Transfer the beef to a plate; cover to keep warm.

- Add the cauliflower, carrots, celery, scallions, and water to the pan. Cover and cook for 4 minutes, or until the cauliflower is tender. Add the beef and reserved marinade. Cook and stir for 1 minute, or until the sauce bubbles and thickens.

PINEAPPLE CABBAGE SLAW

½ cup nonfat plain yogurt
2 tablespoons nonfat mayonnaise
½ teaspoon curry powder
½ head green cabbage, thinly sliced
1 cup drained unsweetened canned crushed pineapple
¼ teaspoon salt
¼ teaspoon ground black pepper

- In a large salad bowl, combine the yogurt, mayonnaise, and curry powder; mix well. Add the cabbage, pineapple, salt, and pepper; toss well.

QUICK SIDE DISH

- **RICE WITH SCALLIONS.** In a large no-stick skillet, warm 4 cups leftover cooked rice with ¼ cup defatted chicken stock over medium-high heat. Add salt and ground black pepper to taste. Sprinkle with 2 tablespoons chopped scallions.

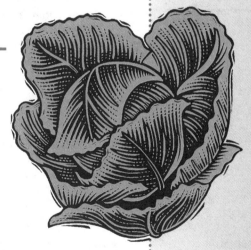

Makes 4 servings

Per serving
Calories 89
Total fat 0.4 g.
Saturated fat 0 g.
Cholesterol 1 mg.
Sodium 277 mg.
Fiber 3.7 g.

Cost per serving

28¢

BISTRO SUPPER

You don't even have to cook the noodles for this easy lasagna. They soften overnight in the refrigerator. This delicious meal serves four, with a bonus of leftover lasagna to freeze for brown-bag lunches.

- Vegetarian Lasagna
- Italian Bread
- Tossed Green Salad

VEGETARIAN LASAGNA

  1 medium onion, thinly sliced
  1 cup shredded carrots
 ¾ cup apple juice
  4 cups shredded zucchini or yellow summer squash
  1 cup chopped broccoli
  2 cups chopped fresh spinach
  1 teaspoon dried basil
 ½ teaspoon dried marjoram
  2 cups nonfat cottage cheese
 ¼ cup grated Parmesan cheese
  1 cup shredded low-fat mozzarella cheese
12 uncooked lasagna noodles
  2 cups reduced-sodium tomato sauce

- Lightly coat a 13" × 9" baking dish with no-stick spray. Set aside.

- In a 10" no-stick skillet, combine the onions, carrots, and apple juice; bring to a boil over medium-high heat. Cook and stir for 2 minutes. Add the zucchini or yellow summer squash and broccoli; cook and stir for 3 minutes, or until the vegetables are soft. Add the spinach, basil, and marjoram. Cover the skillet, remove it from the heat, and let it stand for 2 minutes.

- In a blender, combine the cottage cheese, Parmesan, and ½ cup of the mozzarella. Blend until smooth. Set aside.

- Place 3 uncooked noodles in the bottom of the baking dish. Top with one-third of the cheese mixture and one-third of the vegetable mixture. Repeat layering 2 more times. Top with the remaining 3 noodles, the tomato sauce, and the remaining ½ cup mozzarella. Cover the dish with plastic wrap; refrigerate overnight to soften the noodles.

- Remove the baking dish from the refrigerator and let stand for 30 minutes.

- Preheat the oven to 350°F. Remove the plastic wrap from the baking dish and cover the dish with foil. Bake the lasagna for 40 minutes. Remove the foil and bake for an additional 15 to 20 minutes, or until the noodles are soft and the top is golden brown. Let stand for 5 minutes before serving.

QUICK SIDE DISHES

- **ITALIAN BREAD.** Lightly brush a 1-pound loaf of Italian bread with 1 teaspoon olive oil, then sprinkle it with crushed dried rosemary, salt, and ground black pepper. Place the loaf on a baking sheet and warm it in a 350°F oven for 25 minutes, or until golden brown and steaming.

- **TOSSED GREEN SALAD.** In a large salad bowl combine 2 cups torn romaine lettuce, ½ cup sliced radishes, ½ cup shredded carrots, and 1 tablespoon raisins; drizzle with a mixture of 2 tablespoons lemon juice, 2 tablespoons nonfat plain yogurt, 1 tablespoon honey, and curry powder to taste.

SOUPER ITALIAN SUPPER

This hearty Italian minestrone is a virtual meal in a bowl. It can actually be prepared several days in advance, making it ideal for a weeknight dinner. This recipe makes a big batch, so you can freeze some for lunches. The secret to the minestrone's rich taste is earthy dried beans that flavor and thicken the soup as they soften.

* Hearty Minestrone
* Marinated Vegetable Salad
* Breadsticks

Makes 4 servings

Per serving
Calories 734
Total fat 10 g.
Saturated fat 2.1 g.
Cholesterol 12 mg.
Sodium 1,039 mg.
Fiber 6.8 g.

Cost per serving

78¢

Makes 8 servings

Per serving
Calories 351
Total fat 1.9 g.
Saturated fat 0.4 g.
Cholesterol 6 mg.
Sodium 333 mg.
Fiber 4.7 g.

Cost per serving

39¢

HEARTY MINESTRONE

 1 cup dried navy beans
1½ cups apple juice
 2 cups chopped onions
 2 cups cubed unpeeled red potatoes
 4 teaspoons minced garlic
 4 cups chopped tomatoes
1½ cups chopped carrots
1½ cups chopped celery (with leaves)
 8 cups defatted chicken stock
 2 cups reduced-sodium tomato juice or vegetable juice
 1 cup dried pasta pieces, such as broken spaghetti
 2 teaspoons dried Italian herb seasoning
 ½ teaspoon ground black pepper
 ¼ teaspoon salt

* Place the beans in a bowl and cover with boiling water. Let stand for 30 minutes, then drain well.

* In a Dutch oven, heat the apple juice over medium-high heat. Add the onions, potatoes, and garlic. Cook and stir for 5 minutes, or until the onions are soft. Add the tomatoes, carrots, celery, and 1 cup of the chicken stock. Cook and stir for 5 minutes.

* Add the tomato or vegetable juice, pasta, Italian seasoning, and the remaining 7 cups of stock. Add the beans. Bring to a boil; reduce the heat to medium. Cook, stirring occasionally, for 1½ hours, or until the beans are soft. Add the pepper and salt.

Marinated Vegetable Salad

¼ cup balsamic vinegar
1 tablespoon water
1 teaspoon dark sesame oil
½ teaspoon minced garlic
¼ teaspoon salt
2 cups thinly sliced cabbage
2 carrots, shredded
4 radishes, thinly sliced
½ cup whole corn kernels
¼ cup minced fresh parsley
½ teaspoon ground black pepper

❋ In a large salad bowl, combine the vinegar, water, oil, garlic, and salt; mix well. Add the cabbage, carrots, radishes, corn, and parsley; toss well. Let stand for 45 minutes at room temperature, stirring occasionally. Add the pepper.

Quick Side Dish

❋ **Breadsticks.** Thaw your favorite frozen bread dough overnight in the refrigerator. Break the dough into golf ball–size pieces and then roll into 8″ ropes. Place on a baking sheet. Brush very lightly with olive oil and sprinkle with crushed dried rosemary. Sprinkle lightly with salt, if desired. Bake in a 400°F oven for 10 to 12 minutes, or until golden brown.

Makes 4 servings

Per serving
Calories 70
Total fat 1.3 g.
Saturated fat 0.2 g.
Cholesterol 0 mg.
Sodium 159 mg.
Fiber 2 g.

Cost per serving

27¢

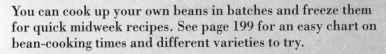

Bean Counters

Would you pay $3.50 a pound for beans? "No way," you say? Well, that's what you're paying when you buy preseasoned bean-soup mix instead of making your own minestrone or bean chili from scratch. Dried beans cost about 69¢ a pound.

You can cook up your own beans in batches and freeze them for quick midweek recipes. See page 199 for an easy chart on bean-cooking times and different varieties to try.

Sometimes you may prefer to add uncooked beans to soup (plan to let the soup simmer while you do other projects around the house). The stock will capture all the flavor released with the starch as the beans cook.

MAMA'S FAVORITE ITALIAN DINNER

Italian cooks use sautéed wedges of polenta with rich-tasting homemade tomato sauce to make a satisfying meal without breaking the bank. Dress up the meal with green beans tossed with pesto and garden vegetables made into a hearty harvest salad.

- **Polenta Wedges with Savory Tomato Sauce**
- **Green Beans with Pesto**
- **Garden Harvest Salad**

POLENTA WEDGES WITH SAVORY TOMATO SAUCE

Savory Tomato Sauce

1¾ cups defatted chicken stock
 1 tablespoon balsamic vinegar
 1 cup chopped onions
⅓ cup chopped celery
 2 teaspoons minced garlic
 2 large tomatoes, diced
 1 green pepper, chopped
¼ teaspoon dried basil
¼ teaspoon dried oregano

Polenta Wedges

1¼ cups yellow cornmeal
 1 cup cold water
 2 cups defatted chicken stock
¼ cup grated Parmesan cheese
¼ cup shredded low-fat extra-sharp Cheddar cheese
 1 tablespoon minced fresh parsley

To make the savory tomato sauce

✸ In a 10″ no-stick skillet, combine the chicken stock and vinegar; bring to a boil over medium-high heat. Add the onions, celery, and garlic. Cook and stir for 5 minutes. Add the tomatoes, peppers, basil, and oregano; bring to a boil. Reduce the heat to low; cook for 30 minutes, or until the sauce is thick. Let cool slightly; puree in a blender or food processor.

To make the polenta wedges

✸ Meanwhile, in a medium saucepan, combine the cornmeal and water; whisk until well-blended. Add the chicken stock; bring to a boil over medium-high heat. Whisking constantly, cook for 10 to 15 minutes, or until the polenta is thick. Remove from the heat and stir in the Parmesan and Cheddar. Spread the polenta in a 9″ round no-stick cake pan. Refrigerate for 20 minutes, or until the polenta is set.

✸ Coat a 10″ no-stick skillet with no-stick spray. Cut the polenta into 4 wedges; place in the skillet. Sauté over medium-high heat for 5 to 8 minutes, or until the polenta wedges are golden brown, turning once. Remove to serving plates.

✸ Reheat the tomato sauce in the skillet. Spoon over the polenta wedges. Sprinkle with the parsley.

QUICK SIDE DISHES

✸ **GREEN BEANS WITH PESTO.** Cook 1 pound fresh green beans in ¼ cup defatted chicken stock just until tender; toss with 1 tablespoon pesto.

✸ **GARDEN HARVEST SALAD.** Combine 3 cups torn lettuce and 1 orange, peeled and chopped. Drizzle with a mixture of 2 tablespoons balsamic vinegar, 1 tablespoon honey, and 1 teaspoon olive oil. Season with salt and ground black pepper to taste.

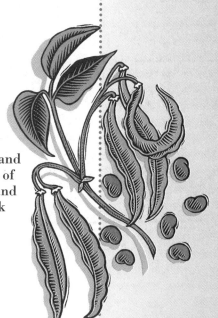

Makes 4 servings

Per serving
Calories 437
Total fat 4.9 g.
Saturated fat 1.2 g.
Cholesterol 74 mg.
Sodium 199 mg.
Fiber 2.2 g.

Cost per serving

$1.37

STUPENDOUS STIR-FRY

Compared to high-priced, fat-laden restaurant fare, homemade Chinese food is healthy for both body and budget. This easy menu features a mildly spicy stir-fry over jasmine rice, with a sweet pineapple dessert.

❋ Szechuan Chicken and Vegetables
❋ Jasmine Rice
❋ Poached Pineapple Rings

Makes 4 servings

Per serving
Calories 192
Total fat 4.5 g.
Saturated fat 1.1 g.
Cholesterol 74 mg.
Sodium 174 mg.
Fiber 1 g.

Cost per serving

76¢

SZECHUAN CHICKEN AND VEGETABLES

2 tablespoons grated fresh ginger
¼ cup water
1 tablespoon cornstarch
1 teaspoon dark sesame oil
4 chicken breast halves, skinned, boned, and cut into strips
½ cup defatted chicken stock
½ cup broccoli florets
½ cup shredded carrots
2 scallions, cut into thin strips
1 teaspoon crushed red-pepper flakes
½ teaspoon honey
2 tablespoons hoisin sauce

❋ In a medium bowl, combine the ginger, water, cornstarch, and oil; mix well. Add the chicken; toss to coat. Cover and refrigerate for 3 hours or overnight, stirring occasionally.

* Drain the chicken, reserving the marinade. Coat a 10″ no-stick skillet with no-stick spray; set it over medium-high heat. When the pan is hot, add the chicken. Cook and stir for 5 minutes, or until the chicken is no longer pink. Transfer the chicken to a plate.

* Add the chicken stock to the skillet; bring to a boil. Add the broccoli, carrots, and scallions; cook and stir for 3 minutes. Add the chicken, reserved marinade, red-pepper flakes, and honey; bring to a boil. Cover and cook for 2 minutes, or until the vegetables are crisp-tender. Add the hoisin sauce; heat through.

QUICK SIDE DISHES

* **JASMINE RICE.** In a medium saucepan, cook 1 cup well-rinsed rice in 2 cups water or defatted chicken stock for 15 minutes, or until all the liquid has been absorbed.

* **POACHED PINEAPPLE RINGS.** In a medium saucepan, combine 1 can (8 ounces) unsweetened pineapple rings (with juice), ¼ cup orange juice, 2 tablespoons raisins, 1 teaspoon honey, and ¼ teaspoon ground cinnamon. Cook for 15 minutes, or until the fruit is soft. Serve hot, topped with nonfat plain yogurt.

CURRY THEIR FAVOR

Curry is to Indian cooks what a stir-fry is to Chinese: a great way to use a variety of vegetables and high-flavor sauces to create delicious dinners. Add a cooling yogurt sauce and steamed rice for a bargain meal fit for a raj.

- ❁ Curried Vegetables
- ❁ Spiced Rice
- ❁ Cucumber-Yogurt Sauce

CURRIED VEGETABLES

1½	cups apple juice
3	cups chopped onions
3	tablespoons grated fresh ginger
1	tablespoon minced garlic
1½	cups cubed unpeeled red potatoes
1	cup chopped carrots
1	cup chopped cauliflower
1	tablespoon ground cumin
1	teaspoon ground turmeric
½	teaspoon ground cloves
½	teaspoon ground cinnamon
¼–½	teaspoon ground red pepper
1	cup peas
1	teaspoon cornstarch
1	tablespoon water

❁ In a 10″ no-stick skillet, bring 1 cup of the apple juice to a boil over medium-high heat. Add the onions, ginger, and garlic. Cook and stir for 5 minutes. Add the potatoes, carrots, cauliflower, cumin, turmeric, cloves, cinnamon, red pepper, and the remaining ½ cup apple juice. Lower the heat to medium. Cook, stirring occasionally, for 25 minutes, or until the potatoes are soft.

❁ Add the peas. Cook for 1 minute. In a small bowl, combine the cornstarch and water; add to the skillet. Cook and stir for 1 minute, or until the sauce thickens slightly.

Quick Side Dishes

❁ **Spiced Rice.** In a medium saucepan, combine 1 cup brown rice with 2 cups defatted chicken stock. Season with ground cinnamon, ground cardamom, and salt to taste. Cook for 40 to 50 minutes, or until all the liquid has been absorbed. Add ground black pepper to taste.

❁ **Cucumber-Yogurt Sauce.** Peel, seed, and shred 1 large cucumber and place in a medium bowl. Add ½ cup nonfat plain yogurt and 1 tablespoon minced fresh cilantro or parsley. Season with salt and ground black pepper to taste.

Makes 4 servings

Per serving
Calories 558
Total fat 13 g.
Saturated fat 3.8 g.
Cholesterol 86 mg.
Sodium 716 mg.
Fiber 10.5 g.

Cost per serving

$1.09

HERE'S THE BEEF!

Beef doesn't have to mean big bucks. Our savory stew dinner uses trimmed chuck roast, an inexpensive cut that turns tender and flavorful as it simmers. The easy dill bread and a colorful salad complete the meal.

- ❀ Beef Stew
- ❀ Dill Bread
- ❀ Cabbage, Tomato, and Spinach Salad

Makes 4 servings

Per serving
Calories 363
Total fat 8.2 g.
Saturated fat 3.1 g.
Cholesterol 59 mg.
Sodium 198 mg.
Fiber 4.7 g.

Cost per serving

65¢

BEEF STEW

12	ounces beef chuck roast, trimmed of fat and cubed
1/3	cup all-purpose flour
1	teaspoon garlic powder
1/4	teaspoon ground cumin
2	cups defatted beef or chicken stock
1	cup chopped onions
2	cups cubed unpeeled potatoes
1	cup chopped broccoli
1	cup whole kernel corn
1/2	teaspoon ground black pepper
1/4	teaspoon salt

❀ In a medium bowl, combine the beef, flour, garlic, and cumin. Toss to coat.

❀ Coat a 10″ no-stick skillet with no-stick spray and set over medium-high heat. Add the coated beef cubes. Cook and stir for 5 minutes, or until the beef is browned. Transfer the beef to a plate.

❀ Add ½ cup of the beef or chicken stock to the skillet; bring to a boil, scraping to loosen any browned bits. Add the onions. Cook and stir for 5 minutes. Add the potatoes, broccoli, corn, red peppers, beef, and the remaining 1½ cups stock. Bring to a boil. Reduce the heat to medium; cook for 25 minutes, or until the potatoes are soft and the beef is tender. Add the pepper and salt.

Dill Bread

Makes 8 slices

Per slice
Calories 156
Total fat 3.4 g.
Saturated fat 0.5 g.
Cholesterol 27 mg.
Sodium 477 mg.
Fiber 4.1 g.

Cost per serving

19¢

¼	cup lukewarm water (about 110°F)
1	tablespoon active dry yeast
1	tablespoon honey
1	cup crumbled reduced-fat firm tofu or nonfat dry-curd cottage cheese
3	tablespoons minced onions
2	tablespoons dill seeds, crushed
1	tablespoon dried dillweed
1	tablespoon oil
¾	teaspoon salt
¼	teaspoon baking soda
1	egg
2–2½	cups whole-wheat flour
1	egg white, lightly beaten

❋ In a small bowl, combine the water, yeast, and honey; cover the bowl with a clean dish towel and let it stand in a warm place for 10 minutes, or until the yeast foams.

❋ Meanwhile, in a medium bowl, combine the tofu or cottage cheese, onions, dill seeds, dillweed, oil, salt, baking soda, and egg; stir well to break up the tofu or cottage cheese. Add the yeast mixture and ½ cup of the flour; stir well. Continue adding the flour ½ cup at a time, stirring well, to make a kneadable dough.

❋ Turn the dough out onto a lightly floured surface. Knead, adding more flour as necessary, for about 10 minutes, or until smooth and elastic. Coat a large bowl with no-stick spray. Add the dough and turn to coat all sides. Cover and set in a warm place for 1 hour, or until doubled in size.

❋ Coat 9" × 5" bread pan with no-stick spray. Stir down the dough; place it in the pan. Cover the pan with a clean dish towel and let the dough rise for 30 minutes in a warm place.

❋ Preheat the oven to 350°F. Brush the top of the loaf with the beaten egg white. Bake for 40 to 50 minutes, or until the loaf is golden brown and sounds hollow when lightly tapped. Remove it from the pan and cool on a wire rack for 10 minutes before slicing.

Quick Side Dish

❋ **Cabbage, Tomato, and Spinach Salad.** In a large bowl, combine 3 cups torn spinach, 1 cup sliced red cabbage, and ¼ cup cherry tomatoes; toss with 3 tablespoons balsamic vinegar and 1 teaspoon olive oil. Season with salt and ground black pepper to taste.

FRENCH COUNTRY SUPPER

Cut costs while you celebrate the harvest season with this economical French menu. Yogurt in the quiche crust keeps fat low and the texture tender.

❀ Vegetable Quiche

❀ Marinated Cucumbers and Tomatoes

❀ French Bread

VEGETABLE QUICHE

Crust

  1 cup all-purpose flour
  2 tablespoons canola oil
  1 tablespoon reduced-calorie margarine or butter
  1 tablespoon nonfat plain yogurt
1–2 tablespoons ice water

Vegetable Filling

1¼ cups sliced mushrooms
 ½ cup shredded carrots
 ½ cup thinly sliced onions
 ¼ cup minced green peppers
 ¼ cup chopped broccoli
 ¼ cup chopped cauliflower
 1 tablespoon reduced-sodium soy sauce
 ½ teaspoon garlic powder
 ½ teaspoon dried thyme
 ⅛ teaspoon dried marjoram
 1 cup low-fat ricotta cheese
 1 cup shredded low-fat extra-sharp Cheddar cheese
 ¾ cup nonfat sour cream
 1 egg

To make the crust

❀ In a food processor, combine the flour, oil, margarine or butter, and yogurt. Pulse briefly until the mixture resembles coarse cornmeal. Add 1 tablespoon of the water and pulse until the dough begins to stick together. Add up to 1 additional tablespoon water if needed. Do not overmix. Flatten the dough into a pancake shape; press into the bottom and up the sides of a 9″ no-stick pie pan. Cover the pan with plastic wrap; place in the freezer while you make the filling.

To make the vegetable filling

❋ Preheat the oven to 350°F. Coat a 10″ no-stick skillet with no-stick spray; set it over medium-high heat. When the skillet is hot, add the carrots, onions, green peppers, broccoli, cauliflower, and 1 cup of the mushrooms; cook and stir for 3 minutes. Add the soy sauce, garlic powder, thyme, and marjoram; cook and stir for 1 minute.

❋ Transfer the mixture to a medium bowl; stir in the ricotta, Cheddar, sour cream, and egg. Pour into the pie shell. Sprinkle the top with the remaining ¼ cup mushrooms.

❋ Bake for 35 to 40 minutes, or until a knife inserted in the center comes out clean. Let the quiche stand on a wire rack for 10 minutes before slicing.

MARINATED CUCUMBERS AND TOMATOES

2 large cucumbers, peeled, seeded, and thinly sliced
2 large tomatoes, sliced
2 tablespoons balsamic vinegar
1 tablespoon minced fresh mint
1 teaspoon minced garlic
½ teaspoon ground black pepper
¼ teaspoon salt

❋ Arrange the cucumbers and tomatoes on a large serving platter. In a small bowl, combine the vinegar, mint, and garlic. Sprinkle over the cucumbers and tomatoes. Cover with plastic wrap; let stand at room temperature for 30 minutes. Sprinkle with the pepper and salt.

QUICK SIDE DISH

❋ **FRENCH BREAD.** Rub a 1-pound loaf of sourdough French bread with 1 teaspoon warmed olive oil, then sprinkle it with dried dillweed, basil, and oregano. Wrap the loaf in foil and heat it in a preheated 350°F oven for 25 minutes, or until warm and crusty.

Makes 4 servings

Per serving
Calories 43
Total fat 0.4 g.
Saturated fat 0.1 g.
Cholesterol 0 mg.
Sodium 144 mg.
Fiber 0.9 g.

Cost per serving

38¢

A Taste of Asia

This Asian menu provides both variety and excitement for dining on a budget. A spicy stir-fry of noodles, vegetables, and a chili-soy sauce is paired with crispy baked strips of wonton.

- ❋ Spicy Thai Noodles with Chinese Vegetables
- ❋ Wonton Strips
- ❋ Summer Fruit Frozen Yogurt Sundaes

Spicy Thai Noodles with Chinese Vegetables

     8 ounces spaghetti
     1 tablespoon minced fresh cilantro or parsley
     1 tablespoon grated fresh ginger
     1 tablespoon minced garlic
     1 tablespoon reduced-sodium soy sauce
     1 teaspoon cornstarch
    ½ teaspoon chili powder
    ¾ cup defatted chicken stock
     3 tablespoons white wine or apple juice
     1 cup peeled, seeded, and sliced cucumbers
    ½ cup diced carrots or sweet red peppers
     1 cup bean sprouts
    ½ cup sliced water chestnuts

❋ Cook the spaghetti according to the package directions; drain.

❋ Meanwhile, in a small saucepan, combine the cilantro or parsley, ginger, garlic, soy sauce, cornstarch, chili powder, and ¼ cup of the chicken stock. Bring to a boil over medium-high heat, stirring constantly. Reduce the heat to medium; cook and stir for 2 minutes, or until the sauce thickens slightly. Set aside.

❀ In a wok or 10″ no-stick skillet, combine the wine or apple juice and the remaining ½ cup stock; bring to a boil over medium-high heat. Add the cucumbers and carrots or red peppers; cook and stir for 2 minutes. Add the sprouts and water chestnuts; cook and stir for 1 minute. Add the cooked spaghetti and sauce; heat through, tossing to coat.

WONTON STRIPS

12 wonton skins
½ teaspoon dark sesame oil
½ teaspoon ground black pepper
¼ teaspoon salt

❀ Preheat the oven to 350°F. Slice the wonton skins into strips. Place on a baking sheet and lightly coat with no-stick spray. Drizzle with the oil, then sprinkle with the pepper and salt.

❀ Bake for 10 to 15 minutes, or until lightly browned and crisp.

Makes 4 servings

Per serving
Calories 75
Total fat 0.9 g.
Saturated fat 0.1 g.
Cholesterol 3 mg.
Sodium 271 mg.
Fiber 0.1 g.

Cost per serving

9¢

SUMMER FRUIT
FROZEN YOGURT SUNDAES

2 cups sliced strawberries
2 cups blueberries
½ cup sugar
½ teaspoon vanilla
2 cups low-fat vanilla frozen yogurt

❀ In a blender, puree 1 cup of the strawberries; set aside.

❀ In a large bowl, combine the blueberries, sugar, vanilla, and the remaining 1 cup strawberries.

❀ Spoon the frozen yogurt into serving bowls; top with the berries, and drizzle with the pureed strawberries.

Makes 4 servings

Per serving
Calories 321
Total fat 3 g.
Saturated fat 1.6 g.
Cholesterol 45 mg.
Sodium 60 mg.
Fiber 3.3 g.

Cost per serving

72¢

Makes 4 servings

Per serving
Calories 541
Total fat 5.9 g.
Saturated fat 1.3 g.
Cholesterol 75 mg.
Sodium 351 mg.
Fiber 6.8 g.

Cost per serving

78¢

MAD ABOUT MEATBALLS

This hearty Italian-American meal of turkey meatballs and savory tomato sauce over spaghetti costs you less than $1 a person to make— and it's skimpy on the fat, too.

* Meatballs in Herbed Tomato Sauce over Spaghetti
* Orange and Spinach Salad

Makes 4 servings

Per serving
Calories 456
Total fat 5 g.
Saturated fat 1.2 g.
Cholesterol 75 mg.
Sodium 305 mg.
Fiber 3.9 g.

Cost per serving

56¢

MEATBALLS IN HERBED TOMATO SAUCE OVER SPAGHETTI

  8 ounces ground turkey breast
  2 slices whole-wheat bread, crumbled
  1 egg
  2 tablespoons minced garlic
  1 teaspoon chopped jalapeño peppers
       (wear plastic gloves when handling)
  ¼ teaspoon dried thyme
  ¼ teaspoon crushed fennel seeds
  ½ cup red wine or defatted chicken stock
  1 cup chopped onions
  1 cup chopped green peppers
  ½ cup chopped celery
  2 cups chopped tomatoes
  2 tablespoons tomato paste
  1 teaspoon dried basil
  ½ teaspoon dried oregano
  ½ teaspoon ground black pepper
  ⅛ teaspoon salt
  8 ounces spaghetti

* In a medium bowl, combine the turkey, bread, egg, garlic, jalapeño peppers, thyme, and fennel seeds. Mix thoroughly and form into 1" balls.

* Coat a 10″ no-stick skillet with no-stick spray; place over medium-high heat. Add the meatballs and cook, turning often, for 5 minutes, or until browned on all sides. Transfer the meatballs to a plate.

* Add the wine or chicken stock, onions, green peppers, and celery to the skillet. Cook and stir for 5 minutes, scraping to loosen any browned bits. Add the tomatoes, tomato paste, basil, and oregano; mix well. Add the meatballs; reduce the heat to medium-low. Cover and simmer for 45 minutes. Add the pepper and salt.

* Cook the spaghetti according to the package directions; drain. Serve topped with the meatballs and sauce.

QUICK SIDE DISH

* **ORANGE AND SPINACH SALAD.** In a medium bowl, combine 3 cups fresh spinach leaves, 1 thinly sliced medium red onion, and 1 cup chopped oranges. Add ¼ cup nonfat plain yogurt, 1 tablespoon lemon juice, 1 tablespoon honey, and ½ teaspoon olive oil; toss well. Season to taste with salt and ground black pepper.

GREEK GETAWAY

This easy menu highlights traditional Greek ingredients: garlic, olive oil, feta cheese, cucumbers, tomatoes, and eggplant. The beef in the main dish lends hearty flavor, but vegetables keep the per-serving cost under $1.

- ❋ Marinated Beef Kabobs
- ❋ Pita Bread
- ❋ Greek Salad

MARINATED BEEF KABOBS

12 ounces beef top round, trimmed of fat and cubed
¼ large eggplant, cubed
½ large onion, cubed
½ green pepper, cubed
2 tablespoons balsamic vinegar
1 tablespoon red wine or reduced-sodium tomato juice
4 cloves garlic, halved
½ teaspoon dried oregano
½ teaspoon ground black pepper
¼ teaspoon salt
4 cherry tomatoes

❋ In a shallow nonmetal dish, combine the beef, eggplant, onions, green peppers, vinegar, wine or tomato juice, and garlic. Cover and refrigerate for 4 hours, stirring frequently.

❋ Preheat the grill or broiler. Drain the beef, vegetables, and garlic cloves; thread onto 4 metal skewers. Lightly coat with no-stick spray; sprinkle with the oregano, pepper, and salt. Grill or broil on a broiler pan 4" from heat for 5 minutes, or until the beef is cooked through and the vegetables are lightly browned. Add the tomatoes and grill or broil for 1 minute longer, or until the tomatoes are hot.

QUICK SIDE DISHES

* **PITA BREAD.** Wrap 4 reduced-sodium whole-wheat pita bread rounds in plastic wrap and warm them in the microwave.

* **GREEK SALAD.** Combine 3 cups chopped fresh tomatoes, 1 cup diced cucumbers, 1 cup chopped lettuce, ¼ cup diced red onions, and 2 tablespoons crumbled low-fat feta cheese. Add 2 tablespoons red wine vinegar, 1 teaspoon olive oil, ½ teaspoon dried oregano, ⅛ teaspoon salt, and ⅛ teaspoon ground black pepper; toss well.

BALSAMIC VINEGAR BOOSTS FLAVOR

Balsamic vinegar is a low-fat cook's dream ingredient. It adds extraordinary flavor to salad dressings and marinades with zero fat. But in the past it's gotten a pricey reputation because only the most expensive varieties were imported from Italy. As balsamic has grown in popularity, supermarkets have begun carrying thriftier brands. You can now buy a 16½-ounce bottle for less than $2. Even if you opt for a more expensive brand, you use only a small amount per recipe so it lasts for months.

CHILI WINTER WARM-UP

Chili is a favorite casual meal, and this three-bean version costs less than $1 a serving. Using dried beans gives it plenty of rich flavor as they cook—and makes it a great dish to simmer on a back burner while you do other projects around the house. With a simple salad and cornbread on the side, this menu will warm up the chilliest winter evening.

* Calico Chili
* Basil Cornbread
* Confetti Salad

CALICO CHILI

1	cup dried chick-peas
1	cup dried kidney beans
1	cup dried pinto beans
1/3	cup red wine or water
1	teaspoon oil
2	large onions, sliced
2	cups chopped tomatoes
1	cup finely chopped red cabbage
1	cup chopped celery
1	cup chopped carrots
1/2	cup sliced mushrooms
4	cloves garlic, minced
1	teaspoon ground cumin
4	cups defatted chicken stock
1/4	cup canned diced green chili peppers
3	tablespoons reduced-sodium tomato paste
1	teaspoon dried basil
2–3	tablespoons chili powder
1/2	teaspoon ground black pepper
1/4	teaspoon salt
2	tablespoons shredded low-fat Cheddar cheese

* Place the chick-peas, kidney beans, and pinto beans in a large bowl; cover with boiling water. Soak for 1 hour. Drain and rinse; set aside.

* In a Dutch oven, combine the wine or water and oil; bring to a boil over medium-high heat. Add the onions; cook and stir for 8 minutes. Add the tomatoes, cabbage, celery, carrots, mushrooms, garlic, and cumin; cook and stir for 5 minutes. Add the stock, beans, chili peppers, tomato paste, basil, and 2 tablespoons of the chili powder; bring to a boil. Lower the heat to medium; cover and cook for 3 hours, or until the beans are soft.

* Add the pepper and salt. Add up to 1 tablespoon more chili powder if desired. Sprinkle each serving with the Cheddar.

QUICK SIDE DISHES

* **BASIL CORNBREAD.** Wrap leftover cornbread (page 250) in plastic wrap and warm it in the microwave.

* **CONFETTI SALAD.** In a medium bowl, combine 2 cups shredded carrots, 2 cups chopped lettuce, 1 cup sliced radishes, and ¼ cup chopped scallions. Add 3 tablespoons wine vinegar, 1 teaspoon olive oil, ⅛ teaspoon salt, and ⅛ teaspoon ground black pepper.

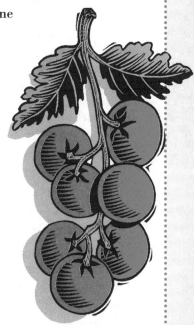

Makes 4 servings

Per serving
Calories 600
Total fat 3.2 g.
Saturated fat 0.6 g.
Cholesterol 5 mg.
Sodium 290 mg.
Fiber 10.1 g

Cost per serving

$1.29

PASSPORT TO MOROCCO

Thrifty cooks around the world rely on grains to boost the value of their meals. Couscous, long a favorite of Moroccan cooks, is topped with grilled vegetables in this easy menu. A simple fruit salad adds spice and sweetness.

- Grilled Vegetables
- Gingery Couscous
- Moroccan Fruit Salad

GRILLED VEGETABLES

Makes 4 servings

Per serving
Calories 79
Total fat 1.6 g.
Saturated fat 0.2 g.
Cholesterol 0 mg.
Sodium 270 mg.
Fiber 1.5 g.

Cost per serving

54¢

1	medium zucchini, cut into 1" chunks
½	large eggplant, cut into 2" chunks
1	green pepper, cut into eighths
4	large mushrooms
2	tablespoons reduced-sodium soy sauce
2	tablespoons frozen apple juice concentrate
1	teaspoon dark sesame oil
1	teaspoon minced garlic
1	cup unsweetened pineapple chunks
4	scallions, ends trimmed

- In a shallow nonmetal dish, combine the zucchini, eggplant, peppers, mushrooms, soy sauce, apple juice concentrate, oil, and garlic; mix well. Refrigerate for 4 hours, stirring occasionally.

- Preheat the grill. Drain the vegetables, reserving the marinade. Thread the vegetables and pineapple chunks onto 4 metal skewers.

- Pour 2 teaspoons of the marinade into a small bowl; set aside. Pour the remaining marinade into a saucepan; cook and stir over medium-high heat for 5 minutes, or until the marinade is reduced by half.

- Grill or broil the kabobs and scallions 4" from the heat for 5 minutes, turning once and brushing occasionally with the reserved 2 teaspoons of marinade. Serve drizzled with the reduced marinade.

GINGERY COUSCOUS

3 cups defatted chicken stock
¼ cup shredded carrots
1 teaspoon grated fresh ginger
1 teaspoon minced garlic
2 cups couscous

❋ In a medium saucepan, combine the chicken stock, carrots, ginger, and garlic; bring to a boil over medium-high heat. Simmer for 1 minute. Add the couscous; stir well. Cover and remove from the heat. Let stand for 5 to 8 minutes, or until the couscous has absorbed all the liquid. Fluff with a fork.

QUICK SIDE DISH

❋ **MOROCCAN FRUIT SALAD.** On a lettuce-lined platter, arrange 2 cups sliced oranges, 1 cup sliced bananas, 1 cup sliced grapefruit, ½ cup sliced kiwifruit, and ½ cup chopped apples. Sprinkle with 2 teaspoons warmed honey and ½ teaspoon ground cinnamon.

Makes 4 servings

Per serving
Calories 362
Total fat 0.9 g.
Saturated fat 0.2 g.
Cholesterol 5 mg.
Sodium 16 mg.
Fiber 4.9 g.

Cost per serving

50¢

KITCHEN TIP

The vegetable kabobs can also be cooked in the broiler for the same amount of time.

Smart Chinese cooks stretch pennies and protein with tofu—which absorbs and extends the flavor of any sauce or seasoning it marinates in. In this stir-fry we mix cubes of tofu and vegetables with a mildly spicy marinade. Serve it alongside steamed brown rice and poached Asian pears.

* Spicy Tofu and Vegetable Stir-Fry
* Poached Asian Pears
* Steamed Brown Rice

Makes 4 servings

Per serving
Calories 405
Total fat 3.5 g.
Saturated fat 0.5 g.
Cholesterol 4 mg.
Sodium 628 mg.
Fiber 4.7 g.

Cost per serving

$1.03

SPICY TOFU AND VEGETABLE STIR-FRY

Makes 4 servings

Per serving
Calories 89
Total fat 1.5 g.
Saturated fat 0.1 g.
Cholesterol 1 mg.
Sodium 597 mg.
Fiber 1.8 g.

Cost per serving

45¢

8 ounces extra-firm reduced-fat tofu, cut into ½" cubes
6 scallions, minced
¼ cup reduced-sodium soy sauce
¼ cup dry sherry or apple juice
5 cloves garlic, minced
1 teaspoon grated fresh ginger
½ teaspoon ground red pepper
⅓ cup defatted chicken stock
½ medium onion, thinly sliced
1 large carrot, julienned
1 cup broccoli florets
½ teaspoon chili oil

* In a shallow nonmetal dish, combine the tofu, scallions, soy sauce, sherry or apple juice, garlic, ginger, and red pepper. Cover and refrigerate for 1 hour, stirring occasionally.

* In a 10" no-stick skillet, bring the chicken stock to a boil over medium-high heat. Add the onions; cook and stir for 2 minutes. Add the carrots; cover and cook for 2 minutes. Add the broccoli; cook and stir for 2 minutes.

* Strain the tofu mixture, reserving 2 tablespoons of the marinade (if desired, save the remainder for another use). Add the tofu mixture to the skillet; cook and stir gently for 1 minute. Add the reserved marinade and chili oil; toss well.

POACHED ASIAN PEARS

4 Asian pears
2 cups apple juice
1 tablespoon vanilla
1 teaspoon ground cinnamon
½ cup nonfat plain yogurt

✱ With an apple corer, core the pears, leaving them whole. In a
large saucepan, combine the pears, apple juice, vanilla, and cinnamon. Bring to a boil over medium-high heat; lower the heat to
medium. Cover and cook for 25 minutes, or until the pears are
soft when pierced with a sharp knife.

✱ Cut the pears into thick slices and top with the yogurt.

QUICK SIDE DISH

✱ **STEAMED BROWN RICE.** In a medium saucepan, cook 1 cup brown
rice in 2 cups defatted chicken stock for 40 to 50 minutes, or
until all the liquid has been absorbed. Serve sprinkled with
2 tablespoons minced scallions.

Makes 4 servings

Per serving
Calories 137
Total fat 0.5 g.
Saturated fat 0.1 g.
Cholesterol 1 mg.
Sodium 25 mg.
Fiber 0.3 g.

Cost per serving

52¢

KITCHEN TIP

The extra marinade
can be used to
flavor chicken, fish,
or vegetables for
another recipe;
it will keep in the
refrigerator for up
to 2 weeks. After
using the marinade
with chicken or
fish, however, be
sure to discard it
because bacteria
can accumulate.
You can also
substitute
⅛ teaspoon of
hot-pepper sauce
for the chili oil.

LEAN AND LUSCIOUS LAMB

Extend lean lamb by combining it with plenty of winter vegetables in a richly flavored stew. Serve with toasted homemade bread and a creamy cabbage salad.

- ❊ Moroccan Vegetable and Lamb Stew
- ❊ Toasted Bread with Apple Butter
- ❊ Cabbage Salad

MOROCCAN VEGETABLE AND LAMB STEW

  8 ounces cubed lamb stew meat, trimmed of fat
  2 cups cubed unpeeled red potatoes
  1 tablespoon all-purpose flour
  1 tablespoon curry powder
 ¼ teaspoon salt
  2 cups defatted chicken stock
  1 cup chopped onions
  1 cup chopped tomatoes
  1 cup chopped carrots
 ½ cup chopped red cabbage
 ¼ cup chopped dried apricots
 ¼ teaspoon ground cinnamon
 ¼ teaspoon crushed red-pepper flakes (optional)

❊ In a medium bowl, combine the lamb, potatoes, flour, curry powder, and salt. Toss to combine.

❊ Coat a Dutch oven with no-stick spray; set it over medium-high heat. When the pan is hot, add the lamb, potatoes, and flour mixture. Cook and stir for 2 minutes (mixture will be dry). Gradually add the chicken stock, stirring constantly. Cook for 5 minutes.

❋ Add the onions, tomatoes, carrots, cabbage, apricots, cinnamon, and red-pepper flakes (if using). Bring to a boil. Reduce the heat to medium; cover and cook for 40 minutes, or until the stew is thick and the potatoes are soft when pierced with a sharp knife.

QUICK SIDE DISHES

❋ **TOASTED BREAD WITH APPLE BUTTER.** Toast 4 slices of French bread or your favorite homemade bread; spread each with 2 teaspoons unsweetened apple butter.

❋ **CABBAGE SALAD.** Combine 2 cups shredded green cabbage, 1 cup shredded red cabbage, 1 cup shredded carrots, and ¼ cup chopped fresh parsley. In a blender, combine ¼ cup low-fat ricotta cheese, 2 tablespoons low-fat buttermilk, and 1 teaspoon cider vinegar; puree. Add to the salad along with ¼ teaspoon ground black pepper and ⅛ teaspoon salt; mix well.

Makes 6 servings

Per serving
Calories 237
Total fat 6.7 g.
Saturated fat 1.9 g.
Cholesterol 91 mg.
Sodium 664 mg.
Fiber 3.6 g.

Cost per serving

$1.25

BREAKFAST FOR DINNER

You may think crêpes, or French pancakes, are too fancy for everyday meals. Actually they are quick and easy, and they make great low-cost wrappers for a variety of sweet and savory fillings. You can make a batch of 12 in less than 30 minutes; extras can be stacked and frozen for up to 4 months.

❋ *Crêpes with Creamy Vegetable Filling*

❋ *Apple-Spinach Salad*

❋ *Canadian Bacon*

Makes 6 servings

Per serving
Calories 121
Total fat 3.8 g.
Saturated fat 1 g.
Cholesterol 72 mg.
Sodium 104 mg.
Fiber 1.7 g.

Cost per serving

31¢

CRÊPES WITH CREAMY VEGETABLE FILLING

Crêpes

1 cup skim milk
½ cup all-purpose flour
2 eggs
1 teaspoon oil
¼ teaspoon ground nutmeg

Creamy Vegetable Filling

1 small clove garlic, minced
1 teaspoon olive oil
2 cups broccoli florets
1 cup sliced mushrooms
½ cup shredded carrots
2 tablespoons defatted chicken stock
⅛ teaspoon ground black pepper
⅓ cup nonfat cottage cheese
2 tablespoons nonfat plain yogurt
1 teaspoon chopped fresh chives or scallion greens
2 teaspoons grated Parmesan cheese

To make the crêpes

❋ In a blender or food processor, combine the milk, flour, eggs, oil, and nutmeg; mix on high speed for 2 minutes. Pour into a bowl and refrigerate for 10 minutes.

❋ Coat a 10″ no-stick skillet with no-stick spray. Place the skillet over medium-high heat until a drop of water sizzles when sprinkled on its surface. Pour 2 tablespoons of the batter into the center of the skillet; swirl to form a very thin circle about 7" across. Immediately pour any excess batter back into the bowl. Cook the crêpe for 1 minute, or until bubbles appear around the edges. Turn and cook the other side for 30 seconds. Continue cooking the crêpes until all the batter is used. You should have 12 crêpes. Stack the cooked crêpes on a plate until ready to fill.

To make the creamy vegetable filling

❋ In a 10" no-stick skillet, combine the garlic and oil; cook and stir over medium-high heat for 1 minute. Add the broccoli, mushrooms, carrots, and stock; cover and cook for 3 minutes. Remove from the heat; add the pepper.

❋ Preheat the broiler. Coat a 13" × 9" baking dish with no-stick spray.

❋ In a blender or food processor, puree the cottage cheese and yogurt until very smooth. Stir into the vegetable mixture. Stir in the chives or scallions. Spoon about 1 tablespoon into each crêpe; roll tightly. Place the crêpes, seam side down, in the baking dish. Sprinkle with the Parmesan; broil for 1 minute, or until the cheese melts.

APPLE-SPINACH SALAD

4 cups fresh spinach leaves
2 cups chopped red apples
2 tablespoons minced red onions
3 tablespoons nonfat plain yogurt
2 tablespoons lemon juice
2 tablespoons honey
½ teaspoon ground black pepper
⅛ teaspoon salt

❋ In a medium bowl, combine the spinach, apples, and onions; toss well. In a small bowl, combine the yogurt, lemon juice, and honey; add the pepper and salt. Pour over the salad; toss well.

QUICK SIDE DISH

❋ **CANADIAN BACON.** Coat a 10" no-stick skillet with no-stick spray and set it over medium-high heat. When the skillet is hot, add 8 thin slices Canadian bacon. Cook for 3 to 5 minutes, or until golden brown. Turn and cook for 3 minutes more.

Makes 6 servings

Per serving
Calories 58
Total fat 0.3 g.
Saturated fat 0.1 g.
Cholesterol 0 mg.
Sodium 80 mg.
Fiber 1.9 g.

Cost per serving

25¢

Makes 6 servings

Per serving
Calories 396
Total fat 5 g.
Saturated fat 1.3 g.
Cholesterol 39 mg.
Sodium 485 mg.
Fiber 5.3 g.

Cost per serving

78¢

WONDERFUL WAFFLES

Sunday-night supper is an under-$1 bargain with these crunchy corn-wheat waffles. Serve them with homemade blueberry syrup and lightly cooked apples, bananas, and strawberries.

- 🌼 **Corn-Wheat Waffles**
- 🌼 **Warm Fruit Compote**
- 🌼 **Blueberry Syrup**

Makes 6 servings

Per serving
Calories 247
Total fat 4.3 g.
Saturated fat 1.1 g.
Cholesterol 39 mg.
Sodium 481 mg.
Fiber 2.3 g.

Cost per serving

28¢

CORN-WHEAT WAFFLES

1½ cups all-purpose flour
½ cup whole-wheat flour
1½ teaspoons baking powder
½ teaspoon salt
½ teaspoon baking soda
¼ teaspoon ground cinnamon
2 cups low-fat buttermilk or skim milk
¼ cup whole kernel corn
1 large egg
2 egg whites, lightly beaten
2 tablespoons honey
1 tablespoon oil

🌼 Into a large bowl, sift together the all-purpose flour, whole-wheat flour, baking powder, salt, baking soda, and cinnamon.

🌼 In a blender or food processor, combine the buttermilk or skim milk, corn, egg, egg whites, honey, and oil; puree.

🌼 Preheat a waffle iron. Lightly coat the surface with no-stick spray. Pour the buttermilk mixture into the flour mixture; stir just until incorporated. Fill the waffle iron two-thirds full with batter; cook for 5 to 6 minutes, or until the waffle is cooked through and golden brown. Continue cooking the batter to make a total of 6 waffles. (The number of waffles may vary with smaller size waffle irons.)

WARM FRUIT COMPOTE

Makes 6 servings

Per serving
Calories 103
Total fat 0.5 g.
Saturated fat 0.2 g.
Cholesterol 0 mg.
Sodium 2 mg.
Fiber 2.2 g.

Cost per serving

34¢

1 cup chopped apples
   Juice of 1 lime or lemon
4 teaspoons packed brown sugar
2 cups sliced bananas
1 cup sliced strawberries

❋ In a medium saucepan, combine the apples, lime or lemon juice, and brown sugar. Cook and stir over medium-high heat for 5 minutes. Add the bananas and strawberries. Cook and stir for 2 minutes, or until the apples are soft when pierced with a sharp knife.

QUICK SIDE DISH

❋ **BLUEBERRY SYRUP.** In a small saucepan combine ¼ cup maple syrup and 1 cup unsweetened frozen blueberries; cook and stir over medium-high heat for 5 to 10 minutes, or until the syrup is warm.

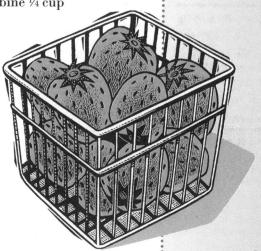

MEXICAN FIESTA

Fajitas appear on every Mexican restaurant menu, but you can save a bundle by making your own at home. They're surprisingly simple and demand just a few ingredients: tortillas, chicken, vegetables, and a cumin-scented marinade.

❀ **Vegetable and Chicken Fajitas**
❀ **Mexican Green Sauce**
❀ **Brown Rice with Cilantro**

VEGETABLE AND CHICKEN FAJITAS

2   chicken breast halves, skinned, boned, and cut into strips
    Juice of 1 lime
2   tablespoons minced garlic
1   teaspoon ground cumin
1   onion, sliced and separated into rings
1   large zucchini, cut into thirds crosswise and then into strips
½   large eggplant, cut into thirds crosswise and then into strips
1   tablespoon defatted chicken stock
8   flour tortillas (6" diameter)
¼   cup nonfat plain yogurt
2   tablespoons minced fresh cilantro

❀ In a shallow nonmetal dish, combine the chicken, lime juice, garlic, and cumin. Cover and refrigerate for 3 hours, stirring occasionally.

❀ Strain the marinade into a 10" no-stick skillet. Return the chicken to the refrigerator. Add the onions to the skillet. Cook and stir over medium-high heat for 5 to 7 minutes, or until the onions are lightly browned; set aside.

❋ Preheat the broiler. Lightly coat the zucchini, eggplant, and chicken with no-stick spray; place on the broiler pan. Broil, turning once, for 5 to 8 minutes, or until the vegetables are golden brown and the chicken is no longer pink in the center when tested with a sharp knife; baste occasionally with the chicken stock.

❋ Meanwhile, wrap the tortillas in plastic wrap and microwave on high power for 1 minute. To serve, spoon the chicken, zucchini, and eggplant onto the tortillas; top with the onions, yogurt, and cilantro. Roll and serve.

QUICK SIDE DISHES

❋ **MEXICAN GREEN SAUCE.** In a 10″ no-stick skillet, combine 2 cups chopped tomatillos, ½ cup chopped green peppers, ⅓ cup defatted chicken stock, 2 teaspoons minced garlic, 1 teaspoon white vinegar, and 1 teaspoon chopped fresh cilantro. Cook and stir over medium-high heat for 10 minutes, or until the sauce is thick. Add ¼ teaspoon salt and ¼ teaspoon ground black pepper.

❋ **BROWN RICE WITH CILANTRO.** In a medium skillet, cook 1 cup brown rice in 2 cups defatted chicken stock for 40 to 50 minutes, or until all the liquid has been absorbed. Sprinkle with 2 tablespoons minced fresh cilantro.

Easy Summertime Meal

Well-seasoned and rich in flavor, this baked egg and vegetable frittata is surprisingly low in cost and calories. You can turn it into a party menu with Caesar salad and a warm summer fruit dessert.

* **Vegetable Frittata**
* **Caesar Salad**
* **Summer Fruit with Yogurt**

Vegetable Frittata

½ medium onion, thinly sliced
3 cloves garlic, minced
½ cup sliced yellow summer squash or zucchini
¼ cup minced fresh parsley
2 scallions, minced
2 tablespoons water
1 tablespoon roasted sweet red peppers
¼ teaspoon salt
¼ teaspoon ground black pepper
4 eggs
6 egg whites
⅓ cup shredded low-fat mozzarella cheese
2 tablespoons grated Parmesan cheese
⅛ teaspoon ground nutmeg

* Preheat the oven to 400°F. Coat an ovenproof 10″ no-stick skillet with no-stick spray; set it over medium-high heat. When the skillet is hot, add the onions and garlic. Cook and stir for 3 minutes. Add the yellow summer squash into the skillet. Bake uncovered for 25 to 35 minutes, or until the frittata is set and golden brown. Cut into 4 wedges.

Caesar Salad

2 tablespoons olive oil
2 tablespoons balsamic vinegar
2 teaspoons grated Parmesan cheese
2 teaspoons lemon juice
2 teaspoons sugar
1 teaspoons Dijon mustard
3 large cloves garlic, pressed
5 cups torn romaine lettuce
¾ cup broccoli florets
¾ cup toasted sourdough bread cubes

✿ In a large salad bowl, combine the oil, vinegar, Parmesan, lemon
   juice, sugar, mustard, and garlic; stir well. Add the lettuce,
   broccoli, and bread cubes; toss well.

Quick Side Dishes

✿ **SUMMER FRUIT WITH YOGURT.** Coat 2 halved nectarines or peaches
   with no-stick spray; place in a 10″ no-stick skillet and cook over
   medium-high heat for 3 minutes, or until golden brown. In a
   small bowl, combine ½ cup nonfat vanilla yogurt and 1 teaspoon
   packed brown sugar; drizzle over the fruit.

Makes 4 servings

Per serving
Calories 120
Total fat 7.6 g.
Saturated fat 1.2 g.
Cholesterol 0.8 mg.
Sodium 91 mg.
Fiber 1.8 g.

Cost per serving

32¢

KITCHEN TIP

Save by making
the bread cubes
from day-old bread
bought on sale.

APPETIZERS AND SNACKS

For many of us, it's unrealistic to think of eating only at meal-times. A well-timed snack can nourish us and keep us cheerful through midafternoon slumps. But traditional packaged snack foods—like chips, candy, and cookies—are unwise in more ways than one. Full of fat, calories, sugar, and sodium, they deprive us of essential nutrients. Making your own between-meal treats saves money and adds nutrition to every snack break.

No longer will you be tempted to pay $3.95 for that plate of nachos when you can make your own healthier version for 48 cents. Or to grab a packaged spinach dip when it costs you only 29 cents a serving to make at home.

Use the recipes in this chapter to create low-cost, healthy snacks and appetizers to enhance your between-meal breaks and family get-togethers.

French Striped Vegetable Mold

Makes 8 servings

Per serving
Calories 115
Total fat 2.2 g.
Saturated fat 0.6 g.
Cholesterol 80 mg.
Sodium 159 mg.
Fiber 4 g.

Cost per serving

19¢

This elegant terrine, striped with subtly seasoned layers of carrots, broccoli, and peas, makes a very pretty party dish. And it can be prepared up to a day before serving.

- 1 pound carrots, chopped
- 1–2 teaspoons red wine vinegar
- 2 cups broccoli florets
- 1 tablespoon all-purpose flour
- 2 cloves garlic, minced
- 1 teaspoon lemon juice
- 2 cups frozen peas
- 2 tablespoons honey
- 3 eggs
- 1/4 teaspoon salt
- 1/4 teaspoon ground black pepper
- 6–9 tablespoons rye bread crumbs
- 4 lettuce leaves

❀ Preheat the oven to 400°F. Lightly coat a 9" × 5" loaf pan with no-stick spray; line it with wax paper.

❀ In a vegetable steamer set over a pot of boiling water, steam the carrots for 5 minutes, or until they are soft but not mushy; drain well. Spoon into a bowl and toss with the vinegar.

❀ Steam the broccoli for 5 minutes, or until it is bright green but not mushy; drain well. Spoon into a second bowl and toss with the flour, garlic, and lemon juice.

❀ Remove the steamer from the pot but keep the water boiling. Add the peas directly to the water. Cook for 30 seconds; drain well. Spoon into a third bowl and toss with the honey.

❀ In a food processor or blender, puree the carrots with 1 egg and 1/8 teaspoon of the salt and 1/8 teaspoon of the pepper. Stir in 2 tablespoons of the bread crumbs to make a mixture with the consistency of peanut butter. If needed, add up to 1 tablespoon more bread crumbs. Spread the carrot mixture in the bottom of the loaf pan.

- Clean the food processor or blender and puree the broccoli mixture with 1 egg and the remaining ⅛ teaspoon salt and ⅛ teaspoon pepper. Thicken with 2 to 3 tablespoons bread crumbs as needed. Spread over the carrots.

- Mash the peas with the remaining egg and thicken with 2 to 3 tablespoons bread crumbs as needed. Spread evenly over the broccoli layer.

- Place the loaf pan in a large baking dish; fill the baking dish with enough hot water to reach halfway up the sides of the loaf pan. Bake for 35 to 45 minutes, or until the loaf is slightly puffed and a toothpick inserted in the center comes out clean. Remove the loaf pan from the hot water.

- Chill for several hours or overnight, then unmold onto a plate lined with the lettuce leaves. Slice into 8 portions.

WARM SPINACH AND CHEESE DIP

Pack a portion of this creamy dip along with vegetables or crackers and you have a great afternoon snack for hectic workdays. It's also a favorite at holiday parties.

2
    1 cup chopped packed fresh spinach
    1 cup canned artichoke hearts, drained
    4 cloves garlic, minced
    1 teaspoon balsamic vinegar
    ⅔ cup shredded low-fat mozzarella cheese
⅔ ⅓ cup nonfat sour cream or nonfat plain yogurt
    ½ teaspoon cornstarch
    4 tablespoons grated Parmesan cheese

- Preheat the oven to 375°F. Coat a 1-quart casserole dish with no-stick spray.

- In a food processor or blender, puree the spinach, artichoke hearts, garlic, and vinegar until smooth. Transfer to a medium bowl. Stir in the mozzarella, sour cream or yogurt, cornstarch, and 2 tablespoons of the Parmesan. Spoon into the casserole dish; sprinkle with the remaining 2 tablespoons Parmesan.

- Bake for 20 minutes, or until the dip is golden brown and bubbling hot.

Makes 2½ cups

Per ¼ cup
Calories 50
Total fat 1.9 g.
Saturated fat 1.3 g.
Cholesterol 6 mg.
Sodium 126 mg.
Fiber 1 g.

Cost per serving

29¢

CURRIED CHICKEN SPREAD

This great party food doubles as a delicious sandwich filling—at half the cost of packaged chicken spreads.

Makes 1¼ cups

Per 2 tablespoons
Calories 50
Total fat 1.2 g.
Saturated fat 0.3 g.
Cholesterol 17 mg.
Sodium 76 mg.
Fiber 0.2 g.

Cost per serving

15¢

¼ cup minced onions
1 tablespoon defatted chicken stock
1 teaspoon olive oil
1 chicken breast, skinned, boned, and chopped
1 teaspoon curry powder
½ cup nonfat sour cream or nonfat plain yogurt
¼ cup sliced scallions
2 teaspoons mango chutney
¼ teaspoon salt

❋ In a 10″ no-stick skillet, combine the onions, stock, and oil; cook and stir over medium-high heat for 3 minutes. Add the chicken and curry powder; cook and stir for 5 to 8 minutes, or until the chicken is no longer pink. Transfer to a food processor; puree until smooth. Spoon into a medium bowl. Stir in the sour cream or yogurt, scallions, chutney, and salt.

❋ Transfer the spread to a decorative bowl; smooth the top with a rubber spatula. Cover and refrigerate for 2 hours. Serve chilled.

Nachos

A favorite snack, quick supper, or crowd-pleasing party dish, our low-fat nachos cost $3.50 less for the entire dish than the popular restaurant version. Quick homemade refried beans and minced chili peppers stretch the value of the cheese topping, without sacrificing good taste.

8 corn tortillas (6" diameter)
2 cups cooked pinto beans (page 199)
¾ teaspoon ground cumin
¼ teaspoon ground red pepper
1 cup shredded nonfat mozzarella cheese
½ cup nonfat sour cream
½ cup diced canned green chili peppers
2 tablespoons minced fresh cilantro

❋ Preheat the oven to 400°F. Using kitchen scissors, cut each tortilla into 6 wedges. Place on a large baking sheet; coat with no-stick spray. Bake for 15 to 20 minutes, or until crisp.

❋ Meanwhile, in a medium no-stick skillet, heat the beans over medium heat. Add the cumin and red pepper; mash well. When the beans are bubbling, remove them from the heat; set aside.

❋ Preheat the broiler. In a small bowl, stir together the mozzarella, sour cream, chili peppers, and cilantro. Drop or spread spoonfuls of the bean mixture on the tortilla chips. Top with the cheese mixture. Broil for 5 minutes, or until the nachos are brown and bubbling. Serve immediately.

Makes 6 servings

Per serving
Calories 199
Total fat 1.2 g.
Saturated fat 0.2 g.
Cholesterol 0 mg.
Sodium 274 mg.
Fiber 4.9 g.

Cost per serving

48¢

CHEESE-VEGETABLE SPREAD WITH RYE CRACKERS

Makes 6 servings

Per serving
Calories 117
Total fat 0.3 g.
Saturated fat 0.1 g.
Cholesterol 1 mg.
Sodium 98 mg.
Fiber 0.2 g.

Cost per serving

33¢

KITCHEN TIP

The liquid drained from the yogurt (called whey) can add a protein punch to home-made bread. Save it in the refrigera-tor or freezer and use it in place of water the next time you make a loaf or two.

Packaged party spreads can cost $3 or more and taste anything but fresh. Make your own spread for a fraction of the cost—and make it delicious with plenty of minced vegetables. This colorful and rich-tasting spread is based on yogurt cheese, a fat-free basic for the low-cost kitchen.

  2 cups nonfat plain yogurt
 ¼ cup apple juice
  2 tablespoons finely minced onions
  2 tablespoons finely minced carrots
  1 teaspoon chopped fresh or dried chives
 12 reduced-sodium low-fat rye crackers

❋ Line a colander with several layers of cheesecloth. Spoon in the yogurt and suspend the colander over a large bowl. Cover and refrigerate overnight, or until all the liquid has drained into the bowl.

❋ Place the yogurt cheese in a medium bowl. Pour the apple juice into a small no-stick skillet; bring to a boil over medium-high heat. Add the onions, carrots, and chives. Cook and stir for 5 minutes, or until the vegetables are soft. Gently stir the vege-tables into the yogurt cheese. Spoon into a decorative bowl; cover and refrigerate for 1 hour. Serve with the rye crackers.

APPETIZERS FOR LESS

❋ *Big Potato Scoop.* Bake 4 baking potatoes; halve lengthwise and scoop out the pulp (reserve for potato soup). Drizzle the skins with ¼ cup reduced-sodium salsa; sprinkle with ½ cup mixed shredded low-fat mozzarella and Cheddar cheese. Bake for 8 to 10 minutes at 350°F, or until the cheese melts and the potato skins are crisp.

❋ *Indonesian Street Fare.* Satay, an Indonesian finger food, can be made low cost and low fat with bulk-purchased chicken tenders. Brush with teriyaki sauce and grill or broil, then serve with nonfat plain yogurt spiced with curry pow-der or with water-thinned mango chutney as a dipping sauce.

(continued)

- *Chinese Champion*. Fill 12 wonton or egg roll skins with 2 cups chopped raw or cooked vegetables and ½ cup shredded low-fat Cheddar cheese; fold. Coat with no-stick spray and bake at 350°F for 25 minutes, or until golden brown and crunchy.

- *Crouton Collection*. Reserve a bag in your freezer for saving bread ends—mix rye, wheat, sourdough, and white breads. Slice thinly and bake at 350°F for 30 minutes for party croutons.

- *Fruit Soup*. For an instant low-cost summer starter course, puree 4 cups chopped fresh fruit (such as cantaloupe, watermelon, berries, peaches, or plums) with 2 cups nonfat plain yogurt, ½ cup honey, and ½ teaspoon ground nutmeg. Chill and serve in glass bowls garnished with mint leaves.

- *Lighten Up*. Cut the cost and high fat of guacamole by adding an equal amount of pureed cooked green beans or cooked peas to each mashed avocado.

- *Meatball Mania*. Stretch 8 ounces of ground lean beef or turkey breast by mixing it with ½ cup bread crumbs. Season with ¼ cup chopped onions, 2 tablespoons minced garlic, 1 teaspoon minced jalapeño peppers (wear plastic gloves when handling), and ½ teaspoon ground cumin or coriander. Form into 1″ balls and bake at 400°F for 20 minutes, or until the meatballs are no longer pink in the center when cut open.

- *Perfect Peppers*. Score big on the fall harvest. Thinly slice sweet red and yellow peppers, brush with olive oil, and broil for 5 minutes, or until soft and browned. Store in freezer bags for winter use. To serve, broil briefly and arrange on a platter with hummus and toasted rye croutons.

- *Take a Quick Dip*. Puree 2 cups leftover steamed broccoli with ¼ cup chopped fresh parsley or fresh basil; add ¼ cup nonfat sour cream, ½ teaspoon ground black pepper, and ¼ teaspoon salt. Serve with French bread.

Appetizers and Snacks

Per serving
Calories 144
Total fat 2.7 g.
Saturated fat 0.3 g.
Cholesterol 9 mg.
Sodium 42 mg.
Fiber 2.6 g.

Cost per serving

47¢

MINIATURE FRUIT KABOBS WITH RASPBERRY CREAM SAUCE

When fruit is on sale, skewer some succulent pieces and serve them with a rosy sauce of sour cream, raspberries, and nutmeg for an unusual party appetizer. Garnish the platter with fresh mint leaves if you have them in your garden.

½ medium cantaloupe, cut into 12 chunks
12 unsweetened canned pineapple chunks, drained and cut in half
 2 bananas, cut into 12 slices
 6 large strawberries, halved
 2 tablespoons lime juice
¼ cup fresh mint leaves
¾ cup low-fat sour cream
¼ cup fresh or frozen unsweetened raspberries
 1 tablespoon packed brown sugar
 1 tablespoon honey
 1 teaspoon ground nutmeg

❋ Thread the cantaloupe, pineapple, bananas, and strawberries onto 12 skewers. Arrange on a platter and sprinkle with the lime juice and mint leaves.

❋ In a blender, puree the sour cream, raspberries, brown sugar, honey, and nutmeg until smooth. Pour into a serving bowl. Serve immediately with the kabobs.

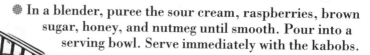

VEGETABLE PIZZA WITH POLENTA RICE CRUST

Rice and polenta make a unique and delicious crust for this easy pizza that both reduces fat and compounds culinary interest.

Makes 8 servings

Per serving
Calories 146
Total fat 2.9 g.
Saturated fat 1.7 g.
Cholesterol 8 mg.
Sodium 195 mg.
Fiber 2.7 g.

Cost per serving
33¢

  2 cups cooked brown rice
  1 cup shredded low-fat mozzarella cheese
  ½ cup yellow cornmeal
3–4 tablespoons water
  4 ounces nonfat cream cheese, softened
  1 teaspoon dried Italian herb seasoning
  2 tomatoes, sliced
  1 green pepper, sliced into rings
  1 cup sliced mushrooms

❀ Preheat the oven to 350°F. Coat a small baking sheet with sides with no-stick spray.

❀ In a large bowl, combine the rice, mozzarella, cornmeal and enough water to form a sticky dough. Spread the rice mixture in the baking sheet in a thin layer. Bake for 15 minutes, or until lightly browned.

❀ In a small bowl, combine the cream cheese and Italian seasoning. Spread on the hot crust. Top with the tomatoes, green peppers, and mushrooms. Cut into 8 pieces.

Minted Hummus with Toasted Pita Wedges

This high-protein chick-pea spread makes a great brown-bag lunch. Reheat the pitas in a toaster oven or microwave.

Makes 4 servings

Per serving
Calories 367
Total fat 6.9 g.
Saturated fat 1.1 g.
Cholesterol 0 mg.
Sodium 453 mg.
Fiber 3.4 g.

Cost per serving

30¢

  4 reduced-sodium pita bread rounds (6" diameter), cut into wedges
  2 cups cooked chick-peas (page 199)
 ¼ cup nonfat plain yogurt
  2 tablespoons low-fat peanut butter
  4 cloves garlic, minced
1–2 teaspoons lemon juice
  2 tablespoons chopped fresh mint
 ½ teaspoon ground black pepper
 ¼ teaspoon salt

✺ Preheat the oven to 400°F. Place the pita wedges on a no-stick baking sheet; coat them with no-stick spray. Bake for 10 minutes, or until golden and crisp.

✺ Meanwhile, in a blender or food processor, combine the chick-peas, yogurt, peanut butter, garlic, and 1 teaspoon of the lemon juice; puree. Stir in the mint, pepper, and salt. Add more lemon juice, if desired. Serve with the pita wedges.

Spicy Honey-Baked Chicken Wings

When chicken wings are on sale at your local supermarket or warehouse store, this sweet-and-spicy marinade makes them shine as finger food or picnic fare. You'll pay less than 30¢ a serving, compared with $2 for the same appetizer at take-out chicken joints.

Makes 6 servings

Per serving
Calories 229
Total fat 6.9 g.
Saturated fat 2 g.
Cholesterol 72 mg.
Sodium 184 mg.
Fiber 0.2 g.

Cost per serving

27¢

 1 pound chicken wings (about 24)
¼ cup honey
2 tablespoons reduced-sodium ketchup
1 tablespoon reduced-sodium soy sauce
1 tablespoon hot-pepper sauce
½ teaspoon ground red pepper
¼ cup nonfat plain yogurt
1 tablespoon minced scallions

- ✤ Remove as much skin as possible from the chicken wings and trim the tips. In a large shallow nonmetal dish, combine the chicken wings, honey, ketchup, soy sauce, hot-pepper sauce, and red pepper. Toss to combine. Cover and refrigerate for 1 hour, turning occasionally.

- ✤ Preheat the oven to 350°F. Line a large baking sheet with foil. Transfer the chicken wings to the baking sheet. Bake for 30 minutes, or until the chicken is no longer pink in the center when tested with a sharp knife.

- ✤ In a small bowl, combine the yogurt and scallions. Serve with the chicken wings.

ROASTED GARLIC SPREAD

Garlic is famous for its low-fat flavor, and slow roasting turns the "stinking rose" into sweet cream. You can make a large batch of this spread at one time, then pack extras into small containers to freeze. It's delicious tossed with pasta or steamed vegetables, as well as spread on French or Italian bread as an appetizer.

4   whole heads garlic (unpeeled)
1   teaspoon olive oil

- ✤ Preheat the oven to 350°F. With a sharp knife, slice the top ¼" off each head of garlic. Lightly brush the heads with the olive oil. Place in a shallow baking dish; cover with foil.

- ✤ Bake for 55 to 60 minutes. Remove the foil and bake for an additional 10 minutes, or until the garlic skin is browned and the interior is very soft. Squeeze the cloves to release the roasted garlic.

Makes ¼ cup

Per 1 tablespoon
Calories 64
Total fat 1.3 g.
Saturated fat 0.2 g.
Cholesterol 0 mg.
Sodium 6 mg.
Fiber 0.8 g.

Cost per serving

35¢

Appetizers
and Snacks

Per 2 burritos
Calories 125
Total fat 1.5 g.
Saturated fat 0.3 g.
Cholesterol 0 mg.
Sodium 123 mg.
Fiber 2 g.

Cost per serving

19¢

MINIATURE BLACK BEAN BURRITOS

Mexican burritos at fast food restaurants cost 99¢ a serving. A comparable amount of ours costs 19¢. This bite-size version gets its flavor from onions, garlic, and plenty of spices instead of high-fat, high-cost cheeses.

⅔ cup minced onions
2 cloves garlic, minced
2 tablespoons defatted chicken stock
2 cups cooked black beans (page 199)
¼ teaspoon ground cumin
⅛ teaspoon ground coriander
⅛ teaspoon crushed red-pepper flakes
4 flour tortillas (6" diameter)
¼ cup reduced-sodium salsa
¼ cup nonfat sour cream
¼ cup chopped fresh cilantro

❋ In a 10" no-stick skillet, combine the onions, garlic, and chicken stock; cook and stir over medium heat for 3 minutes. Add the beans, cumin, coriander, and red-pepper flakes; cook and stir for 1 minute. Remove from the heat and mash the beans.

❋ Wrap the tortillas in plastic wrap; microwave on high power for 1 minute, or until warm. Spread each tortilla with the bean mixture. Roll up; cut each roll into 4 pieces. Top with dollops of salsa and sour cream. Sprinkle with the cilantro.

WHITE BEAN AND LENTIL SPREAD

Beans boost fiber in your meals and, at less than 59¢ a pound, are basic to low-fat, low-cost cooking. They taste anything but basic in this simple spread, featuring lentils, curry spices, and aromatic vegetables.

¼ cup dry sherry or defatted chicken stock
1 small onion, finely minced
2 cloves garlic, minced
2 cups cooked lentils (page 199)
1 cup cooked navy beans (page 199)
1 egg
¼ cup chopped fresh parsley
1 teaspoon curry powder
½ teaspoon dried basil
½ teaspoon ground paprika
½ teaspoon salt
¼ teaspoon ground nutmeg
1 cup soft rye bread crumbs
¼ cup grated Parmesan cheese

❋ Preheat the oven to 350°F. Coat a 9″ × 5″ loaf pan with no-stick spray.

❋ In a medium saucepan, bring the sherry or stock to a boil over medium-high heat; add the onions and garlic. Cook and stir for 3 minutes; remove from the heat.

❋ In a medium bowl, mash the lentils, white beans, and egg. Stir in the onion mixture, parsley, curry powder, basil, paprika, nutmeg, and salt. Add the bread crumbs and Parmesan; mix well. Spoon into the loaf pan; smooth the top with a rubber spatula.

❋ Bake for 40 minutes, or until the spread is slightly browned. Cool for 20 minutes before serving. Spoon into a serving bowl.

Makes 2⅔ cups

Per ⅓ cup
Calories 143
Total fat 2 g.
Saturated fat 0.9 g.
Cholesterol 29 mg.
Sodium 233 mg.
Fiber 4 g.

Cost per serving

17¢

Per serving
Calories 203
Total fat 6.1 g.
Saturated fat 1.1 g.
Cholesterol 0 mg.
Sodium 212 mg.
Fiber 0.8 g.

Cost per serving

28¢

KITCHEN TIP

For an even tastier dish, grill the whole eggplant over low coals on a charcoal grill. The skin will blacken and can be peeled off after the eggplant cooks and cools.

BABA GHANOUSH WITH PITA WEDGES

Middle Eastern cooks use this rich-tasting eggplant and garlic spread as a dip, in sandwiches, and even as a baste for grilled foods.

  1 medium eggplant
  1 teaspoon olive oil
 ½ cup minced onions
  3 large cloves garlic, minced
 ¼ cup lemon juice
  3 tablespoons peanut butter
  1 tablespoon minced fresh parsley
 ½ teaspoon ground black pepper
  4 reduced-sodium pita bread rounds (6" diameter)

❋ Preheat the oven to 400°F. Pierce the eggplant in several places with a fork; place on a baking sheet. Bake for 1 hour, or until the eggplant is very soft and has collapsed. Cool. Scoop out the flesh into a blender or food processor; discard the skin.

❋ In a small no-stick skillet, heat the oil over medium-high heat; add the onions and garlic. Cook and stir for 3 minutes, or until the onions are soft. Transfer to the blender or food processor. Add the lemon juice and peanut butter. Process until smooth. Stir in the parsley and pepper.

❋ Cut each pita round into 6 wedges; toast. Serve with the baba ghanoush.

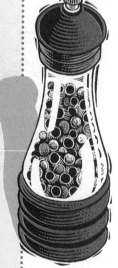

RANCHERO BEAN DIP WITH WHEAT BREAD

Black beans are traditional penny stretchers in New Mexican cuisine. They pack a lot of flavor and richness for very little cost.

½–¾ cup water
½ cup minced onions
5 large cloves garlic, minced
2 cups cooked black beans (page 199)
⅓ cup salsa
1 tablespoon minced jalapeño peppers
    (wear plastic gloves when handling)
½ teaspoon ground cumin
⅓ cup chopped fresh cilantro
½ teaspoon ground black pepper
1 round loaf whole-wheat bread

✽ In a 10″ no-stick skillet, bring ½ cup of the water to a boil over medium-high heat; add the onions and garlic. Cook and stir for 3 minutes, or until the onions are tender.

✽ In a medium bowl, mash the beans until nearly smooth. Add the beans, salsa, jalapeño peppers, and cumin to the skillet. Cook and stir for 5 minutes, or until thick. If necessary, add enough to the remaining ¼ cup water to attain a good dip consistency. Remove from the heat; add the pepper.

✽ Spoon the bean mixture into a serving bowl set on a large plate. Slice the bread and arrange around the bowl.

Makes 10 servings

Per serving
Calories 167
Total fat 2 g.
Saturated fat 0.4 g.
Cholesterol 0 mg.
Sodium 302 mg.
Fiber 1.8 g.

Cost per serving

18¢

Makes 36

Per 3 pieces
Calories 85
Total fat 1.2 g.
Saturated fat 0.1 g.
Cholesterol 0 mg.
Sodium 374 mg.
Fiber 1.6 g.

Cost per serving

25¢

BROWN RICE VEGETARIAN SUSHI

No need to run to the nearest Japanese restaurant for a sushi break—you can make your own in minutes for a fraction of the cost. This satisfying vegetarian version uses brown rice in the traditional sweet marinade and toasted sheets of nori seaweed for wrappers. If desired, you can easily substitute lettuce leaves for the nori or simply serve the sushi rice in a bowl with the vegetables on top.

1	cup brown rice
2	cups water
¼	cup cider vinegar
3	tablespoons honey
5	teaspoons apple juice
¾	teaspoon salt
6	sheets nori seaweed
4	spinach leaves, cut into thin strips
½	large cucumber, peeled, seeded, and cut into thin strips
¼	small avocado, cut into thin strips
¼	small sweet red pepper, cut into thin strips
1	teaspoon reduced-sodium soy sauce

✱ In a medium saucepan, combine the rice and water; bring to a boil over medium-high heat. Cook, uncovered, for 20 minutes. As needed, add water to equal the level of the rice. Lower the heat to medium; cover and cook for 25 minutes, or until all the water has been absorbed. Remove from the heat. Transfer to a large bowl.

✱ In a small saucepan, combine the vinegar, honey, apple juice, and salt. Bring to a boil over medium heat; cook for 2 minutes. Add to the cooked rice; stir continuously for 5 minutes, or until the rice reaches room temperature.

✱ Toast each sheet of nori in a large no-stick skillet over high heat for 2 minutes, or until crisp and fragrant. Place 1 sheet at a time on a clean dry dish towel. Top with approximately ¾ cup of the rice; spread with your fingertips to make a thin layer, leaving ½" around the edges uncovered. Make a crosswise (left to right) groove in the center of the rice and layer with strips of spinach, cucumber, avocado, and red peppers; sprinkle lightly with soy sauce.

* Lift the edge of the towel and roll the nori away from you, tucking firmly as you roll and being careful not to catch the towel in the roll. When rolled, moisten the edge of the nori with water and press to seal the roll. Place the roll, seam side down, on a firm surface and cut into 6 pieces with a sharp knife. Repeat with the remaining nori and rice mixture.

VEGETABLE PLATTER WITH YOGURT-HERB SAUCE

At your next party, raid the garden for this elegant, low-cost appetizer. We borrow an old trick from caterers and serve the yogurt-herb sauce in a hollowed-out red cabbage. (After serving, rinse the cabbage "bowl" and chop up for soup later in the week.)

Makes 8 servings

Per serving
Calories 60
Total fat 0.5 g.
Saturated fat 0.1 g.
Cholesterol 1 mg.
Sodium 43 mg.
Fiber 1.9 g.

Cost per serving

49¢

        1 cup nonfat plain yogurt
    ½–1 tablespoon packed brown sugar
        2 teaspoons minced fresh chives
        1 teaspoon dried tarragon
        1 teaspoon mustard
        1 small red cabbage
        1 cup cherry tomatoes
        1 cup broccoli florets
        1 cup snow peas, trimmed
        2 small zucchini or yellow summer squash, sliced
        1 cup green beans, trimmed
        1 cup halved mushrooms

* In a small bowl, combine the yogurt, chives, tarragon, mustard, and ½ tablespoon of the brown sugar. Add up to ½ tablespoon more brown sugar to taste if desired.

* Cut a thin slice off the bottom of the cabbage so it will sit flat. Cut a circle in the top and with a sharp knife scoop out the interior sections of the cabbage, leaving a thin shell. Place on a platter. (Save the interior of the cabbage for another use.) Spoon the yogurt sauce into the cabbage.

* Arrange the tomatoes, broccoli, snow peas, zucchini or yellow squash, beans, and mushrooms around the cabbage. Serve immediately.

79

Cucumber Sesame Salad

Makes 4 servings

Per serving
Calories 40
Total fat 2.5 g.
Saturated fat 0.4 g.
Cholesterol 0 mg.
Sodium 137 mg.
Fiber 0.2 g.

Cost per serving

20¢

Make this refreshing appetizer when cucumbers are in season—and at their cheapest—in late summer. The strong flavor of dark sesame oil, an Asian staple, allows you to use less, cutting both cost and fat for this recipe.

2 tablespoons rice vinegar
2 teaspoons dark sesame oil
1 teaspoon honey or sugar
½ teaspoon crushed red-pepper flakes
¼ teaspoon salt
1 large cucumber, peeled, seeded, and thinly sliced
4 lettuce leaves
¼ teaspoon toasted sesame seeds

❋ In a large bowl, combine the vinegar, oil, honey or sugar, red-pepper flakes, and salt. Add the cucumbers; toss well. Cover and let stand at room temperature for 30 to 45 minutes; stir occasionally.

❋ Line a large platter with the lettuce leaves; top with the cucumber salad. Sprinkle with the sesame seeds. Serve at room temperature.

Cheddar Toast with Black Bean Relish

Makes 12 servings

Per serving
Calories 150
Total fat 3.2 g.
Saturated fat 1.3 g.
Cholesterol 5 mg.
Sodium 300 mg.
Fiber 0.9 g.

Cost per serving

19¢

Rich in flavor and visual appeal, these bite-size appetizers are surprisingly lean in cost and calories. We combine hot-from-the-oven Cheddar toast with a chilled, slightly spicy black bean and vegetable relish for a delightful combination of tastes and temperatures.

1 cup cooked black beans (page 199)
¼ cup minced peeled pears or mangoes
¼ cup chopped scallions
¼ cup chopped tomatoes
1 teaspoon minced fresh jalapeño peppers
(wear plastic gloves when handling)
1 teaspoon olive oil
1 teaspoon ground cumin
1–2 tablespoons lime juice
1 medium loaf Italian bread
½ cup shredded low-fat extra-sharp Cheddar cheese

* In a medium bowl, combine the beans, pears or mangoes, scallions, tomatoes, jalapeño peppers, oil, cumin, and 1 tablespoon of the lime juice; mix well. Cover and refrigerate for 45 minutes, stirring occasionally. Add up to 1 tablespoon more lime juice if desired.

* Preheat the oven to 350°F. Cut the bread into 12 slices; place in a single layer on a baking sheet. Bake for 10 minutes. Sprinkle with the Cheddar. Bake for 5 minutes, or until the cheese has melted. Top with the black bean relish.

QUICK-PICKLED VEGETABLE APPETIZER

Japanese cooks serve homemade pickles as traditional appetizers—a thrifty way to add variety and interest to family and company meals. We like the colorful combination of radishes, cucumbers, and carrots, but you can substitute any crisp vegetables. You can easily double or triple the recipe.

  1 cup sliced radishes
½ cup peeled and sliced cucumbers
½ cup diagonally sliced carrots
½ teaspoon salt
  6 tablespoons water
  2 tablespoons cider vinegar
  4 lettuce leaves

* In a medium bowl, toss together the radishes, cucumbers, carrots, and salt. Let stand at room temperature for 2 hours. Place the vegetables in a colander and press gently to drain off any liquid. Return the vegetables to the bowl.

* In a small saucepan, bring the water and vinegar to a boil. Remove from the heat; let cool. Pour over the vegetables; toss well. Cover and refrigerate for 24 hours. Serve on the lettuce leaves.

Makes 4 servings

Per serving
Calories 18
Total fat 0.3 g.
Saturated fat 0 g.
Cholesterol 0 mg.
Sodium 284 mg.
Fiber 1.2 g.

Cost per serving

23¢

Appetizers
and Snacks

BROILED POLENTA WITH TOMATO TOPPING

Thrifty Italian families serve polenta, or cooked cornmeal, as a substitute for pasta, as a grilled breakfast, or as a lunch with steamed vegetables. Here it is cooked, cooled, and sliced, then broiled to a golden brown. Topped with garden tomatoes and basil, it makes a delicious and inexpensive at-home snack.

Polenta

1¼ cups yellow cornmeal
1 cup cold water
2 tablespoons grated Parmesan cheese

Tomato Topping

2 cups chopped tomatoes
¼ cup minced fresh basil
1 tablespoon chopped roasted sweet red peppers
2 teaspoons olive oil
1 teaspoon minced garlic
⅛ teaspoon crushed red-pepper flakes
¼ teaspoon ground black pepper
⅛ teaspoon salt

To make the polenta

❋ In a medium saucepan, combine the cornmeal and water; bring to a boil over medium-high heat. Cook and stir for 10 to 15 minutes, or until the polenta is thick. Remove from the heat; stir in the Parmesan.

❋ Line a tray with wax paper; spoon the polenta onto the tray and spread to ½" thickness. Cover with plastic wrap and refrigerate for 20 minutes.

❋ Preheat the broiler. Cut the polenta into 12 small squares; place on a baking sheet. Coat with no-stick spray. Broil for 2 minutes. Turn and coat the other side with cooking spray. Broil for 2 minutes, or until the polenta turns slightly golden.

To make the tomato topping

❋ In a small bowl, combine the tomatoes, basil, roasted red peppers, oil, garlic, and red-pepper flakes. Let stand at room temperature for 20 minutes, stirring occasionally. Add the pepper and salt. Serve over the polenta.

ONION AND TOMATO QUESADILLAS

Traditional Mexican "sandwiches," quesadillas are fun and easy to serve to a crowd.

Makes 16

Per wedge
Calories 133
Total fat 3.5 g.
Saturated fat 1.2 g.
Cholesterol 4 mg.
Sodium 224 mg.
Fiber 1.2 g.

Cost per serving

71¢

2 medium onions, sliced
1 teaspoon olive oil
1 cup chopped tomatoes
⅓ cup chopped fresh cilantro or parsley
2 tablespoons minced jalapeño peppers
   (wear plastic gloves when handling)
8 flour tortillas (12" diameter)
¾ cup shredded low-fat Monterey Jack cheese

❋ Coat a 10" no-stick skillet with no-stick spray; set over medium-high heat. When the skillet is hot, add the onions and oil; cook and stir for 8 minutes, or until the onions are very soft and golden brown. Add the tomatoes, cilantro or parsley, and peppers; cook and stir for 5 minutes.

❋ Place 4 tortillas on a large baking sheet. Divide the onion mixture among them. Top with the Monterey Jack and the remaining tortillas.

❋ Preheat the broiler and broil the quesadillas until the cheese melts. (Alternatively, place each quesadilla on a microwave-safe plate and microwave on high power for 1 minute, or until the cheese melts.) Cut into wedges.

Appetizers
and Snacks

ONE
ONION

1/3 c.
CELERY

1/2 c.
APPLE JUICE

2 CLOVES
GARLIC

JUICE OF
2 ORANGES

Soups, Stews, and Chowders

These days, good soup recipes are hoarded as carefully as mutual funds. That's because a big bowl of comforting soup is one of the few ways to serve a table of hungry people for less than $1 a serving. Soup is the backbone of all good cooking, relying as it does on inexpensive ingredients, simple seasonings, and a richly flavored stock.

This chapter provides you with great recipes to stock up your refrigerator and freezer. See the recipes on pages 98 and 99 for three essential soup stocks to make first—each cup of homemade saves you 47 cents a serving over canned broths or instant bouillon cubes, besides trimming excess sodium and fat from your soup.

Add nutrient value, taste, and texture to the bowl with plenty of vegetables, beans, and whole grains flavored with small amounts of lean meat or poultry. All through the year, make soup a staple in your low-cost cooking repertoire.

Per serving
Calories 57
Total fat 0.4 g.
Saturated fat 0.1 g.
Cholesterol 2 mg.
Sodium 26 mg.
Fiber 1.6 g.

Cost per serving

58¢

SAVORY PUMPKIN SOUP

This surprisingly easy soup transforms a jack-o'-lantern into an autumn feast. Made from pureed sugar pumpkin, it's a great way to take advantage of Halloween sales and encourage your family to carve some nutrition from this vegetable that's rich in beta-carotene. Add festive flavor to the table by serving the soup in the scooped-out pumpkin. It'll stay hotter if you warm the pumpkin tureen in a 200°F oven for 20 minutes while you make the soup.

　1　large sugar pumpkin
　2　cups defatted chicken stock
　　　Juice of 2 oranges
　½　cup apple juice
　1　small onion, diced
　⅓　cup diced celery
　2　cloves garlic, minced
1½　teaspoons curry powder
　½　teaspoon ground cumin
　½　cup nonfat plain yogurt
　¼　cup chopped fresh parsley

❋ With a heavy knife, cut off the top third of the pumpkin. Scoop out the seeds; discard or reserve for another use. With a large kitchen spoon, scoop out 2½ cups of pumpkin pulp; place in a blender or food processor. Add the chicken stock and orange juice; puree.

❋ In a Dutch oven, bring the apple juice to a boil over medium-high heat. Add the onions, celery, and garlic; cook and stir for 10 minutes, or until the onions are soft but not browned. Add the curry powder and cumin; cook and stir for 1 minute. Add the pumpkin mixture; bring to a boil. Cook, stirring occasionally, for 10 minutes.

❋ Let the soup cool slightly; puree in batches in a blender or food processor. Stir in the yogurt. Serve sprinkled with the parsley.

TOAST THOSE SEEDS

Toasted pumpkin seeds make a great snack. Separate the seeds from the stringy membranes that surround them. Rinse and spread on a baking sheet; coat with no-stick spray and sprinkle with a small amount of reduced-sodium soy sauce. Bake at 300°F for 45 minutes, or until the seeds are golden brown and crunchy. Store in an airtight container.

SUNDAY CHICKEN SOUP

Chicken soup is Grandma's favorite for what ails you—and it's easy on the budget, too. This robust soup easily serves a family of four for dinner, plus it provides sumptuous leftovers for another meal. We keep it lean by removing the chicken skin (where two-thirds of the fat is) before making the soup.

Makes 8 servings

Per serving
Calories 133
Total fat 3.2 g.
Saturated fat 0.9 g.
Cholesterol 43 mg.
Sodium 188 mg.
Fiber 1.3 g.

Cost per serving

38¢

- 6 cups water
- 1 broiler-fryer chicken (3 pounds), skin and giblets removed
- 1 large carrot, coarsely chopped
- 1 large onion, quartered
- 1 stalk celery, coarsely chopped
- 2 bay leaves
- 1 large potato, thinly sliced
- 1 cup chopped canned reduced-sodium tomatoes (with juice)
- 1 cup chopped green cabbage
- ½ cup chopped celery leaves
- 1 teaspoon dried marjoram
- ¼ teaspoon ground coriander
- 1 teaspoon ground black pepper
- ½ teaspoon salt

❋ In a Dutch oven, combine the water, chicken, carrots, onions, celery, and bay leaves. Bring to a boil over medium-high heat. Reduce the heat to medium; cover and cook for 1 hour.

❋ Let the stock cool slightly, then strain it into a large bowl. As soon as the chicken is cool enough to handle, remove the meat from the bones. Cut the chicken and vegetables into small pieces; return to the Dutch oven along with the bay leaves. Add the potatoes, tomatoes (with juice), cabbage, celery leaves, marjoram, and coriander. Bring to a boil over medium-high heat; reduce the heat to medium. Cook, stirring occasionally, for 30 minutes, or until the potatoes are tender when pierced with a sharp knife. Remove and discard the bay leaves. Add the pepper and salt.

Soups, Stews, and Chowders

Per serving
Calories 247
Total fat 2.6 g.
Saturated fat 0.5 g.
Cholesterol 23 mg.
Sodium 226 mg.
Fiber 7.8 g.

Cost per serving

54¢

TURKEY AND VEGETABLE CHILI

This quick chili easily saves you $3 a serving over restaurant versions, plus it's got less than half the fat of most restaurant versions because lean turkey replaces the beef.

    8 ounces ground turkey breast
    ½ cup minced onions
    2 cloves garlic, minced
    2 cups cooked kidney beans (page 199)
    2 cups chopped canned reduced-sodium tomatoes
         (with juice)
    1 cup sliced carrots
    ½ cup diced red potatoes
    ½ cup defatted chicken stock
    4 teaspoons chili powder
    1 jalapeño pepper, seeded and chopped
         (wear plastic gloves when handling)
    ½ teaspoon ground black pepper
    ¼ teaspoon salt

❋ Coat a Dutch oven with no-stick spray; set it over medium-high heat. When the Dutch oven is hot, add the turkey; cook and stir for 5 minutes, or until no longer pink. Add the onions and garlic; cook and stir for 1 minute. Add the beans, tomatoes (with juice), carrots, potatoes, chicken stock, chili powder, and jalapeño peppers; bring to a boil. Lower the heat to medium; cover and cook for 20 minutes, or until the vegetables are soft. Add the pepper and salt.

Per serving
Calories 67
Total fat 3 g.
Saturated fat 0.9 g.
Cholesterol 113 mg.
Sodium 52 mg.
Fiber 0.2 g.

Cost per serving

29¢

GARLIC EGG-DROP SOUP

There are no out-of-the-ordinary or costly ingredients in this rich-tasting recipe from Asian cuisine—just items found in your local supermarket. A whole head of garlic creates a buttery flavor for the brothy soup. For an exotic touch, replace the soy sauce with an equal amount of Thai fish sauce.

    1 head garlic, broken into unpeeled cloves
    4 cups defatted chicken stock
    2 large eggs, lightly beaten
    ½ cup chopped fresh cilantro
    ¼ teaspoon ground red pepper
    ¼ teaspoon reduced-sodium soy sauce

* In a Dutch oven, combine the garlic and chicken stock. Bring to a boil over medium-high heat. Cook for 15 minutes. Remove the garlic with a slotted spoon; reserve for another use.

* With a chopstick or fork, stir the beaten eggs into the boiling stock. Add the cilantro, red pepper, and soy sauce.

GARLICKY PORK, POTATO, AND BEAN STEW

Call the garlic-lovers in your family! This stew delivers great flavor for just pennies. Only 8 ounces of lean pork is needed to serve 4 people when hearty potatoes and beans are used to extend the meat.

8   ounces boneless pork loin roast, trimmed of fat and cut into ½" cubes
1   cup chopped onions
1   cup chopped carrots
1   cup diced red potatoes
1   cup cooked pinto beans (page 199)
4   large cloves garlic, minced
¼   cup all-purpose flour
3   cups defatted chicken stock
½   teaspoon dried thyme
½   teaspoon ground black pepper
¼   teaspoon salt
½   cup nonfat sour cream

* Coat a Dutch oven with no-stick spray; set it over medium-high heat. When the Dutch oven is hot, add the pork and onions; cook and stir for 5 minutes. Add the carrots, potatoes, beans, garlic, and flour; cook and stir for 1 minute. Add ½ cup of the chicken stock; cook and stir for 2 minutes. Add the thyme and the remaining 2½ cups stock; bring to a boil. Cook for 20 minutes, or until the stew is thick and the pork is no longer pink in the center. (Check by cutting into 1 cube.) Add the pepper and salt. Top each serving with the sour cream.

Makes 4 servings

Per serving
Calories 258
Total fat 3.7 g.
Saturated fat 1.2 g.
Cholesterol 29 mg.
Sodium 188 mg.
Fiber 4.8 g.

Cost per serving

51¢

Soups, Stews, and Chowders

Northwoods Soup

Canadian northwoods folk rely on this warming cheese soup to revive them after a day spent outdoors. The creamy base is made from aromatic vegetables, flour, and milk, cutting the amount of cheese needed in half and reducing the fat.

Makes 4 servings

Per serving
Calories 197
Total fat 5.7 g.
Saturated fat 2.6 g.
Cholesterol 18 mg.
Sodium 519 mg.
Fiber 1.9 g.

Cost per serving

32¢

¼ cup minced onions
¼ cup minced carrots
¼ cup minced celery
2 tablespoons apple juice
1 teaspoon oil
¼ cup all-purpose flour
2 cups skim milk
2 cups defatted chicken stock
½ cup cooked navy beans (page 199)
½ teaspoon ground black pepper
¼ teaspoon salt
½ cup shredded low-fat extra-sharp Cheddar cheese
¼ cup grated Parmesan cheese
½ teaspoon paprika

✿ In a Dutch oven, combine the onions, carrots, celery, apple juice, and oil; cook and stir over medium-high heat for 3 to 5 minutes, or until the vegetables soften slightly. Reduce the heat to low. Add the flour; cook and stir for 2 minutes. Gradually add the milk, whisking constantly; cook and stir for 2 minutes, or until the soup thickens slightly.

✿ Add the chicken stock, beans, pepper, and salt; cook and stir for 10 minutes, watching carefully to avoid scorching. Add the Cheddar and Parmesan; cook and stir for 2 minutes, or until the cheeses melt. Serve sprinkled with the paprika.

ORANGE-CARROT SOUP WITH GINGER

Soup this elegant can cost $3 a bowl in a restaurant; you save over $2.50 per person serving it at home. The rich stock is made extra flavorful by simmering whole garlic in it for 20 minutes. A great inexpensive starter for a company meal, this soup goes well with broiled fish or chicken, a large green salad, and crusty French bread.

2 heads garlic, broken into unpeeled cloves
4 cups defatted chicken stock
1 cup chopped onions
1 cup chopped carrots
1 cup diced potatoes
¼ cup chopped raw almonds
1 tablespoon frozen orange juice concentrate
1 tablespoon honey
2 teaspoons grated fresh ginger

❁ Place the garlic cloves in a large metal teaball or wrap in a small piece of cheesecloth and tie with kitchen string. Place in a Dutch oven. Add the chicken stock, onions, carrots, and potatoes; bring to a boil over medium-high heat. Reduce the heat to medium; cover and cook for 20 minutes.

❁ Let the soup cool slightly. Remove the garlic; reserve for another use. Pour the soup into a blender or food processor. Add the almonds; puree until very smooth. Return the soup to the pot; heat through. Add the orange juice concentrate, honey, and ginger.

Makes 4 servings

Per serving
Calories 190
Total fat 4.9 g.
Saturated fat 0.6 g.
Cholesterol 6 mg.
Sodium 24 mg.
Fiber 3.5 g.

Cost per serving

43¢

KITCHEN TIP

Most frozen juice concentrates have snap-off metal lids, so spoonfuls of frozen concentrate can be measured right out of the container. Replace the lid and keep the rest frozen right in the original container.

Soups, Stews, and Chowders

Per serving
Calories 73
Total fat 0.9 g.
Saturated fat 0.1 g.
Cholesterol 2 mg.
Sodium 144 mg.
Fiber 3.6 g.

Cost per serving

55¢

TOMATO DILL SOUP

Instead of donating your abundant tomato harvest to the neighbors, spend a few minutes making enough of this summery soup to freeze for winter menus. Each time you use this gourmet recipe, you save 10¢ per serving over store-bought versions—and get a better product.

4 cups chopped fresh tomatoes
2 cups defatted chicken or vegetable stock
2 onions, minced
1 cup diced sweet red peppers
¼ cup diced celery
2 tablespoons chopped mild green chili peppers,
     such as Anaheim
2 cloves garlic, minced
2 tablespoons chopped fresh parsley or cilantro
2 teaspoons chopped fresh dill
½ teaspoon ground red pepper
½ teaspoon salt
¼ teaspoon ground black pepper
¼ teaspoon ground cumin

❋ In a Dutch oven, combine the tomatoes, chicken stock, onions, red peppers, celery, chili peppers, and garlic; bring to a boil over medium-high heat. Reduce the heat to medium; cover and cook for 35 minutes.

❋ Let the soup cool slightly. Pour into a blender or food processor; puree in batches. Add the parsley or cilantro, dill, ground red pepper, salt, pepper, and cumin. Process briefly to combine. Return the mixture to the Dutch oven. Cook over medium-high heat for 2 to 3 minutes to heat through.

COOK IT QUICKER

Using a large surface speeds sautéing and cooking of most soups; that's why the recipes in this book call for a Dutch oven—a large, double-handled cooking pot. The heavy-bottomed pot distributes the heat evenly. Dutch ovens like these last a lifetime and are worth the initial investment.

WINTER PESTO SOUP

Unless it's home grown, fresh basil can be a scarce ingredient in thrifty menus. So we developed a basil-flavored spinach and parsley pesto for this sensational Mediterranean soup. You won't even taste the difference, but you'll save 50¢ a serving.

1 cup diced potatoes
1 cup diced butternut squash
1 large carrot, chopped
1 large onion, thinly sliced
½ cup chopped celery leaves
⅓ cup chopped scallions
1 teaspoon olive oil
4 cups defatted chicken stock
1 cup cooked navy beans (page 199)
1 cup cooked chick-peas (page 199)
½ cup broken spaghetti
2 tablespoons tomato paste
1 cup chopped spinach leaves
½ cup minced fresh parsley
2 tablespoons dried basil
2 cloves garlic, minced
1 tablespoon grated Parmesan cheese

❀ In a Dutch oven, combine the potatoes, squash, carrots, onions, celery leaves, scallions, and oil; cook and stir over medium-high heat for 3 minutes. Add the chicken stock, beans, and chick-peas; bring to a boil. Lower the heat to medium; cover and cook, stirring occasionally, for 30 minutes, or until the potatoes and squash are soft when pierced with a sharp knife.

❀ Stir in the spaghetti and tomato paste; cook and stir for 5 minutes, or until the spaghetti is tender.

❀ Meanwhile, in a food processor or blender, combine the spinach, parsley, basil, garlic, and Parmesan; puree. Stir into the soup.

Makes 4 servings

Per serving
Calories 312
Total fat 3.9 g.
Saturated fat 0.8 g.
Cholesterol 7.4 mg.
Sodium 134 mg.
Fiber 7.3 g.

Cost per serving

48¢

Per serving
Calories 105
Total fat 2.6 g.
Saturated fat 0.7 g.
Cholesterol 6 mg.
Sodium 92 mg.
Fiber 1.7 g.

Cost per serving

24¢

PEANUT SOUP WITH CURRY

To reduce the fat in this traditional African soup, we replace all but a tablespoon of peanut butter with low-fat buttermilk and plenty of spices, which create a creamy base with rich flavor.

¼ cup apple juice
1 cup chopped onions
1 cup chopped carrots
½ cup diced potatoes
2 cloves garlic, minced
1 tablespoon sugar
1 teaspoon curry powder
1 teaspoon ground cumin
½ teaspoon ground red pepper
½ teaspoon ground cinnamon
¼ teaspoon ground cloves
4 cups defatted chicken stock
1 tablespoon peanut butter
1½ cups low-fat buttermilk
¼ cup chopped fresh parsley
½ teaspoon chopped raw peanuts

❀ In a Dutch oven, bring the apple juice to a boil over medium-high heat. Add the onions, carrots, potatoes, and garlic; cook and stir for 3 minutes. Add the sugar, curry powder, cumin, red pepper, cinnamon, and cloves; cook and stir for 1 minute. Add the chicken stock and peanut butter; bring to a boil. Lower the heat to medium; cook, stirring occasionally, for 30 minutes.

❀ Let the soup cool slightly; pour into a blender or food processor. Add the buttermilk; puree in batches. Return the soup to the pot; heat through. Top each serving with the chopped parsley and peanuts.

WHY SAUTÉ SOUP VEGETABLES?

Many chefs versed in low-fat cooking recommend quickly sautéing soup vegetables before adding them to stock. Why? Because certain aromatic vegetables, like onions, garlic, carrots, and celery, only release their sweeter flavors when sautéed. With low-fat cooking, there's less fat to make vegetables taste rich, so a five-minute sauté fills in background flavor and keeps your hand away from the salt shaker.

CHILLED BEET SOUP WITH ORANGE

Makes 4 servings

Per serving
Calories 264
Total fat 2.3 g.
Saturated fat 0.4 g.
Cholesterol 7 mg.
Sodium 285 mg.
Fiber 10.6 g.

Cost per serving

94¢

Beat the heat during the dog days of summer with this easy puree of root vegetables sweetened with orange. If you can wait that long, let it stand overnight in the refrigerator. It gets even more flavorful as the seasonings blend. Scrub the beets well but don't bother peeling them—they cook up soft and sweet.

⅓ cup apple juice
 1 teaspoon olive oil
 4 cups chopped beets
 2 cups chopped onions
 1 cup chopped carrots
 2 cloves garlic, minced
 4 cups defatted chicken stock
 2 tablespoons honey or sugar
 1 teaspoon cider vinegar
 4 large oranges
½ teaspoon ground black pepper
⅛ teaspoon salt
½ cup nonfat plain yogurt

❋ In a Dutch oven, bring the apple juice and oil to a boil over medium-high heat. Add the beets, onions, carrots, and garlic; cook and stir for 5 minutes, or until the onions are soft but not browned. Add the chicken stock, honey or sugar, and vinegar; bring to a boil. Lower the heat to medium and cook for 30 minutes, or until the beets are very soft when pierced with a sharp knife.

❋ Meanwhile, grate 1 tablespoon of orange rind and reserve. Squeeze the juice from the oranges and set aside.

❋ Let the soup cool slightly; pour into a blender or food processor. Add the orange juice; puree. Refrigerate for 3 hours, or until cold. Add the pepper and salt. Stir yogurt into each serving, swirling slightly. Sprinkle each serving with the orange rind.

Per serving
Calories 143
Total fat 2 g.
Saturated fat 0.3 g.
Cholesterol 49 mg.
Sodium 135 mg.
Fiber 1.4 g.

Cost per serving

97¢

KITCHEN TIP

You can substitute
3 cups of defatted
chicken stock and
3 cups of water
for the fish stock.

FISH CHOWDER WITH CUCUMBERS

This clear chowder is a favorite summer meal for savings-conscious Ukrainians, who serve it with hearty slices of rye bread and homemade pickles. You can use any fish that's on sale—the simple seasonings of tomato, onion, and cucumber enhance any mild white fish.

1½	pounds cod or haddock
⅔	cup chopped onions
⅔	cup chopped celery
⅔	cup chopped carrots
1	teaspoon olive oil
6¾	cups fish stock
¼	cup white wine or water
1	cup chopped tomatoes
1	cup peeled, seeded, and sliced cucumbers
2	tablespoons lemon juice
¼	teaspoon ground black pepper
⅛	teaspoon salt

✺ In a Dutch oven, combine the fish, onions, celery, carrots, and oil; cook and stir over medium-high heat for 1 minute. Add ¾ cup of the stock and the wine or water; cook and stir for 5 minutes. Add the remaining 6 cups stock; bring to a boil. Cook for 20 minutes, stirring occasionally, or until the vegetables are soft.

✺ Remove from the heat; add the tomatoes, cucumbers, lemon juice, pepper, and salt.

Per serving
Calories 124
Total fat 0.7 g.
Saturated fat 0.2 g.
Cholesterol 1 mg.
Sodium 32 mg.
Fiber 2.1 g.

Cost per serving

49¢

SWEET CHILLED STRAWBERRY SOUP

Our favorite soup to make in June when strawberries are less than $1 a pint at the local U-Pick, this 5-minute mix of yogurt, bananas, fruit juices, and sweet berries is as refreshing as a cool breeze.

4	cups sliced strawberries
2	cups apple juice
¼	cup sugar
½	cup low-fat buttermilk
½	cup orange juice
½	tablespoon lemon juice
¼	cup nonfat plain yogurt
1	tablespoon chopped fresh mint

In a medium saucepan, combine the strawberries, apple juice, and sugar; bring to a boil over medium-high heat. Cook and stir for 5 minutes. Let the soup cool slightly; pour into a blender or food processor. Add the buttermilk and orange juice; puree. Refrigerate for 2 hours, or until the soup is very cold. Add the lemon juice. Top each serving with a dollop of the yogurt and a sprinkle of the mint.

SPICY WINTER SQUASH AND CHICKEN STEW

Orange winter squash gives plenty of flavor and a bonus of beta-carotene to this hearty cold-weather stew. To make it easy to peel the squash, pierce it and microwave it on high power for 10 minutes.

½ cup apple juice
1 teaspoon olive oil
4 chicken thighs, skinned, boned, trimmed of fat, and cubed
1 cup chopped onions
1 tablespoon minced garlic
3 cups peeled and cubed butternut squash
2 cups defatted chicken stock
1 cup cubed red potatoes
½ cup chopped carrots
¼ cup pitted prunes
1 tablespoon canned diced green chili peppers
2 teaspoons curry powder
¼ teaspoon ground red pepper
½ teaspoon salt
½ teaspoon ground black pepper

In a Dutch oven, combine the apple juice and oil; bring to a boil over medium-high heat. Add the chicken, onions, and garlic; cook and stir for 5 minutes. Add the squash, chicken stock, potatoes, carrots, prunes, chili peppers, curry powder, and red pepper; bring to a boil. Lower the heat to medium; cover and cook for 35 minutes, or until the stew is thick and the vegetables are tender. Add the salt and pepper.

Makes 4 servings

Per serving
Calories 307
Total fat 7.3 g.
Saturated fat 1.8 g.
Cholesterol 52 mg.
Sodium 328 mg.
Fiber 5.8 g.

Cost per serving

74¢

HOMEMADE STOCKS FOR SOUPS AND STEWS

Making your own stock not only saves money but also lets you control the sodium and fat content of your soups. Cook the stock in an uncovered Dutch oven to allow some of the water to evaporate and the flavors to concentrate. Each of the following recipes will provide you with about 12 cups of soup stock. You can save time by cooking a double batch and freezing the extra stock in 1-cup containers.

VEGETABLE STOCK

14 cups water
4 stalks celery (with leaves), chopped
4 carrots, chopped
1 cup chopped green cabbage
1 cup mushrooms
1 onion, chopped
12 cloves garlic
10 sprigs parsley
2 bay leaves

⬤ In a Dutch oven, combine the water, celery, carrots, cabbage, mushrooms, onions, garlic, parsley, and bay leaves; bring to a boil over medium-high heat. Lower the heat to medium; cook for 1 hour, or until the stock is golden brown. Strain the stock through a colander, pressing the vegetables lightly to extract their flavor. Discard the vegetables.

CHICKEN STOCK

14 cups water
4 pounds chicken pieces (thighs, drumsticks, backs, and necks)
2 large carrots, quartered
2 small onions, unpeeled
6 cloves garlic
2 bay leaves

(continued)

Makes 12 cups

Per 1 cup
Calories 2
Total fat 0 g.
Saturated fat 0 g.
Cholesterol 0 mg.
Sodium 2 mg.
Fiber 0.1 g.

Cost per serving

3¢

Makes 12 cups

Per 1 cup
Calories 14
Total fat 0.4 g.
Saturated fat 0.1 g.
Cholesterol 6 mg.
Sodium 6 mg.
Fiber 0.1 g.

Cost per serving

13¢

Soups, Stews, and Chowders

In a Dutch oven, combine the water, chicken, carrots, onions, garlic, and bay leaves; bring to a boil over medium-high heat. Skim the foam from the top; reduce the heat to low. Cook for 2 hours, or until the stock has a rich chicken flavor.

Strain the stock through a colander, pressing the ingredients to extract their flavor. Save the chicken for another use; discard the vegetables. Refrigerate the stock overnight; skim off and discard any solidified fat before using.

FISH STOCK

14 cups water
 2 pounds fish heads or fish bones
 2 large carrots, quartered
 2 small onions, unpeeled
 6 cloves garlic
 2 bay leaves

In a Dutch oven, combine the water, fish heads or bones, carrots, onions, garlic, and bay leaves; bring to a boil over medium-high heat. Skim the foam from the top; reduce the heat to low. Cook for 2 hours, or until the stock has a rich fish flavor.

Strain the stock through a colander, pressing the ingredients to extract their flavor. Discard the solids. Refrigerate the stock overnight; skim off any solidified fat before using.

Makes 12 cups

Per 1 cup
Calories 10
Total fat 0.3 g.
Saturated fat 0 g.
Cholesterol 0 mg.
Sodium 0 mg.
Fiber 0 g.

Cost per serving
2¢

KITCHEN TIP

Ask for free fish bones or fish heads at your fish market. Shrimp shells also make a flavorful stock. Use in addition to or in place of the fish bones.

KITCHEN TIP

Cornstarch is stirred into low-fat or nonfat sour cream before adding it to hot soups in order to keep the sour cream from separating. It's a chef's trick that works every time.

RUSSIAN POTATO AND BEAN STEW

Sauerkraut gives authentic Russian flavor to this hearty winter stew. Look for reduced-sodium sauerkraut in the supermarket, then rinse and drain it before using. Serve for lunch or supper with whole-grain bread and salad.

½ cup water or apple juice
1 teaspoon olive oil
3 russet potatoes, cubed
1 large onion, thinly sliced
5 cups defatted chicken stock
8 ounces green beans, cut into 1" pieces
⅓ cup low-fat sour cream
2 tablespoons all-purpose flour
1 teaspoon cornstarch
¾ cup reduced-sodium sauerkraut, rinsed and drained
1 teaspoon dried dillweed
¾ teaspoon ground black pepper

* In a Dutch oven, bring the water or apple juice and oil to a boil over medium-high heat; add the potatoes and onions. Cook and stir for 5 minutes. Add the chicken stock and beans; bring to a boil. Lower the heat to medium; cover and cook for 1 hour.

* In a small bowl, combine the sour cream, flour, and cornstarch. Add to the hot stew by spoonfuls, stirring with a large spoon. Add the sauerkraut and dillweed; cook for 15 minutes, or until the stew is thick. Add the pepper.

STORING SOUPS

Most soups have a long storage life in the freezer. You can keep vegetable soups 4 months, poultry or fish soups 3 months, and meat soups 2 months without loss of flavor. Be sure to avoid thawing and refreezing, because bacteria can develop. Thaw frozen soups overnight in the refrigerator. Red potatoes tend to get mushy when frozen; use baking potatoes if you're making soup to freeze.

VEGETABLE BORSCHT

Try this favorite Russian way to harvest leftover vegetables at summer's end—or to clean out the vegetable drawer. Borscht's satisfying flavor comes from a careful combination of honey, vinegar, and spices. The hearty texture comes from plenty of potatoes and beets—and you don't need to peel the beets first.

Makes 8 servings

Per serving
Calories 156
Total fat 0.6 g.
Saturated fat 0.1 g.
Cholesterol 4 mg.
Sodium 141 mg.
Fiber 4.8 g.

Cost per serving

42¢

3	cups chopped green cabbage
2	cups thinly sliced onions
1½	cups diced beets
1½	cups diced red potatoes
1	cup diced carrots
¼	cup dry sherry or orange juice
5	cups defatted chicken stock
1	cup canned reduced-sodium tomato puree
½	cup chopped celery
½	cup whole kernel corn
2	tablespoons vinegar
2	tablespoons honey or sugar
1	teaspoon crushed caraway seeds
½	teaspoon ground black pepper
¼	teaspoon salt
½	cup nonfat plain yogurt
¼	teaspoon dried dillweed

✺ In a Dutch oven, combine the cabbage, onions, beets, potatoes, carrots, and sherry or orange juice; cook and stir over medium-high heat for 3 minutes. Add the chicken stock, tomato puree, celery, corn, vinegar, honey or sugar, and caraway seeds; bring to a boil. Reduce the heat to medium; cook, stirring occasionally, for 30 minutes, or until the beets are very soft when pierced with a sharp knife.

✺ Add the pepper and salt. Top each serving with a dollop of the yogurt and a sprinkle of the dillweed.

101

Per serving
Calories 214
Total fat 2 g.
Saturated fat 0.3 g.
Cholesterol 6 mg.
Sodium 105 mg.
Fiber 3 g.

Cost per serving

67¢

MEXICAN CORN STEW

Corn season in many regions gives a dozen delicious ears for $1.99, so you have plenty of reason to make this hearty, slightly spicy stew for dinner. We cook the beans with the stock to take advantage of the robust flavor released in the starch—but if you're in a hurry, make this soup with precooked beans and cut the cooking time in half.

- 1 teaspoon olive oil
- 1 cup chopped onions
- ½ cup thinly sliced carrots
- ½ cup thinly sliced celery
- 1 small sweet red pepper or green pepper, diced
- 3 small jalapeño peppers, seeded and diced (wear plastic gloves when handling)
- 1 tablespoon minced garlic
- 6 cups defatted chicken stock
- 2 cups whole kernel corn
- 1 cup dried pinto beans
- 3 tablespoons minced fresh parsley or cilantro
- 2 teaspoons ground cumin
- 2 teaspoons ground coriander
- ½ teaspoon ground red pepper
- ⅛ teaspoon salt
- ⅛ teaspoon ground black pepper

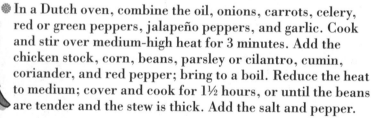

❋ In a Dutch oven, combine the oil, onions, carrots, celery, red or green peppers, jalapeño peppers, and garlic. Cook and stir over medium-high heat for 3 minutes. Add the chicken stock, corn, beans, parsley or cilantro, cumin, coriander, and red pepper; bring to a boil. Reduce the heat to medium; cover and cook for 1½ hours, or until the beans are tender and the stew is thick. Add the salt and pepper.

HOLD THE SALT!
SEASONING TIPS
FOR SUPER SOUPS

Seasoning mixes from the store are not only three times more expensive than home-made but also salted with a heavy hand, making them too high in sodium for everyday use. Skilled cooks learn how to season homemade soups and stews with combinations of fresh or dried herbs and spices, augmented with small amounts of salt when needed. A pinch or a dash of any of these seasoning mixes can turn a simple stock into a wonderful soup.

Seasoning mixes keep for about 6 months in a dark cupboard at room temperature; or store them for up to 1 year in the freezer in small sealed containers.

* *French.* Combine 1 teaspoon dried tarragon, 1 teaspoon dried parsley, ½ teaspoon garlic powder, ½ teaspoon ground black pepper, and ¼ teaspoon salt. Use in creamy vegetable soups.

* *Indian.* Combine 1 tablespoon mild curry powder, ½ teaspoon ground cinnamon, ½ teaspoon ground cumin, ½ teaspoon ground coriander, ¼ teaspoon turmeric, and ¼ teaspoon ground red pepper. Use in winter squash or vegetable soups.

* *Mediterranean.* Combine 1 tablespoon dried basil, 2 teaspoons dried oregano, 1 teaspoon dried marjoram, ½ teaspoon ground black pepper, and 1 teaspoon garlic powder. Use in tomato-based soups and stews.

* *Middle Eastern.* Combine 1 tablespoon paprika, ½ teaspoon turmeric, ½ teaspoon ground black pepper, ¼ teaspoon ground red pepper, and ¼ teaspoon salt. Use in chicken, pork, beef, bean, and grain-based stews.

* *Southwestern.* Combine 1 tablespoon paprika, 2 teaspoons ground coriander, 2 teaspoons ground cumin, 2 teaspoons dried oregano, 1 teaspoon chili powder, ½ to 1 teaspoon ground red pepper, and 1 teaspoon garlic powder. Use in chicken, beef, or vegetable soups and stews.

Per serving
Calories 89
Total fat 1.8 g.
Saturated fat 0.3 g.
Cholesterol 0 mg.
Sodium 156 mg.
Fiber 2 g.

Cost per serving

50¢

RATATOUILLE STEW

Garden alert! Raid the vines for this savory dish: a thick Mediterranean stew of fresh vegetables and herbs. Add French bread and a green salad for a great meal at under $1 a serving.

  1 teaspoon olive oil
  ½ cup chopped onions
  1 green pepper, chopped
  3 cloves garlic, minced
  1 can (28 ounces) reduced-sodium tomatoes (with juice)
  2 cups peeled and cubed eggplant
  1 medium zucchini, chopped
  1 cup water
  ½ cup broken spaghetti
  1 teaspoon dried basil
  ¾ teaspoon dried oregano
  ¼ teaspoon salt
  ¼ teaspoon ground black pepper

❀ Coat a Dutch oven with no-stick spray; add the oil and set it over medium-high heat. When the oil is hot, add the onions, green peppers, and garlic; cook and stir for 5 minutes. Add the tomatoes (with juice), eggplant, zucchini, water, spaghetti, basil, and oregano. Bring to a boil; lower the heat to medium. Cover and cook for 25 minutes, or until the stew is thick, stirring occasionally. Add the salt and pepper.

Makes 4 servings

Per serving
Calories 172
Total fat 1.3 g.
Saturated fat 0.5 g.
Cholesterol 8 mg.
Sodium 219 mg.
Fiber 2.8 g.

Cost per serving

31¢

POTATO, LEEK, AND PARSLEY CHOWDER

This economical chowder gets its creamy texture from pureed potatoes rather than cream or butter. We recommend yellow potatoes (often on sale in the fall) because of their buttery flavor, but red potatoes work equally well.

  4 cups defatted chicken stock
  2 cups chopped yellow or red potatoes
  1 cup sliced leeks
  1 medium onion, finely chopped
  1 cup low-fat buttermilk
  ⅓ cup chopped fresh parsley
  ½ teaspoon ground black pepper
  ¼ teaspoon salt
  1 tablespoon chopped fresh chives

* In a Dutch oven, combine the chicken stock, potatoes, leeks, and onions; bring to a boil over medium-high heat. Cover and cook, stirring occasionally, for 35 minutes, or until the potatoes are very soft when pierced with a sharp knife.

* Let the soup cool slightly. Pour into a blender or food processor; puree. Add the buttermilk, parsley, pepper, and salt. Serve sprinkled with the chives.

Spicy Black Bean Stew

At less than 15¢ a cup, cooked beans are a thrifty, low-fat protein. This stylish stew sells for $4 a bowl in San Francisco restaurants. At home it costs you less than $1 a serving.

¼ cup orange juice
1½ cups chopped onions
 1 small sweet red pepper, chopped
 2 tablespoons minced garlic
 3 cups defatted chicken stock
 3 cups diced canned reduced-sodium tomatoes
      (with juice)
 2 cups cooked black beans (page 199)
 1 cup diced carrots
 1 cup diced red potatoes
 1 stalk celery, diced
 1 cup tomato juice
 1 tablespoon chili powder
½ teaspoon ground red pepper
⅓ cup minced fresh parsley
¼ cup shredded low-fat mozzarella cheese
½ cup crushed baked tortilla chips

* In a Dutch oven, combine the orange juice, onions, red peppers, and garlic; cook and stir over medium-high heat for 5 minutes. Add the chicken stock, tomatoes (with juice), beans, carrots, potatoes, celery, tomato juice, chili powder, and ground red pepper; bring to a boil. Lower the heat to medium; cover and cook for 1 hour, or until the stew is thick. Add the parsley. Top each serving with the mozzarella and chips.

Kitchen Tip

How do you clean a leek? It's easy. Slice off the root end, then slit the leek from top to bottom. Holding the cut side under running water, fan the layers and allow any sand to rinse out. Then slice each half into thin half-circles.

Makes 4 servings

Per serving
Calories 349
Total fat 3.4 g.
Saturated fat 1.1 g.
Cholesterol 8 mg.
Sodium 366 mg.
Fiber 10.5 g.

Cost per serving

78¢

CHAPTER 5

POULTRY AND EGG DISHES

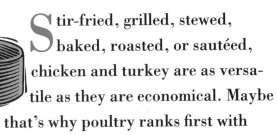

Stir-fried, grilled, stewed, baked, roasted, or sautéed, chicken and turkey are as versatile as they are economical. Maybe that's why poultry ranks first with families looking for affordable main dishes full of lean protein. Poultry can be dressed up with sauces or kept simple—and offered every night of the week without serving the same dish twice.

And it's hard to beat eggs for economy or nutrition. For less than 10 cents apiece, you get all the essential amino acids, only 5 grams of fat, and a versatile protein that can be cooked in a variety of ways. According to the American Heart Association, you can safely eat up to four eggs a week. Eggs are rising to the top of the value charts again as an occasional addition to a well-balanced eating plan.

Bring chicken, turkey, and egg dishes to the dinner table any night of the week, and you get sure value for your food dollar.

Per serving
(with white meat)
Calories 368
Total fat 5.5 g.
Saturated fat 1.2 g.
Cholesterol 55 mg.
Sodium 543 mg.
Fiber 5.2 g.

Per serving
(with dark meat)
Calories 356
Total fat 6.7 g.
Saturated fat 1.6 g.
Cholesterol 41 mg.
Sodium 533 mg.
Fiber 5.2 g.

Cost per serving

76¢

LOUISIANA CHICKEN AND BEANS

This Creole-style dinner is especially warming on a cold night. Instead of expensive filé powder (the traditional gumbo spice of ground sassafras leaves), we substitute chili pepper, bay leaf, and thyme.

- 1 broiler-fryer chicken (about 3 pounds)
- 2 tablespoons all-purpose flour
- 1 teaspoon vegetable oil
- ¼ cup white wine or apple juice
- 1 medium onion, chopped
- 5 scallions, chopped
- ½ dried red chili pepper
- 1 bay leaf
- 1 clove garlic, minced
- 1 teaspoon dried thyme
- 3 cups defatted chicken stock
- 3 cups hot cooked pinto beans (page 199)
- ¼ cup chopped fresh parsley
- ¼ cup medium-hot salsa
- ¾ teaspoon ground black pepper
- ½ teaspoon salt
- ½ loaf French bread, sliced

❋ Skin and cut the chicken into 6 serving pieces, saving any extra pieces for stock. Dredge the chicken in the flour; set aside. Coat a Dutch oven with no-stick spray; set it over medium-high heat. Add the oil; when the oil is hot, add the chicken. Cook for 5 minutes; turn and cook for 3 minutes more, or until light brown. Transfer the chicken to a plate.

❋ Add the wine or apple juice, scraping to loosen any browned bits. Add the onions, scallions, chili pepper, bay leaf, garlic, and thyme; cook and stir for 5 minutes. Add the chicken and chicken stock; cover and cook for 1 hour.

❋ Add the beans, parsley, and salsa; cook for 1 minute. Add the pepper and salt. Remove and discard the bay leaf. Serve with the French bread.

ROAST CHICKEN WITH LEMON-GINGER SAUCE

Lemons and fresh ginger lend extraordinary flavor to this easy roast chicken; the lemon juice also keeps the chicken moist while roasting. There's no need to peel fresh ginger before grating it, especially if it's thin-skinned.

1 roasting chicken (about 3 pounds)
2 tablespoons grated fresh ginger
¾ teaspoon ground black pepper
¼ teaspoon salt
2 lemons, halved
4 cloves garlic, halved
2 tablespoons reduced-sodium soy sauce

✳ Preheat the oven to 400°F. Wash the chicken and pat it dry; place it in a roasting pan. Rub the chicken with the ginger, pepper, and salt. Squeeze the lemons over the chicken; pack the lemon halves and garlic into the chicken cavity. Drizzle the chicken with the soy sauce.

✳ Roast the chicken for 2 hours, or until it is no longer pink in the center. Check by inserting a sharp knife in the thigh joint. Transfer the chicken to a platter and cover to keep warm. Skim the fat from the roasting pan. Add ¼ cup water to the pan, stirring to loosen any browned bits. Transfer the pan juices to a saucepan; cook and stir over medium-high heat for 5 minutes, or until reduced by half.

✳ Remove the chicken skin; discard. Serve the pan juices over the chicken.

Makes 4 servings

**Per serving
(with white meat)**
Calories 183
Total fat 4.4 g.
Saturated fat 1.2 g.
Cholesterol 78 mg.
Sodium 471 mg.
Fiber 0.7 g.

**Per serving
(with dark meat)**
Calories 164
Total fat 6.1 g.
Saturated fat 1.6 g.
Cholesterol 56 mg.
Sodium 456 mg.
Fiber 0.7 g.

Cost per serving

82¢

BALSAMIC CHICKEN THIGHS WITH VEGETABLES

Makes 4 servings

Per serving
Calories 441
Total fat 11.1 g.
Saturated fat 3.1 g.
Cholesterol 94 mg.
Sodium 115 mg.
Fiber 4.6 g.

Cost per serving

86¢

Your whole house will smell like Thanksgiving dinner is cooking with this roast chicken dinner. You can easily double this recipe and freeze extra portions for up to one month for fast weeknight dinners.

8 bone-in chicken thighs, skinned
1 cup thinly sliced onions
1 cup defatted chicken stock
2 cups quartered red potatoes
2 medium carrots, quartered
¼ cup balsamic vinegar
1 tablespoon minced garlic
1 teaspoon dried thyme
¼ teaspoon dried sage
2 cups yolk-free egg noodles

✸ Preheat the oven to 400°F. Coat a Dutch oven with no-stick spray; set it over medium-high heat. When the Dutch oven is hot, add the chicken thighs, onions, and ¼ cup of the chicken stock. Cook for 3 minutes; turn and cook for 3 minutes more. Add the potatoes, carrots, vinegar, garlic, thyme, sage, and the remaining ¾ cup stock.

✸ Bake for 40 minutes, or until the chicken is no longer pink in the center and the vegetables are soft. Check by inserting the tip of a sharp knife into 1 thigh.

✸ Meanwhile, cook the noodles according to the package directions.

✸ To serve, divide the chicken and vegetables among 4 plates; arrange the noodles alongside. Drizzle with the cooking liquid.

CHICKEN SATAY WITH CURRY SAUCE

This Indonesian street food is a favorite summer dinner because it's so easy and inexpensive to make. Start the satay kabobs marinating the night before, then grill or broil them the next evening. When reduced in a saucepan over high heat, the marinade becomes the base for a creamy curry-flavored dipping sauce.

Makes 4 servings

Per serving
Calories 371
Total fat 4.4 g.
Saturated fat 1.2 g.
Cholesterol 74 mg.
Sodium 233 mg.
Fiber 1.4 g.

Cost per serving

73¢

- 1 tablespoon reduced-sodium soy sauce
- 1 tablespoon honey
- 1 teaspoon lemon juice or lime juice
- ¼ teaspoon crushed red-pepper flakes
- 1 teaspoon peanut butter
- ½ teaspoon cornstarch
- 1 teaspoon curry powder
- 4 chicken breast halves, skinned, boned, and cut into ½" strips
- ½ small onion, diced
- 1 carrot, diced
- 3 cups defatted chicken stock
- 1 cup long-grain white rice
- ½ cup nonfat plain yogurt

✱ In a shallow nonmetal dish, combine the soy sauce, honey, lemon or lime juice, red-pepper flakes, peanut butter, cornstarch, and curry powder; mix well. Add the chicken; toss to coat. Cover and refrigerate for at least 4 hours, or up to 24; stir occasionally.

✱ Coat a medium saucepan with no-stick spray; set it over medium-high heat. Add the onions and carrots; cook and stir for 5 minutes. Add the chicken stock and rice; bring to a boil. Reduce the heat to low; cover and cook for 15 minutes, or until the stock is absorbed and the rice is tender.

✱ Meanwhile, preheat the grill or broiler. Thread the chicken onto skewers; save the marinade. Grill or broil 4" from the heat for 5 minutes; turn and cook for 5 minutes more, or until the chicken is no longer pink in the center. Check by inserting the tip of a sharp knife into 1 breast.

✱ While the chicken is cooking, transfer the marinade to a saucepan; cook and stir over high heat for 5 minutes, or until the marinade is reduced by half. Cool slightly; add the yogurt. Serve the satay over the rice with the yogurt sauce on the side.

Per serving
Calories 237
Total fat 5.4 g.
Saturated fat 1.2 g.
Cholesterol 69 mg.
Sodium 347 mg.
Fiber 1.5 g.

Cost per serving

96¢

SESAME CHICKEN SAUTÉ WITH NOODLES

A tiny amount of dark sesame oil creates outstanding flavor in this simple supper dish. To keep the flavor fresh, store the oil in the refrigerator after opening.

  2 tablespoons reduced-sodium soy sauce
1½ tablespoons sugar
  2 teaspoons dark sesame oil
  2 teaspoons vinegar
  1 teaspoon cornstarch
  2 drops hot chili oil (optional)
  2 chicken breasts, skinned, boned, and cut into ½" strips
¼ cup orange juice
  1 cup shredded carrots
½ cup sliced scallions
½ cup diagonally sliced celery
  2 cloves garlic, minced
  4 ounces spaghetti

❋ In a shallow nonmetal dish, combine the soy sauce, sugar, sesame oil, vinegar, cornstarch, and chili oil (if using); mix well. Add the chicken; toss to coat. Cover and refrigerate for 1 hour, stirring occasionally.

❋ Coat a 10" no-stick skillet with no-stick spray; set it over medium-high heat. When the skillet is hot, remove the chicken from the marinade and add it to the skillet; cook and stir for 3 to 5 minutes, or until the chicken is no longer pink. Check by inserting the tip of a sharp knife into a piece of chicken. Transfer the chicken to a plate; cover to keep warm.

❋ Add the orange juice to the skillet; bring to a boil, scraping to loosen any browned bits. Add the carrots, scallions, celery, and garlic; cover and cook for 3 minutes, or until the carrots are crisp-tender. Add the marinade and chicken; cook and stir for 1 minute, or until the mixture bubbles and thickens.

❋ Meanwhile, cook the spaghetti according to the package directions; drain well. Add the spaghetti to the skillet; cover and cook for 1 minute.

CARIBBEAN CHICKEN AND FRUIT KABOBS

Sweet and spicy flavors taste exotic in Caribbean island cooking, but the ingredients are as close as your supermarket. Serve this easy summer entrée with hot rice and wedges of grilled pita bread.

- 1 can (8 ounces) unsweetened pineapple chunks (with juice)
- 2 chicken breasts, skinned, boned, and cut into 1" pieces
- 2 tablespoons molasses
- 2 tablespoons reduced-sodium soy sauce
- ½ teaspoon ground allspice
- 2 drops hot-pepper sauce
- 1 small green pepper, cut into 1" pieces

❋ Drain the pineapple chunks, reserving the juice. In a shallow nonmetal dish, combine the reserved pineapple juice, chicken, molasses, soy sauce, allspice, and hot-pepper sauce; mix well. Cover and refrigerate for 1 hour, stirring frequently.

❋ Preheat the grill or broiler. Drain the chicken, reserving the marinade. Thread the chicken onto skewers (12" long), alternating with the pineapple chunks and peppers. Grill or broil the kabobs 4" from the heat for 5 minutes, basting with the reserved marinade. Turn and cook for 5 minutes more, or until the chicken is no longer pink in the center. Check by inserting the tip of a sharp knife into a piece of chicken.

5 FAST IDEAS FOR SKINNED AND BONED CHICKEN

❋ Coat the chicken with mixed dried herbs, then broil it.

❋ Cut the chicken into 1" cubes and marinate in fruit juice; skewer and grill.

❋ Pound the chicken into thin cutlets; sprinkle with shredded low-fat cheese. Roll up and secure with toothpicks. Microwave on high power until the chicken is no longer pink in the center.

❋ Add cubed cooked chicken and chopped cooked vegetables to defatted chicken broth for instant soup.

❋ Broil the chicken and brush it with mustard; layer with sliced vegetables between slices of rye bread.

Makes 4 servings

Per serving
Calories 185
Total fat 3 g.
Saturated fat 0.8 g.
Cholesterol 69 mg.
Sodium 335 mg.
Fiber 0.8 g.

Cost per serving

97¢

KITCHEN TIP

Skewers come in various sizes and materials. Double the number of kabobs if you have 6" skewers. Bamboo skewers need to be soaked in salted cold water to cover for 30 minutes to keep them from scorching during cooking.

Makes 4 servings

Per serving
Calories 340
Total fat 6.4 g.
Saturated fat 1.5 g.
Cholesterol 82 mg.
Sodium 351 mg.
Fiber 0.5 g.

Cost per serving

96¢

PINEAPPLE CHICKEN

Chicken drumsticks are basted with honey-soy marinade and then baked for an hour, bringing the exotic flavors of Hawaii to your dinner table for less than you'd pay at the cheapest fast food drive-through.

    1 can (8 ounces) unsweetened crushed pineapple (with juice)
       Juice of 1 lime
    2 tablespoons reduced-sodium soy sauce
    4 cloves garlic, minced
    2 tablespoons honey or packed brown sugar
    1 teaspoon olive oil
    ½ teaspoon ground coriander
    8 chicken drumsticks, skinned
    2 cups long-grain white rice

❋ In a glass 8" × 8" baking dish, combine the pineapple (with juice), lime juice, soy sauce, garlic, honey or brown sugar, oil, and coriander; mix well. Add the chicken and turn to coat. Cover and refrigerate for 1 hour, turning occasionally.

❋ Preheat the oven to 375°F. Bake the chicken in the marinade for 40 minutes, or until it is no longer pink in the center. Check by inserting the tip of a sharp knife into 1 drumstick.

❋ While the chicken is baking, cook the rice according to the package directions. Serve the chicken with the rice.

SKINNING AND BONING TIPS

❋ Save the butcher's labor cost—often 50¢ per pound—by skinning and boning your own chicken breasts and thighs.

❋ Chicken skin is easy to remove by hand. Just pull it off and discard. For boning, use a sharp knife. Poultry bones easiest when slightly frozen.

❋ To bone chicken breasts, make a shallow cut by the edge of the breast. Use your knife to scrape the meat off the bone (scrape against the bone, not the meat). To bone chicken thighs, make a deep cut on the back of the thigh along the bone. Peel away the meat. Save the bones in the freezer for your next batch of stock.

GLAZED CHICKEN WITH ONIONS

Balsamic vinegar is a delicious addition to your low-cost pantry—especially now that it's available for less than $1.99 a bottle in most supermarkets. You'll love the sweet glaze it gives this marinated chicken.

½ cup balsamic vinegar
2 teaspoons olive oil
1 tablespoon packed brown sugar or honey
1 tablespoon frozen orange juice concentrate
2 cloves garlic, minced
8 chicken thighs, skinned
2 large onions, thinly sliced

❀ In a shallow nonmetal dish, combine the vinegar, oil, brown sugar or honey, orange juice concentrate, and garlic; mix well. Add the chicken; turn to coat. Cover and refrigerate for 1 hour, turning frequently.

❀ Preheat the grill or broiler. Drain the chicken, reserving the marinade. Grill or broil the chicken 4″ from the heat for 8 to 10 minutes; turn and cook, basting frequently with 2 tablespoons of the marinade, for 8 minutes more, or until no longer pink in the center. Check by inserting the tip of a sharp knife into 1 thigh.

❀ Meanwhile, coat a 10″ no-stick skillet with no-stick spray; set it over medium-high heat. When the pan is hot, add the onions. Cook and stir for 5 to 8 minutes, or until golden brown. Place them on a plate; cover to keep warm.

❀ Pour the remaining marinade into the skillet and set over high heat. Cook and stir for 5 minutes, or until the marinade is reduced by half. Serve over the chicken and onions.

Makes 4 servings

Per serving
Calories 321
Total fat 13.7 g.
Saturated fat 3.5 g.
Cholesterol 98 mg.
Sodium 101 mg.
Fiber 365 g.

Cost per serving

85¢

Poultry and Egg Dishes

Per serving
Calories 166
Total fat 3 g.
Saturated fat 0.8 g.
Cholesterol 69 mg.
Sodium 60 mg.
Fiber 1.4 g.

Cost per serving

96¢

RASPBERRY-BASTED CHICKEN BREASTS

Making your own raspberry vinegar marinade for this quick-cooking French entrée saves you $3.50 a bottle over buying it ready-made. You can assemble the chicken before work and let it marinate all day in the refrigerator, for a fast-cooking dinner on a rushed night.

¾ cup cider vinegar
1 cup frozen raspberries
1 tablespoon honey or sugar
4 bone-in chicken breast halves, skinned

❀ In a medium saucepan over medium-high heat, bring the vinegar to a boil. Add the raspberries and honey or sugar; remove from the heat and pour into a shallow nonmetal dish. Cool to room temperature. Add the chicken breasts; turn to coat. Cover and refrigerate for at least 3 hours but no longer than 10 hours, turning occasionally.

❀ Preheat the grill or broiler. Broil or grill the chicken for 7 minutes, basting frequently with the raspberry marinade. Turn and cook for 5 to 7 minutes more, or until the chicken is no longer pink in the center. Check by inserting the tip of a sharp knife into 1 breast. Discard the remaining marinade.

TURKEY TACOS

Leaner and quicker to make than traditional beef tacos, these spicy roll-ups of ground turkey and Southwestern seasonings are stuffed into soft tortilla shells.

½ cup defatted chicken stock
1 cup minced onions
2 tablespoons minced jalapeño peppers
    (wear plastic gloves when handling)
1 teaspoon minced garlic
1 pound ground turkey breast
¼ cup diced celery
¼ cup mild salsa
½ teaspoon ground cumin
2 tablespoons honey or sugar
2 tablespoons minced fresh cilantro
1 tablespoon reduced-sodium soy sauce
¼ teaspoon salt
¼ teaspoon ground black pepper
8 flour tortillas (8" diameter)

❋ In a 10" no-stick skillet, bring the chicken stock to a boil over medium-high heat. Add the onions, peppers, and garlic; cook and stir for 5 minutes. Add the turkey, celery, salsa, and cumin; cook and stir for 3 minutes. Add the honey or sugar, cilantro, and soy sauce; cook and stir for 5 minutes, or until the liquid has evaporated. Add the salt and pepper.

❋ Meanwhile, wrap the tortillas in plastic wrap and microwave on high power for 1 minute to warm. Divide the turkey mixture among the tortillas; roll up.

Makes 4 servings

Per serving
Calories 396
Total fat 7.6 g.
Saturated fat 1.6 g.
Cholesterol 45 mg.
Sodium 860 mg.
Fiber 1.4 g.

Cost per serving

$1.01

117

Makes 4 servings

Per serving
Calories 271
Total fat 6.6 g.
Saturated fat 2 g.
Cholesterol 48 mg.
Sodium 403 mg.
Fiber 1.4 g.

Cost per serving

72¢

Cheddar Turkey Burgers

Stuffing each burger with Cheddar cheese adds flavor to the mild turkey and gives diners a delightful surprise, for only 6¢ more per serving.

- 1 pound ground turkey breast
- ¼ cup fresh bread crumbs
- 1 tablespoon stone-ground mustard
- ⅛ teaspoon dried thyme
- ⅛ teaspoon dried sage
- ¼ cup shredded low-fat extra-sharp Cheddar cheese
- 1 large red onion, sliced crosswise
- 4 whole-wheat hamburger buns, split and toasted
- 1 medium tomato, sliced
- 4 lettuce leaves

✻ In a medium bowl, combine the turkey, bread crumbs, mustard, thyme, and sage; mix well. Form into 4 balls. Make an indentation in the center of each ball; stuff with one-fourth of the Cheddar. Close the indentation by pressing the turkey around it to seal in the Cheddar. Form into patties.

✻ Preheat the grill or broiler. Coat the onions with no-stick spray; grill or broil the onions and burgers 4" from the heat for 5 to 7 minutes, or until the onions are golden, turning the onions as needed. Place the onions on a plate; cover to keep warm. Turn the burgers and cook for 5 minutes more, or until they are no longer pink near the center. Check by inserting the tip of a sharp knife in the center of the burger. Place the burgers in the buns and top with the onions, tomatoes, and lettuce.

4 EASY SAUCES FOR POULTRY

Keep these sauces in your refrigerator or freezer to dress up cooked poultry for a crowd… or a couple. Freeze in ½-cup amounts.

❀ *Light and Lean Cheese Sauce.* In a 10″ no-stick skillet, gradually stir 2 tablespoons all-purpose flour into ¼ cup defatted chicken stock. Bring to a boil over medium-high heat. Cook and whisk for 2 minutes to prevent lumping. Gradually add 1 cup skim milk; cook and whisk for 5 minutes, or until the sauce is thick. Add 1 cup shredded low-fat extra-sharp Cheddar cheese; cook and stir for 1 minute. Makes about 1½ cups.

❀ *Mushroom Madness Sauce.* In a 10″ no-stick skillet, combine 2 cups sliced mushrooms, ½ cup minced onions, 2 teaspoons minced garlic, and 1 teaspoon olive oil; cook and stir over medium-high heat for 10 minutes. Add ⅓ cup defatted chicken stock mixed with 1 teaspoon cornstarch; cook and stir for 5 minutes, or until the sauce is slightly thickened. Add ¼ teaspoon salt and ¼ teaspoon ground black pepper. Makes about 1 cup.

❀ *Roasted Garlic Sauce.* Bake 2 whole heads of garlic for 30 minutes at 400°F. Let cool, then extract the garlic paste by squeezing each clove. Mash the garlic paste. In a 10″ no-stick skillet, whisk 1 tablespoon flour into ¼ cup apple juice; cook and stir over medium-high heat for 2 minutes. Add the garlic paste and 1 cup defatted chicken stock; cook and stir for 3 to 5 minutes, or until the sauce is thick. Add ½ teaspoon salt and ½ teaspoon ground black pepper. Makes about 1 cup.

❀ *Sweet and Tangy Sauce.* In a 10″ no-stick skillet, combine 2 cups sliced onions and ¼ cup defatted chicken stock; cook and stir over medium heat for 15 minutes, or until the onions are very soft. Add ¼ cup balsamic vinegar; cook and stir for 5 minutes, or until the liquid has evaporated. Add ¼ teaspoon salt and ¼ teaspoon ground black pepper. Makes about 1 cup.

Per serving
Calories 217
Total fat 4.9 g.
Saturated fat 1.6 g.
Cholesterol 88 mg.
Sodium 345 mg.
Fiber 0.1 g.

Cost per serving

82¢

THYME AND GARLIC ROAST TURKEY

An inexpensive alternative to holiday feasts, this herb-rubbed turkey breast roasts in just 90 minutes. The skin acts as an envelope to seal in the cooking juices. It's removed before serving to keep the fat content low.

2 teaspoons dried thyme
4 cloves garlic, minced
½ teaspoon dried oregano
½ teaspoon salt
½ teaspoon ground black pepper
1 bone-in turkey breast half (about 2 pounds)

❋ Preheat the oven to 400°F. Coat a 13" × 9" baking pan with no-stick spray. In a small bowl, combine the thyme, garlic, oregano, salt, and pepper.

❋ Remove the skin from the turkey breast; reserve. Place the turkey in the pan. Rub the thyme mixture over the turkey; replace the skin and secure with toothpicks. Lightly coat the turkey skin with no-stick spray.

❋ Bake for 1½ hours, or until the turkey is no longer pink in the center. Check by inserting the tip of a sharp knife into the turkey. Remove the skin before serving.

TURKEY TIME LEFTOVERS

Buying and roasting a large turkey breast is an economical way to get plenty of Thanksgiving-style leftovers in the house without cooking all day. Shred and store any leftover turkey in small freezer containers for up to two months. Leftover turkey breast is great in tacos or enchiladas instead of ground beef. You can add it to salads for a lean protein boost, or chop and add it to soups.

ROAST TURKEY DRUMSTICKS WITH ASIAN SPICES

Tropical flavors of citrus, garlic, and chili peppers are slow-cooked into the lean turkey drumsticks, making them extra moist and tender.

Juice of 2 limes or lemons
2 tablespoons sugar
1 teaspoon minced jalapeño peppers
    (wear plastic gloves when handling)
1 teaspoon minced garlic
½ teaspoon ground coriander
½ teaspoon ground cumin
2 turkey drumsticks (1 pound each), skinned

❋ Preheat the oven to 400°F. In a small bowl, combine the lime juice or lemon juice, sugar, peppers, garlic, coriander, and cumin.

❋ Coat a medium roasting pan with no-stick spray. Place the turkey in the pan; drizzle it with the spice mixture. Cover and roast, basting frequently with the cooking liquid, for 1 hour, or until the turkey is no longer pink in the center. Check by inserting the tip of a sharp knife into the thickest part of 1 drumstick.

Makes 4 servings

Per serving
Calories 183
Total fat 4.2 g.
Saturated fat 1.4 g.
Cholesterol 107 mg.
Sodium 93 mg.
Fiber 0.1 g.

Cost per serving

76¢

Per serving
Calories 498
Total fat 11.5 g.
Saturated fat 2.7 g.
Cholesterol 186 mg.
Sodium 584 mg.
Fiber 6.9 g.

Cost per serving

79¢

HAM AND TOMATO QUICHE

This quiche is made with a crust of shredded raw potatoes, which eliminates a lot of the work and fat of a regular crust. Potato crusts are thicker than pastry crusts, so you can use fewer eggs in the quiche filling.

Crust

4 cups peeled and shredded potatoes
¼ cup minced onions
1 egg
¼ cup all-purpose flour

Filling

2 medium zucchini, thinly sliced
1 ounce chopped lean ham
¼ cup apple juice
1 teaspoon olive oil
1 large tomato, thinly sliced
2 eggs
1 cup nonfat cottage cheese
1 cup low-fat sour cream
¼ cup grated Parmesan cheese
¼ teaspoon dried thyme
¼ teaspoon salt
⅛ teaspoon ground red pepper

To make the crust

❀ Preheat the oven to 400°F. In a medium bowl, combine the potatoes, onions, egg, and flour; mix well. Press into the bottom and up the sides of a 9″ pie pan. Bake for 20 minutes, or until the crust is golden brown. Set aside. Reduce the heat to 350°F.

To make the filling

❀ In a 10″ no-stick skillet, combine the zucchini, ham, apple juice, and oil; cook and stir over medium-high heat for 3 minutes, or until the zucchini is slightly soft. Remove from the heat. Spread the zucchini mixture in the crust. Add the tomato, overlapping the slices as necessary.

❀ In a blender or food processor, combine the eggs, cottage cheese, sour cream, Parmesan, thyme, salt, and ground red pepper; puree. Pour over the vegetables.

❀ Bake for 40 minutes, or until the quiche is golden brown and set. Let it stand for 5 minutes before slicing.

CURRIED VEGETABLE OMELET

The golden hue of the curried vegetable filling complements the bright green spinach in this omelet. Make it spicier with a sprinkle of ground red pepper or a dash of hot-pepper sauce.

⅓ cup apple juice
½ cup thinly sliced zucchini or yellow summer squash
¼ cup diced green or sweet red peppers
¼ cup thinly sliced mushrooms
2 tablespoons minced scallions
2 tablespoons minced fresh parsley
1 teaspoon curry powder
8 egg whites
¼ teaspoon salt
½ teaspoon ground black pepper
½ cup chopped fresh spinach
1 teaspoon canola oil
⅓ cup shredded low-fat Swiss cheese

❁ In a 10″ no-stick skillet, bring the apple juice to a boil over medium-high heat. Add the zucchini or yellow summer squash, peppers, mushrooms, and scallions; cook and stir for 3 minutes. Add the parsley and curry powder. Transfer the vegetables to a bowl; cover to keep warm. Wash and dry the skillet.

❁ In a large bowl, beat the egg whites with electric beaters until soft peaks form. Add the salt and pepper. Fold in the spinach.

❁ Heat the oil in the skillet over medium-high heat; add the egg white mixture. Cook and stir for 1 minute, or until the egg whites begin to set. Add the vegetables and Swiss; fold the omelet over the filling. Cut into 4 wedges.

Makes 4 servings

Per serving
Calories 96
Total fat 3 g.
Saturated fat 1.1 g.
Cholesterol 7 mg.
Sodium 276 mg.
Fiber 1 g.

Cost per serving

28¢

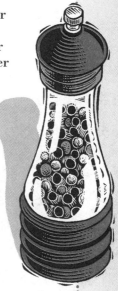

Sedona Black Bean Huevos Rancheros

Makes 6 servings

Per serving
Calories 213
Total fat 5.1 g.
Saturated fat 1.6 g.
Cholesterol 110 mg.
Sodium 266 mg.
Fiber 3 g.

Cost per serving

25¢

For your next Southwestern brunch, try this colorful egg dish, served ranch-style with lightly scrambled eggs. It's a northern Arizona tradition for only 25¢ a serving.

2 tablespoons dry sherry or apple juice
1 teaspoon olive oil
2 cups cooked black beans (page 199)
¼ cup minced green peppers
¼ cup minced red onions
1 teaspoon minced garlic
1 teaspoon ground cumin
1 tablespoon minced fresh parsley or cilantro
6 corn tortillas (6" diameter)
3 eggs, lightly beaten
½ cup medium-hot salsa
¼ cup shredded low-fat Monterey Jack cheese
¼ cup nonfat sour cream

❋ In a 10" no-stick skillet, combine the sherry or apple juice and oil; bring to a boil over medium-high heat. Add the beans, peppers, onions, garlic, and cumin; cook and stir for 5 minutes. Add the parsley or cilantro; remove from the heat. With a wooden spoon, mash the beans into the vegetables. Spoon onto a plate; cover to keep warm.

❋ Rinse the skillet; set it over medium-high heat. Add the tortillas, overlapping if necessary. Cook for 1 minute, then turn. Place ¼ cup of the bean mixture on each tortilla. Add the eggs. Spoon on the salsa and sprinkle with the Monterey Jack. Cover and cook for 2 minutes, or until the eggs are set and the cheese has melted. Top with dollops of the sour cream. Cut into 6 wedges.

VEGETABLE SKILLET FRITTATA

We combine whole eggs with egg whites and plenty of vegetables and seasonings to reduce the total fat and calories in this family brunch favorite.

Makes 4 servings

Per serving
Calories 158
Total fat 4.7 g.
Saturated fat 1.9 g.
Cholesterol 114 mg.
Sodium 522 mg.
Fiber 2.3 g.

Cost per serving

45¢

1 cup low-fat cottage cheese
2 eggs
4 egg whites
¼ cup defatted chicken stock
1 cup chopped onions
1 cup sliced green beans
1 cup chopped broccoli
¼ cup shredded carrots
2 cloves garlic, minced
½ teaspoon ground black pepper
⅛ teaspoon salt
⅓ cup shredded low-fat sharp Cheddar cheese

✸ In a blender or food processor, combine the cottage cheese, eggs, and egg whites; puree until very smooth. Set aside.

✸ In a 10″ no-stick skillet, bring the chicken stock to a boil over medium-high heat; add the onions. Cook and stir for 5 minutes, or until the onions soften. Add the beans, broccoli, carrots, and garlic; cover and cook for 2 minutes. Add the pepper and salt; stir well. Add the egg mixture and Cheddar; reduce the heat to low. Cover and cook for 15 minutes, or until the eggs are set. Cut into 6 wedges.

CRACKING THE EGG MYTH

Eggs have gotten a bad rap, but they're essentially good food when enjoyed in moderation without the accompanying high-fat breakfast meats. One egg delivers only about 5 grams of fat, and fat is more of a concern than cholesterol. (A traditional bacon-and-three-egg breakfast weighs in at a whopping 50 grams of fat.) A combination of whole eggs and egg whites, plus plenty of vegetables and seasonings, makes a low-fat breakfast entrée. Eggs are a good deal—cost-wise and nutrient-wise.

Yolks provide all of an egg's fat and cholesterol, so many recipes call for egg whites—which contain neither. What can you do with the leftover yolks? Scramble them lightly and add to pet food.

Per serving
Calories 210
Total fat 6.6 g.
Saturated fat 3.3 g.
Cholesterol 117 mg.
Sodium 440 mg.
Fiber 1.1 g.

Cost per serving

50¢

Mozzarella Mushroom Soufflé

Mushrooms add earthy flavor to this ethereal soufflé if you sauté them slowly until they release their flavor.

¼ cup dry sherry or defatted chicken stock
2 cups chopped mushrooms
½ cup minced onions
3 tablespoons all-purpose flour
1 cup skim milk
½ cup grated Parmesan cheese
½ cup shredded nonfat mozzarella cheese
¼ cup sliced scallions
2 eggs
3 egg whites

❋ Preheat the oven to 375°F. Coat a 1½-quart soufflé dish with no-stick spray.

❋ Coat a 10″ no-stick skillet with no-stick spray; set it over medium heat. Add the sherry or chicken stock; bring to a boil. Add the mushrooms and onions; cook and stir for 10 minutes, or until the liquid has evaporated.

❋ Reduce the heat to low. Add the flour; cook and stir for 1 minute. (The mixture will be dry.) Gradually add the milk; cook and stir for 2 minutes, or until the sauce is thick. Remove from the heat; add the Parmesan, mozzarella, scallions, and eggs.

❋ In a medium bowl, beat the egg whites with electric beaters until stiff peaks form. Fold the egg whites into the sauce. Spoon into the soufflé dish.

❋ Bake for 45 minutes, or until the soufflé is puffed and golden brown.

MOUTHWATERING MARINADES

These marinades are easy to make and turn ordinary poultry into a gourmet meal—with practically no work on your part! Be sure to discard the marinade afterward, or else bring it to a full boil before using it as a sauce. Each recipe is great for marinating 1 pound of skinned, boned poultry, whether you broil or grill it.

❋ *Chinese Plum.* Combine 2 plums (peeled and finely chopped), ⅓ cup cider vinegar, ¼ cup apple juice, 2 tablespoons honey, and 1 tablespoon minced garlic.

❋ *Currying Favor.* Combine 1 cup apple juice, ¼ cup cider vinegar, 1 teaspoon curry powder, 1 teaspoon minced garlic, and ¼ teaspoon crushed red-pepper flakes.

❋ *Great Grilling.* Combine ½ cup balsamic vinegar, ½ cup orange juice, ¼ cup chopped onions, 1 tablespoon honey, 1 teaspoon chopped fresh cilantro, ½ teaspoon olive oil, and ⅛ teaspoon crushed red-pepper flakes.

❋ *Mighty Minty.* Bring ¼ cup grape jelly and ¼ cup cider vinegar to a boil; add ¼ cup chopped fresh mint and 2 tablespoons reduced-sodium soy sauce. Let cool before using.

❋ *Orange You Glad?* Combine ½ cup orange juice, 1 teaspoon grated orange rind, 1 teaspoon grated fresh ginger, 1 teaspoon minced garlic, and ¼ teaspoon dark sesame oil.

❋ *Pucker Up.* Combine ½ cup dry sherry or defatted chicken stock, 2 tablespoons lemon juice, 1 teaspoon minced garlic, 1 teaspoon stone-ground mustard, and ½ teaspoon prepared horseradish.

❋ *Teriyaki Treat.* Combine ½ cup unsweetened pineapple juice, ¼ cup reduced-sodium soy sauce, 1 teaspoon grated fresh ginger, and 1 teaspoon minced garlic.

Per serving
Calories 99
Total fat 3.7 g.
Saturated fat 1.6 g.
Cholesterol 59 mg.
Sodium 200 mg.
Fiber 2 g.

Cost per serving

45¢

BROCCOLI SOUFFLÉS IN TOMATOES

Only one whole egg and two egg whites are needed for these inexpensive airy soufflés. Hollowed-out tomatoes make delicious baking and serving "dishes."

4 ripe but firm large tomatoes
⅛ teaspoon salt
½ cup minced broccoli
1 tablespoon minced onions
½ teaspoon olive oil
2 teaspoons all-purpose flour
¼ cup skim milk
⅓ cup shredded low-fat mozzarella cheese
1 egg, lightly beaten
1 tablespoon dried chives or minced fresh chives
¼ teaspoon dried thyme
2 egg whites

❀ Slice the top ½" off the tomatoes; scoop out the seeds and pulp, leaving a ½" shell. Reserve the pulp for another use. Sprinkle the insides of the tomato shells with the salt; invert over a paper towel and let drain for 20 minutes.

❀ Meanwhile, coat a 10" no-stick skillet with no-stick spray; set it over medium-high heat. Add the broccoli, onions, and oil; cook and stir for 5 minutes. Transfer the vegetables to a plate; cover to keep warm.

❀ Reduce the heat to medium; coat the skillet with no-stick spray. Add the flour; cook and stir for 2 minutes. Gradually add the milk; cook and stir for 5 minutes. Stir in the vegetables, mozzarella, egg, chives, and thyme; immediately remove from the heat.

❀ Preheat the oven to 400°F. Coat an 8" × 8" baking dish with no-stick spray. Arrange the tomato shells in the dish.

❀ In a large bowl, beat the egg whites with electric beaters just until they hold stiff peaks. Fold into the vegetable mixture. Spoon into the tomato shells, mounding slightly on top.

❀ Bake for 15 to 20 minutes, or until the soufflés are puffed and golden.

VEGETABLE BREAKFAST CUSTARDS

There's nothing cheap about these oven-baked custards—except the price. The hearty sautéed vegetables are lightened with beaten egg whites.

½ cup defatted chicken stock
1 teaspoon olive oil
3 tablespoons minced red onions
3 cups diced peeled eggplant
1 green pepper, diced
1 sweet red pepper, diced
½ cup sliced zucchini
2 large cloves garlic, minced
½ teaspoon ground black pepper
⅛ teaspoon salt
¼ cup nonfat plain yogurt
2 eggs
2 tablespoons grated Parmesan cheese
1 tablespoon minced fresh parsley
4 egg whites

❋ Preheat the oven to 350°F. Coat four (4-ounce) custard cups or gratin dishes with no-stick spray.

❋ In a 10″ no-stick skillet, bring the chicken stock and oil to a boil over medium-high heat. Add the onions; cook and stir for 1 minute. Add the eggplant, green peppers, red peppers, zucchini, and garlic; cook and stir for 10 minutes, or until the peppers are soft. Add the pepper and salt. Remove from the heat; divide among the 4 custard cups or gratin dishes.

❋ In a large bowl, combine the yogurt, eggs, Parmesan, and parsley.

❋ In a medium bowl, beat the egg whites with electric beaters until soft peaks form. Fold into the yogurt mixture; spoon evenly over the vegetables. Bake for 15 minutes, or until the custards are puffed and set.

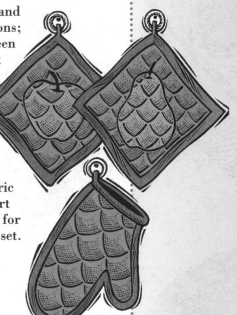

Makes 4 servings

Per serving
Calories 137
Total fat 5 g.
Saturated fat 1.6 g.
Cholesterol 110 mg.
Sodium 226 mg.
Fiber 1.7 g.

Cost per serving

53¢

CHAPTER 6

BEEF, PORK, AND LAMB

Lean beef, pork, and lamb give good return for the dollar as flavorful, nutritious protein that's quick to prepare. Few sources of protein are as versatile as meat, and most markets now sell a wide range of leaner cuts to cater to the consumer's growing demand for less fat.

To save the most from lean cuts, plan your meat purchases to take advantage of weekly supermarket specials and warehouse-store bulk buys. Buying most of your meat on sale can cut your weekly bill up to 25 percent. Also look for savings in bigger cuts of meat, often called "family packs." Buying more than a pound of pork chops or chicken breasts at a time usually saves an extra 5 to 10 percent.

Recipes in this chapter show you how to enrich meat entrées with plenty of vegetables, grains, and legumes—foods that are robust enough to satisfy big appetites, yet never fail to expand the value of your protein dollar.

Per serving
Calories 334
Total fat 7.7 g.
Saturated fat 2.4 g.
Cholesterol 51 mg.
Sodium 143 mg.
Fiber 5.9 g.

Cost per serving

85¢

PORK AND PEPPER CURRY

This authentic Indian curry relies on onions, potatoes, peppers, and sweet potatoes to allow less than a pound of lean pork to serve 4 hungry diners. Slow cooking tenderizes the meat and keeps the curry moist. Serve the curry over rice.

1 pound pork roast, trimmed of fat and cut into 1" cubes
1 teaspoon lemon juice
1 teaspoon olive oil
½ teaspoon ground cumin
½ teaspoon stone-ground mustard
¼ teaspoon ground black pepper
⅛ teaspoon salt
1 large onion, thinly sliced
3 cloves garlic, minced
1 cup diced unpeeled red potatoes
1 cup diced peeled sweet potatoes
1 cup diced green peppers
1 small jalapeño pepper, seeded and minced
   (wear plastic gloves when handling)
1 teaspoon curry powder
1 cup defatted chicken stock
1 teaspoon honey

❋ In a shallow nonmetal dish, combine the pork, lemon juice, oil, cumin, mustard, pepper, and salt; toss well. Cover and refrigerate for 2 hours, stirring occasionally.

❋ Coat a 10″ no-stick skillet with no-stick spray; set it over medium-high heat. When the skillet is hot, add the onions and garlic; cook and stir for 5 minutes. Add the red potatoes, sweet potatoes, green peppers, jalapeño peppers, curry powder, and pork mixture; cook and stir for 5 minutes. Add the chicken stock and honey; bring to a boil. Reduce the heat to medium; cook, stirring occasionally, for 45 minutes, or until the curry is thick.

What's in Curry Powder?

Most Indian cooks make their own curry powder, and you can too, at a savings of about 26¢ per ounce over buying it premade. More importantly, fresh curry powder has a dramatic depth of flavor and sweetness that many packaged curry powders lose while sitting on the supermarket shelves.

Get together a group of friends and make a big batch. This recipe can be doubled or tripled. Combine ¼ cup ground cumin, ¼ cup ground coriander, ¼ cup ground cinnamon, 2 tablespoons ground turmeric, and 1 tablespoon ground red pepper; stir well. Makes about 1 cup. Store in a tightly closed container in a dark cupboard for up to 1 year.

Citrus-Marinated Pork Chops

Pork loin chops are lean yet filling—a good deal when you can find them on sale. Plenty of garlic and seasonings are rubbed into these lean chops before grilling or broiling. Serve them with Mashed Pesto Potatoes (page 227) and corn on the cob for a great harvest dinner.

- 2 tablespoons minced garlic
- 1 teaspoon ground paprika
- ½ teaspoon ground cumin
- ¼ teaspoon salt
- ¼ teaspoon ground red pepper
- 4 small bone-in pork loin chops (about 6 ounces each), trimmed of fat
- 1 tablespoon frozen orange juice concentrate, thawed

✤ In a small bowl, combine the garlic, paprika, cumin, salt, and red pepper. Place the chops in a shallow container. Lightly brush the chops with the orange juice concentrate; spread with the spice mixture. Cover and refrigerate for 4 hours.

✤ Preheat the grill or broiler. Grill or broil 4″ from the heat for 8 minutes; turn and cook for 8 minutes more, or until the chops are browned, crisp, and no longer pink in the center. Check by inserting the tip of a sharp knife in the center of 1 pork chop.

Makes 4 servings

Per serving
Calories 225
Total fat 10.9 g.
Saturated fat 3.7 g.
Cholesterol 54 mg.
Sodium 189 mg.
Fiber 0.2 g.

Cost per serving

$1.63

Beef, Pork, and Lamb

Makes 4 servings

Per serving
Calories 514
Total fat 9.6 g.
Saturated fat 2.9 g.
Cholesterol 75 mg.
Sodium 267 mg.
Fiber 2.2 g.

Cost per serving

42¢

CHINESE CURRIED PORK AND PASTA

This curried pork stir-fry gets its incredible flavor from only three spices: dry mustard, curry powder, and paprika.

- 1 pound pork shoulder, trimmed of fat and cut into 1" strips
- 1 tablespoon apple juice
- 1 tablespoon packed brown sugar
- 2 teaspoons curry powder
- 1 teaspoon dry mustard
- ½ teaspoon paprika
- 8 ounces spaghetti
- 1 medium onion, sliced
- 1 teaspoon minced garlic
- 1 teaspoon grated fresh ginger
- ½ cup shredded carrots
- ½ cup diagonally sliced celery
- ½ cup sliced scallions
- 1 cup defatted chicken stock
- 1 tablespoon reduced-sodium soy sauce
- 1 teaspoon cornstarch

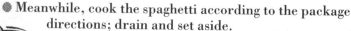 In a shallow nonmetal dish, combine the pork, apple juice, brown sugar, curry powder, dry mustard, and paprika; stir well. Cover and refrigerate for 15 minutes.

❋ Meanwhile, cook the spaghetti according to the package directions; drain and set aside.

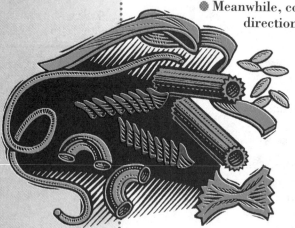

✿ Coat a 10″ no-stick skillet with no-stick spray; set it over medium-high heat. When the skillet is hot, add the onions, garlic, and ginger; cook and stir for 5 minutes, or until the onions turn golden brown. Add the carrots, celery, scallions, ½ cup of the chicken stock, and the pork mixture; cook and stir for 10 minutes, or until the liquid has almost evaporated and the pork is no longer pink. Check by inserting the tip of a sharp knife in a pork cube.

✿ In a small bowl, combine the soy sauce, cornstarch, and the remaining ½ cup stock. Add to the skillet; cook and stir for 2 to 3 minutes, or until the sauce thickens. Add the spaghetti; toss well. Cover and cook for 1 minute, or until the spaghetti is hot.

STIR-FRY SECRET FROM ASIAN CHEFS

Stir-fries require medium-high heat and quick cooking to maintain top-quality flavor and bring out the bright colors of the vegetables. Most Asian chefs cut and measure out all the ingredients before starting to cook—this makes the fast cooking process safer and less stressful, especially for beginning cooks.

GINGERED PORK STIR-FRY WITH VEGETABLES

Makes 4 servings

Per serving
Calories 200
Total fat 6.1 g.
Saturated fat 2.2 g.
Cholesterol 50 mg.
Sodium 447 mg.
Fiber 2.4 g.

Cost per serving

73¢

A stir-fry dinner can cost over $5 per person at even inexpensive Chinese restaurants, but you can make your own for a fraction of the price. Serve this one over cooked rice.

 1 pound pork roast, trimmed of fat and cut into ½" strips
 ¼ cup apple juice or white wine
 2 tablespoons minced garlic
 2 tablespoons minced fresh ginger
 1 tablespoon cornstarch
 3 tablespoons reduced-sodium soy sauce
 1 onion, thinly sliced
1½ cups shredded carrots
 ⅓ cup defatted chicken stock
 ⅓ cup diagonally sliced scallions

❋ In a shallow nonmetal dish, combine the pork, apple juice or wine, garlic, ginger, cornstarch, and 1 tablespoon of the soy sauce; toss well. Cover and refrigerate for 1 hour, stirring occasionally.

❋ Coat a 10" no-stick skillet with no-stick spray; set it over medium-high heat. When the skillet is hot, add the onions; cook and stir for 2 minutes. Add the carrots and chicken stock; cook and stir for 1 minute. Drain the pork, reserving the marinade; add the pork to the skillet. Cook and stir for 3 minutes, or until the pork is no longer pink in the center when pierced with the tip of a sharp knife. Transfer the pork and vegetables to a plate; cover to keep warm.

❋ Add the marinade to the skillet; bring to a boil. Cook and stir for 3 minutes, or until the marinade thickens. Add the pork and vegetables, scallions, and the remaining 2 tablespoons soy sauce; cook and stir for 1 minute.

BEST BUYS ON RICE

Shop Asian markets for the best bulk buys on basmati, jasmine, and other really flavorful long-grain white rices as well as some brown rices. Most Asian markets carry five to ten varieties, often at savings of 25¢ to 50¢ a pound over supermarket boxed rices.

PAPRIKA PORK BRAISED WITH APPLES

This German-style one-pot meal relies on mustard, apples, and apple juice to enliven the simple flavors of economical pork shoulder. The slow cooking, or braising, tenderizes it. Serve it with rye bread and boiled red potatoes or cooked noodles.

Makes 4 servings

Per serving
Calories 394
Total fat 8.5 g.
Saturated fat 2.8 g.
Cholesterol 74 mg.
Sodium 300 mg.
Fiber 4 g.

Cost per serving

80¢

1	pound pork shoulder, trimmed of fat and cut into 1" cubes
1	tablespoon honey
1	tablespoon paprika
1	teaspoon Dijon mustard
¼	teaspoon salt
¼	teaspoon ground black pepper
1	cup apple juice
1	cup chopped green cabbage
1	cup sliced carrots
1	cup sliced potatoes
1	onion, thinly sliced
1½	tablespoons minced garlic
1	large tart apple, peeled and sliced
½	cup nonfat sour cream

❋ In a shallow nonmetal dish, combine the pork, honey, paprika, mustard, salt, and pepper; toss well. Cover and refrigerate for 30 minutes.

❋ Meanwhile, in a Dutch oven, bring ½ cup of the apple juice to a boil over medium-high heat; add the cabbage, carrots, potatoes, onions, and garlic. Cook and stir for 8 minutes, or until the liquid has almost evaporated. Transfer the vegetables to a plate.

❋ Preheat the oven to 350°F. Coat the Dutch oven with no-stick spray; set it over medium-high heat. When the Dutch oven is hot, add the pork mixture. Cook and stir for 5 minutes, or until the mustard mixture begins to brown. Add the remaining ½ cup apple juice, scraping to loosen any browned bits. Add the apples and vegetables; stir well.

❋ Cover and bake for 1 hour, or until the potatoes are soft when pierced with a sharp knife. Stir in the sour cream.

Pork Chops
with Herbed Apple Dressing

Makes 4 servings

Per serving
Calories 320
Total fat 11.6 g.
Saturated fat 3.9 g.
Cholesterol 55 mg.
Sodium 272 mg.
Fiber 2.6 g.

Cost per serving

$1.36

Family packs of pork chops reduce your cost to less than $1 per serving; wrap the remaining chops in butcher paper or plastic wrap and store them in the freezer for up to 2 months.

½ cup apple juice
2 cups peeled and diced tart apples
1 cup diced celery
½ cup diced onions
1 cup toasted whole-wheat bread cubes or croutons
¼ cup chopped pitted prunes
1 cup defatted chicken stock or water
½ teaspoon dried sage
½ teaspoon dried thyme
4 small bone-in pork loin chops (about 6 ounces each), trimmed of fat
½ teaspoon ground black pepper
¼ teaspoon salt

❀ Preheat the oven to 350°F. Coat a 2-quart casserole dish with no-stick spray.

❀ In a 10″ no-stick skillet, bring the apple juice to a boil over medium-high heat. Add the apples, celery, and onions; cook and stir for 5 minutes, or until the onions soften. Add the bread cubes or croutons, prunes, and ½ cup of the chicken stock or water; cook and stir for 1 minute. Add the sage and thyme; mix well. Spoon into the casserole dish.

❀ Bake for 25 minutes, or until the dressing is golden brown and all the liquid is absorbed.

❀ While the dressing is baking, add the remaining ½ cup stock or water to the skillet; cook and stir for 1 minute, scraping to loosen any browned bits. Sprinkle the pork chops with the pepper and salt; add them to the skillet. Cover and cook for 5 minutes; turn and cook for 5 to 8 minutes more, or until the chops are no longer pink in the center. Check by inserting the tip of a sharp knife in 1 pork chop. Serve with the apple dressing.

MUSTARDY HAM WITH PAN GRAVY

Ham steak is a great Southern favorite for Sunday dinner and a real money-saver at less than 50¢ a serving. It can also be a healthy choice if you keep the pan gravy lean by straining off all the fat.

- 1 pound lean reduced-sodium ham steak, trimmed of fat
- 2 tablespoons molasses
- 1 tablespoon Dijon mustard
- 2 cloves garlic, minced
- 1½ cups defatted chicken stock
- 1 teaspoon reduced-calorie butter or margarine
- 2 tablespoons all-purpose flour
- ¼ teaspoon ground black pepper

❋ In a shallow nonmetal dish, combine the ham, molasses, mustard, and garlic; cover and refrigerate for 1 hour, turning frequently.

❋ Coat a 10″ no-stick skillet with no-stick spray; set it over medium-high heat. When the skillet is hot, add the ham and marinade; cook the ham for 5 to 7 minutes, or until browned. Turn and cook for 5 minutes more. Place the ham on a cutting board; let it stand for 5 minutes.

❋ Meanwhile, drain any fat from the skillet; add the chicken stock. Bring it to a boil, scraping to loosen any browned bits. In a small bowl, mash the margarine into the flour; add to the pan. Cook and stir for 5 minutes, or until the gravy thickens. Add the pepper. Cut the ham into 4 wedges; serve with the gravy.

Makes 4 servings

Per serving
Calories 187
Total fat 5.7 g.
Saturated fat 1.8 g.
Cholesterol 51 mg.
Sodium 936 mg.
Fiber 0.2 g.

Cost per serving

48¢

Beef, Pork, and Lamb

Per serving
Calories 583
Total fat 4.6 g.
Saturated fat 1 g.
Cholesterol 21 mg.
Sodium 460 mg.
Fiber 2.4 g.

Cost per serving

85¢

NEW ORLEANS RED BEANS AND RICE

Red beans and rice comes from New Orleans, where the dish was tradition-ally made on Monday. It took about as much time to cook as Monday's laundry did to dry, and it made thrifty use of Sunday dinner's ham bone.

2 cups dried kidney beans
4 cups boiling water
6 cups defatted chicken stock
4 ounces reduced-sodium lean ham, cubed
1 bay leaf
1 large onion, diced
2 stalks celery, diced
2 teaspoons minced garlic
1 teaspoon olive oil
1 large tomato, diced
2 tablespoons tomato paste
1 teaspoon dried thyme
¼ teaspoon crushed red-pepper flakes
1 cup long-grain white rice
¼ teaspoon salt
¼ teaspoon ground black pepper
3 tablespoons minced fresh parsley

❋ Rinse the beans and place them in a medium bowl; add the water. Set aside for 1 hour. Drain and rinse.

❋ Meanwhile, in a Dutch oven combine the chicken stock, ham, and bay leaf. Bring to a boil over medium-high heat. Reduce the heat to medium. Simmer for 30 minutes.

❋ Remove and discard the bay leaf. Add the beans. Bring to a boil. Reduce the heat to medium. Cook for 30 minutes.

❋ In a 10″ skillet, combine the onions, celery, garlic, and oil; cook and stir over medium-high heat for 10 minutes, or until the onions are golden brown. Add to the beans. Add the tomatoes, tomato paste, thyme, and red-pepper flakes; cover and cook, stirring occasionally, for 45 minutes, or until the beans are soft. Check by pressing a bean against the side of the saucepan with a large spoon.

❋ Meanwhile, cook the rice according to the package directions.

❋ Add the salt and pepper to the beans. Serve over the rice. Sprinkle with the parsley.

BEEF BURGUNDY

French cooks transform inexpensive cuts of beef by simmering them in fragrant sauces of wine, stock, and spices. Serve this traditional dish from the wine-growing regions of Burgundy with cooked noodles.

2 cups sliced mushrooms
1 cup diced onions
½ cup dry red wine (optional)
3 cups defatted chicken stock
1 pound lean chuck roast, trimmed of fat and cut into 2" cubes
1 tablespoon tomato paste
2 cloves garlic, chopped
¼ teaspoon dried thyme
1 bay leaf
2 tablespoons all-purpose flour
2 teaspoons reduced-calorie butter or margarine
¾ teaspoon ground black pepper
½ teaspoon salt

❋ Coat a Dutch oven with no-stick spray; set it over medium-high heat. When the Dutch oven is hot, add the mushrooms, onions, wine (if using), and ½ cup of the chicken stock; cook and stir for 8 minutes, or until the liquid has almost evaporated. Transfer the vegetables to a plate.

❋ Add the beef and ½ cup of the remaining stock; cook and stir for 5 minutes, scraping to loosen any browned bits. Add the tomato paste, garlic, thyme, bay leaf, and the remaining 2 cups stock; bring to a boil. Reduce the heat to medium low; add the vegetables. Cover and cook for 30 minutes, or until the beef is tender.

❋ Using a slotted spoon, transfer the beef and vegetables to a plate; cover to keep warm. Increase the heat to high; bring the sauce to a boil. In a small bowl, combine the flour and margarine (the mixture will be crumbly). Add by spoonfuls; cook and stir for 5 minutes, or until the sauce thickens. Remove and discard the bay leaf. Add the pepper and salt; stir well. Add the beef and vegetables; cook for 1 minute, or until the beef and vegetables are hot.

Makes 4 servings

Per serving
Calories 220
Total fat 8 g.
Saturated fat 2.7 g.
Cholesterol 65 mg.
Sodium 420 mg.
Fiber 1.6 g.

Cost per serving

98¢

Per serving
Calories 189
Total fat 3.5 g.
Saturated fat 1.2 g.
Cholesterol 72 mg.
Sodium 252 mg.
Fiber 1.5 g.

Cost per serving

51¢

Kitchen Tip

To remove the cabbage leaves without tearing them, cut out the core with a sharp knife. Cutting away part of the thick rib of each leaf allows the cabbage to fold around the filling more easily. You can use either green cabbage or Savoy cabbage for this recipe.

Swedish Beef and Cabbage Rolls

A year-round favorite, cabbage costs less than 12¢ a serving, making it one of the most economical vegetables you can buy. These Swedish-style rolls are filled with beef and rice in a sweet sauce. If you have leftover cooked rice, use 1½ cups.

½ cup long-grain white rice
12 large cabbage leaves
1 pound extra-lean beef ground round
1 egg, lightly beaten
¼ cup skim milk
¼ cup minced onions
½ teaspoon salt
¼ teaspoon ground black pepper
1 can (8 ounces) reduced-sodium tomato sauce
1 tablespoon molasses
1 tablespoon lemon juice
1 teaspoon reduced-sodium Worcestershire sauce

❋ Cook the rice according to the package directions. Let cool.

❋ Preheat the oven to 350°F. Coat a 13″ × 9″ baking dish with no-stick spray.

❋ Bring a large pot of water to a boil. Cook the cabbage leaves for 3 minutes, or until they are limp; drain well.

❋ In a large bowl, combine the cooked rice, beef, egg, milk, onions, salt, and pepper; stir well. Place about 3 tablespoons of the meat mixture in the center of each cabbage leaf; fold in the sides and roll tightly. Place the cabbage rolls seam side down in the baking dish.

❋ In a medium bowl, combine the tomato sauce, molasses, lemon juice, and Worcestershire sauce. Pour over the cabbage rolls.

❋ Bake for 1 hour, or until the sauce is thick and the beef is no longer pink. Check by inserting the tip of a sharp knife in 1 roll.

Ground Beef and Tomato Skillet Dinner with Noodles

A quick and delicious way to double the value of ground beef is to serve it in this savory tomato sauce with noodles. In less than 15 minutes, you have a satisfying meal for under $1.25 a serving.

Makes 4 servings

Per serving
Calories 444
Total fat 4.2 g.
Saturated fat 1.3 g.
Cholesterol 55 mg.
Sodium 406 mg.
Fiber 5 g.

Cost per serving

$1.18

- 8 ounces yolk-free egg noodles
- 1 pound extra-lean beef ground round
- 1 cup chopped sweet red peppers
- ½ cup minced onions
- 1 teaspoon minced garlic
- ½ teaspoon chili powder
- 1 cup whole kernel corn
- 2 cans (8 ounces each) reduced-sodium tomato sauce
- 1 cup canned diced reduced-sodium tomatoes (with juice)
- ½ cup mild salsa

❀ Cook the noodles according to the package directions; drain well.

❀ Meanwhile, coat a 10″ no-stick skillet with no-stick spray; set it over medium-high heat. Add the beef, red peppers, onions, garlic, and chili powder; cook and stir for 5 to 8 minutes, or until the beef is browned. Drain off any excess fat. Add the tomato sauce, tomatoes (with juice), and salsa. Cook and stir for 5 minutes. Add the noodles. Cover and cook for 1 minute, or until the noodles are hot.

143

Thai Beef Kabobs with Garden Vegetable Sauté

Makes 4 servings

Per serving
Calories 302
Total fat 13.9 g.
Saturated fat 4.4 g.
Cholesterol 75 mg.
Sodium 204 mg.
Fiber 2.1 g.

Cost per serving

$1.00

A lemony sweet-and-sour marinade works flavor magic on lean beef as it waits for the grill. The kabobs are served with a colorful fresh vegetable medley.

2 tablespoons lemon juice
1 tablespoon reduced-sodium soy sauce
1 tablespoon packed brown sugar
1 tablespoon minced garlic
1 teaspoon crushed red-pepper flakes
1 teaspoon ground black pepper
1 pound beef chuck, trimmed of fat and cut into 2" cubes
1 cup julienned yellow summer squash or zucchini
½ cup sliced scallions
½ cup whole kernel corn
½ cup sliced green beans
1 tablespoon olive oil
½ pint cherry tomatoes, halved
1 tablespoon minced fresh parsley or cilantro

✹ In a shallow nonmetal dish, combine the vinegar, soy sauce, brown sugar, garlic, red-pepper flakes, and black pepper; mix well. Add the beef; toss well. Cover and refrigerate for 2 hours, stirring frequently.

✹ Preheat the grill or broiler. Drain the beef, reserving the marinade. Thread the beef onto 8 skewers. Grill or broil the kabobs 4" from the heat for 12 to 15 minutes, or until the beef is lightly browned on all sides and no longer pink in the center. Check by inserting the tip of a sharp knife into 1 beef cube.

✹ Meanwhile, coat a 10" no-stick skillet with no-stick spray; set it over medium-high heat. Add the yellow summer squash or zucchini, scallions, corn, beans, and oil; cook and stir for 5 minutes, or until the beans are crisp-tender. Add the tomatoes and 2 tablespoons of the reserved marinade (discard any remaining marinade); cook and stir for 2 minutes. Add the parsley or cilantro. Serve with the beef.

GARLIC BEEF BURGERS ON TOASTED BUNS

Adding a small amount of grated Parmesan and garlic to burgers lifts them above the ordinary, for only 79¢ a serving.

- 1 pound extra-lean beef ground round
- ¼ cup soft bread crumbs
- 2 tablespoons grated Parmesan cheese
- 1 tablespoon minced garlic
- ½ teaspoon ground black pepper
- 1 tablespoon nonfat mayonnaise
- 1 teaspoon Dijon mustard
- 4 whole-wheat hamburger buns, split and toasted
- 4 large lettuce leaves

❀ Preheat the grill or broiler. In a small bowl, combine the beef, bread crumbs, Parmesan, garlic, and pepper; mix well. Form into 4 burgers. Grill or broil 4″ from the heat for 4 minutes; turn and cook for 5 to 8 minutes more, or until the burgers are no longer pink in the center. Check by inserting the tip of a sharp knife in 1 burger.

❀ Spread the mayonnaise and mustard on the buns. Top with the burgers and lettuce.

Makes 4 servings

Per serving
Calories 289
Total fat 7.7 g.
Saturated fat 2.6 g.
Cholesterol 57 mg.
Sodium 425 mg.
Fiber 0.4 g.

Cost per serving

79¢

Beef, Pork,
and Lamb

BEEF VEGETABLE STROGANOFF

Makes 4 servings

Per serving
Calories 324
Total fat 10.8 g.
Saturated fat 4 g.
Cholesterol 75 mg.
Sodium 629 mg.
Fiber 4 g.

Cost per serving

$1.16

Trim a bulk buy of beef chuck or top round into cubes for this family favorite—updated with colorful chopped vegetables. Serve it over cooked rice to soak up the tasty sauce.

1 pound beef chuck or top round, trimmed of fat and
      cut into 1" cubes
1 tablespoon all-purpose flour
1 tablespoon paprika
1 teaspoon ground black pepper
½ teaspoon salt
½ cup defatted chicken stock
2 cups sliced mushrooms
1 cup thinly sliced carrots
1 large onion, diced
1 green or sweet red pepper, chopped
1 teaspoon minced garlic
1 teaspoon caraway seeds
1 cup tomato puree
1 cup nonfat sour cream

❋ In a medium bowl, combine the beef, flour, paprika, pepper, and salt; toss well.

❋ Coat a Dutch oven with no-stick spray; set it over medium-high heat. When the Dutch oven is hot, add the beef; cook and stir for 5 minutes, or until the beef is lightly browned. Transfer the beef to a plate.

❋ Add the chicken stock to the skillet; bring to a boil, scraping to loosen any browned bits. Add the mushrooms, carrots, onions, peppers, garlic, and caraway seeds; cook and stir for 5 minutes, or until the liquid has almost evaporated. Add the tomato puree and beef; bring to a boil. Lower the heat to medium; cover and cook for 15 to 20 minutes, or until the sauce is thick, stirring occasionally. Stir in the sour cream.

Texas Beef and Bean Chili

Chili is a favorite Southwestern way to jazz up humble ground beef. Keep evenings simple with this easy one-pot meal of beef and beans in a spicy tomato sauce.

- 8 ounces extra-lean beef ground round
- 8 ounces turkey sausage
- ½ medium onion, diced
- 1 can (28 ounces) reduced-sodium stewed tomatoes (with juice)
- ¼ cup diced canned green chili peppers
- 3 cups cooked pinto or kidney beans (page 199)
- 1 teaspoon dried oregano
- ½ teaspoon ground cumin
- 2–3 tablespoons chili powder
- ½ teaspoon ground black pepper

❋ Coat a Dutch oven with no-stick spray; set it over medium-high heat. When the Dutch oven is hot, add the beef, turkey sausage, and onions. Cook and stir for 8 minutes, or until the meat is no longer pink. Drain well. Add the tomatoes, beans, peppers, oregano, cumin, and 2 tablespoons of the chili powder; bring to a boil. Reduce the heat to medium. Cover and cook for 25 minutes, or until the chili is thick. Add the pepper. Add up to 1 tablespoon more chili powder to taste if desired.

Makes 4 servings

Per serving
Calories 393
Total fat 8.1 g.
Saturated fat 2 g.
Cholesterol 63 mg.
Sodium 687 mg.
Fiber 13.5 g.

Cost per serving

$1.04

Cooking Beans Quicker

Cooking dried beans can save you up to $1 over 2 cups of canned beans. To save time, try this easy tip: Cover the dried beans with boiling water and let them soak for 1 hour. Drain and rinse, then continue with the recipe. It reduces the cooking time and still saves you that $1.

Per serving
Calories 414
Total fat 9.3 g.
Saturated fat 3.7 g.
Cholesterol 52 mg.
Sodium 197 mg.
Fiber 2.8 g.

Cost per serving

$1.89

MOROCCAN BEEF WITH LEMON COUSCOUS

Flank steak is known for its hearty flavor and low cost. In this recipe we dress it up in a sweet marinade of ginger, garlic, soy sauce, and sugar, then grill it. Slicing it against the grain gives melt-in-your-mouth texture.

Beef

- 2 tablespoons minced fresh ginger
- 1 tablespoon molasses
- 1 tablespoon reduced-sodium soy sauce
- 2 cloves garlic, minced
- 1 pound beef flank steak, trimmed of fat

Couscous

- 1/2 teaspoon olive oil
- 1/4 cup chopped scallions
- 1/4 cup minced sweet red peppers
- 1 clove garlic, minced
- 1 1/2 cups defatted chicken stock
- 1 cup couscous
- 1/4 cup lemon juice
- 2 tablespoons minced fresh parsley

To make the beef

❋ In a shallow nonmetal dish, combine the ginger, molasses, soy sauce, and garlic; mix well. Add the beef; turn to coat. Cover and refrigerate for at least 4 hours or up to 12 hours, turning occasionally.

❋ Preheat the grill or broiler. Grill or broil the beef 4″ from the heat for 5 minutes; turn and cook for 5 minutes more, basting frequently with the marinade. Let the beef stand for 5 minutes before slicing it against the grain.

To make the couscous

❋ While the beef is cooking, in a 10″ no-stick skillet, combine the oil, scallions, red peppers, and garlic. Cook and stir over medium-high heat for 1 minute. Add the chicken stock, couscous, and lemon juice; bring to a boil. Cover and remove from the heat. Let stand for 5 minutes, or until the liquid has been absorbed. Add the parsley and fluff with a fork. Serve with the beef.

Italian Meatball Sandwiches

Stuffed with flavor, these subs will satisfy even hungry teens. You save $3 a serving when you make them at home rather than buying them from a fast-food restaurant.

```
 1  pound extra-lean beef ground round
¼  cup dry bread crumbs
 1  cup coarsely chopped onions
 4  cloves garlic, minced
 1  can (14 ounces) reduced-sodium whole tomatoes
      (with juice), chopped
 2  tablespoons tomato paste
 1  tablespoon sugar
 1  teaspoon dried basil
½  teaspoon dried oregano
 1  long loaf (16 ounces) Italian or French bread,
      halved horizontally
½  cup shredded low-fat mozzarella cheese
```

❋ In a medium bowl, combine the beef, bread crumbs, and ¼ cup of the onions; mix well. Form into 1″ meatballs.

❋ Coat a 10″ no-stick skillet with no-stick spray; set over medium-high heat. When the skillet is hot, add the garlic and the remaining ¾ cup onions; cook and stir for 5 minutes, or until the onions are golden brown. Add the meatballs; cook for 5 minutes, or until the meatballs are browned on the bottom. Turn the meatballs; add the tomatoes (with juice), tomato paste, sugar, basil, and oregano. Cover and cook for 10 minutes, or until the meatballs are no longer pink in the center. Check by inserting the tip of a sharp knife in the center of 1 meatball.

❋ Scoop out the bread from the bottom half of the loaf; reserve the bread crumbs for another use. Spoon the meatballs and sauce into the bread shell; top with the mozzarella and the top half of the bread. Cut into 8 sandwiches.

Makes 8 servings

Per serving
Calories 324
Total fat 10.3 g.
Saturated fat 4 g.
Cholesterol 39 mg.
Sodium 479 mg.
Fiber 0.9 g.

Cost per serving

42¢

Kitchen Tip

You can grind the bread crumbs in a blender, then freeze in a plastic bag for adding to soups, topping casseroles, and toasting to sprinkle on salads. It's a smart use for stale bread as well as the soft crumbs scooped from the center of this loaf.

Easy Marinades for Meat

Marinades are the most effective way to flavor and moisten extra-lean cuts of meat which can often be dry due to lack of fat. Use about 1 pound of lean beef or pork with any of the following marinades. For the best results, marinate the meat in the refrigerator for at least 1 hour. To keep meats moist during cooking, baste them frequently with the marinade.

❀ *Chinese Cheer.* Combine 3 tablespoons honey, 1 tablespoon reduced-sodium soy sauce, 1 tablespoon dry sherry (optional), 1 tablespoon minced jalapeño peppers (wear plastic gloves when handling), 1 teaspoon dark sesame oil, and 1 teaspoon minced garlic. Makes about ⅓ cup.

❀ *Citrus Glaze.* Combine ¼ cup lemon juice, 1 tablespoon honey, 1 teaspoon grated lemon rind, ¼ teaspoon salt, and ¼ teaspoon ground black pepper. Makes about ⅓ cup.

❀ *Curry Yogurt.* Combine ½ cup nonfat plain yogurt, 1 table-spoon packed brown sugar, 1 teaspoon curry powder, and 1 teaspoon olive oil. Makes about ½ cup.

❀ *Honey and Spice.* Combine 3 tablespoons honey, 2 tablespoons Dijon mustard, 1 tablespoon lemon juice, 1 tablespoon frozen orange juice concentrate, and 1 teaspoon ground cinnamon. Makes about ⅓ cup.

❀ *Latin Salsa.* Combine ⅓ cup mild salsa, 1 tablespoon packed brown sugar, ½ teaspoon ground cumin, ¼ teaspoon ground red pepper, and a pinch of salt. Makes about ⅓ cup.

❀ *Maple Madness.* Combine ¼ cup balsamic vinegar, 3 tablespoons maple syrup, 1 teaspoon minced garlic, and 1 teaspoon olive oil. Makes about ½ cup.

❀ *Tomato Bliss.* Combine ¼ cup tomato puree, ¼ cup nonfat plain yogurt, 1 tablespoon reduced-sodium soy sauce, 1 teaspoon chili powder, 1 teaspoon minced garlic, and 1 teaspoon sugar. Makes about ½ cup.

❀ *Zippy Mustard.* Combine ¼ cup lemon or lime juice, 1 tablespoon Dijon mustard, 1 tablespoon chopped fresh parsley or cilantro, 1 teaspoon minced garlic, and 1 teaspoon grated lime or lemon rind. Makes about ⅓ cup.

MINTED ROAST LAMB

A leg of lamb is a traditional Sunday supper for many savings-conscious families around the world, because the leftovers can be used in so many ways all week long. On sale it can cost as little as $1.30 a serving.

½ cup mint-flavored apple jelly
2 teaspoons minced garlic
½ cup chopped fresh mint
1 leg of lamb (about 4 pounds), trimmed of fat
1½ cups defatted chicken stock
1 cup couscous
¼ cup minced scallions

❋ Preheat the oven to 450°F. In a small bowl, combine the jelly, garlic, and ¼ cup of the mint. Set the lamb on a rack in a roasting pan. With a sharp knife, make deep slits in the lamb. Spread the jelly mixture in the slits.

❋ Reduce the temperature to 350°F. Cover and roast for 2 hours, or until a thermometer inserted in the thickest part registers 140°F for medium rare. Remove from the oven; let stand for 5 minutes.

❋ Slice the lamb; arrange about 3 slices on each plate. (Reserve the remaining lamb for another use.)

THREE MEALS IN ONE

Buying large cuts, like the leg of lamb in this recipe, reduces the per-serving costs from $4 (for loin chops) to less than $1.30. You can freeze the leftover cooked lamb for up to 6 weeks. Use it in the Greek Lamb Kabobs over Confetti Rice (page 152) or Moussaka (page 153).

Makes 12 servings

Per 3 ounces
Calories 241
Total fat 6.1 g.
Saturated fat 2.2 g.
Cholesterol 58 mg.
Sodium 56 mg.
Fiber 0.2 g.

Cost per serving

$1.59

KITCHEN TIP

You can serve minted couscous with the lamb. In a medium saucepan, combine 1½ cups defatted chicken stock, 1 cup couscous, and ¼ cup minced scallions; bring to a boil over medium-high heat. Remove from the heat; cover and let stand for 5 minutes, or until the liquid has been absorbed. Add ¼ cup chopped fresh mint and fluff with a fork.

Beef, Pork, and Lamb

Per serving
Calories 235
Total fat 4.8 g.
Saturated fat 1.7 g.
Cholesterol 52 mg.
Sodium 354 mg.
Fiber 1.4 g.

Cost per serving

97¢

KITCHEN TIP

If you don't have 12" skewers, you can use 8 short skewers (6" long).

GREEK LAMB KABOBS OVER CONFETTI RICE

Lamb kabobs are traditional picnic fare in Greece, often cooked over a charcoal brazier. Topping the cooked lamb with a yogurt sauce gives it a delicious tangy flavor.

- 1 cup long-grain white rice
- 1 cup nonfat plain yogurt
- ½ cup minced red onions
- 1 tablespoon honey
- 2 cloves garlic, minced
- 1 teaspoon curry powder
- ¼ cup defatted chicken stock
- 2 tablespoons chopped scallions
- 2 tablespoons whole kernel corn
- 2 tablespoons diced carrots
- ½ teaspoon salt
- ½ teaspoon ground black pepper
- 2 cups 1" cubes cooked leg of lamb, trimmed of fat (page 151)
- 1 green pepper, cut into 1" pieces
- 4 cherry tomatoes

❋ Preheat the grill or broiler. Cook the rice according to the package directions.

❋ In a medium bowl, combine the yogurt, onions, honey, garlic, and curry powder; stir well. Let stand at room temperature for 15 minutes, stirring occasionally.

❋ Coat a 10" no-stick skillet with no-stick spray; set it over medium-high heat. When the pan is hot, add the stock, scallions, corn, and carrots. Cook and stir for 5 minutes, or until the carrots are soft. Add the rice. Cover and cook for 3 minutes, stirring occasionally. Remove from the heat. Add the salt and pepper.

❋ Meanwhile, thread the lamb and green peppers onto 4 skewers (12" long). Coat with no-stick spray. Grill or broil 4" from the heat for 5 minutes. Turn and cook for 2 minutes more, or until the lamb has browned on all sides. Add the tomatoes to the skewers; cook for 1 minute, or until the tomatoes are hot. Serve the kabobs over the rice mixture. Top with the sauce.

MOUSSAKA

Middle Eastern cooks designed this dish to use up leftover lamb or beef by combining it with eggplant and tomatoes in a baked cheese custard. Salting, then rinsing, the eggplant slices softens them so they don't absorb oil while cooking.

2 medium eggplants, thinly sliced
1 tablespoon salt
2 medium onions, diced
1 teaspoon minced garlic
2 cups diced cooked leg of lamb, trimmed of fat (page 151)
¼ cup defatted chicken stock
1 can (14 ounces) reduced-sodium tomatoes (with juice), chopped
1 teaspoon ground black pepper
1 cup nonfat cottage cheese
½ cup nonfat plain yogurt
2 eggs
¼ cup shredded nonfat mozzarella cheese

❋ Preheat the oven to 350°F. Coat a 13" × 9" baking dish with no-stick spray.

❋ Arrange the eggplant in a colander in several layers, sprinkling each layer with salt. Cover with a plate and weight it with a heavy can. Set the colander in the sink for 30 minutes.

❋ Meanwhile, coat a 10" no-stick skillet with no-stick spray. Set it over medium-high heat. When the skillet is hot, add the onions and garlic. Cook and stir for 5 minutes. Add the lamb and chicken stock. Cook and stir for 1 minute. Add the tomatoes (with juice); bring to a boil. Reduce the heat to medium. Cook, stirring occasionally, for 20 minutes. Add the pepper.

❋ In a blender or a food processor, combine the cottage cheese, yogurt, eggs, and mozzarella. Set aside.

❋ Rinse the eggplant until all traces of salt are gone; pat dry. Arrange half the eggplant in the baking dish. Top with the lamb mixture and the remaining eggplant. Add the cheese mixture.

❋ Bake for 35 to 45 minutes, or until the moussaka is golden brown. Cool slightly before cutting it into 6 squares.

Makes 6 servings

Per serving
Calories 219
Total fat 5.3 g.
Saturated fat 1.7 g.
Cholesterol 105 mg.
Sodium 566 mg.
Fiber 1.3 g.

Cost per serving

83¢

FISH AND SHELLFISH

Fresh from the sea: Fish and shellfish are nutritious additions to any diet, but they can often be prohibitively expensive—unless you know how to find the bargains that wait for the smart seafood shopper. Experts recommend two plans: (1) shop the sales and (2) replace the type of fish in your recipe with the often-discounted catch of the day. You can also experiment with regional varieties, which are often delicious and lower in price.

Surprisingly, shellfish can be a bargain too—if you buy it frozen in bulk at your warehouse store and rethink its position on the plate. In these recipes, we make seafood go further. A few ounces of shrimp or scallops added to a vegetable or pasta stir-fry give you seafood's high-quality protein and minerals, but the cost stays reasonable. So enjoying the delicious recipes in this chapter couldn't be simpler.

Per serving
Calories 209
Total fat 4.1 g.
Saturated fat 0.9 g.
Cholesterol 78 mg.
Sodium 495 mg.
Fiber 1.8 g.

Cost per serving

50¢

NEW ENGLAND FISH CAKES

Codfish cakes are a New England staple, but you don't have to be a thrifty Yankee to enjoy this nutritious dish. Leftover mashed potatoes work beautifully in this recipe. (Use about 1½ cups.)

1 large baking potato, peeled and cubed
1 teaspoon olive oil
1 large onion, minced
8 ounces cod fillets, coarsely chopped
1 large egg, lightly beaten
3 drops hot-pepper sauce
2 tablespoons minced scallions
½ teaspoon dry mustard
½ teaspoon salt
¼ teaspoon ground black pepper
¾ cup dry bread crumbs

❋ Cook the potatoes in boiling water for 15 minutes, or until they are soft. Check by inserting the tip of a sharp knife. Drain, then mash. Cool.

❋ In a 10″ no-stick skillet, combine the oil and onions; cook and stir over medium-high heat for 5 minutes, or until the onions are soft.

❋ In a medium bowl, gently combine the onions, potatoes, cod, egg, hot-pepper sauce, scallions, mustard, salt, and pepper. Form into 4 fish cakes; press each fish cake in the bread crumbs to cover both sides. Place the fish cakes on a plate. Cover and refrigerate for 30 minutes.

❋ Coat a 10″ no-stick skillet with no-stick spray. Set it over medium-high heat. When the skillet is hot, add the fish cakes. Cover and cook for 5 to 7 minutes. Turn and cook for 5 minutes more, or until the fish cakes are firm and golden brown. Serve immediately.

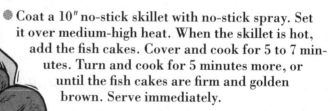

Baked Cod with Lemon and Herbs

You won't miss those restaurant meals with this gourmet recipe. We use a foolproof French method—cooking in foil—for keeping fish flavorful and moist. You can also use a very tightly covered pan for the same moisture-sealing effect, which turns ordinary fish into an extraordinary dinner with only the simplest seasonings.

¼ cup chopped scallions
3 tablespoons chopped fresh parsley
2 tablespoons lemon juice
1 tablespoon grated lemon rind
2 cloves garlic, minced
1 teaspoon olive oil
4 cod fillets (4 ounces each)

❋ Preheat the oven to 450°F. Place a 12″ × 12″ piece of foil on a baking sheet.

❋ In a small bowl, combine the scallions, parsley, lemon juice, lemon rind, garlic, and oil. Arrange the fish on the foil in a single layer. Top with the lemon mixture. Fold the sides of the foil over the fish, creating a sealed packet.

❋ Bake for 8 minutes, or until the fish flakes when lightly pressed with a fork and is opaque in the center. Check by inserting the tip of a sharp knife in the center of 1 fillet. Serve with the cooking liquid.

Makes 4 servings

Per serving
Calories 110
Total fat 1.9 g.
Saturated fat 0.3 g.
Cholesterol 49 mg.
Sodium 71 mg.
Fiber 0.2 g.

Cost per serving

84¢

Good Nutrition from the Sea

Most inexpensive white fish—especially cod, haddock, and pollack—is extremely low in fat. Fillets of orange roughy, red snapper, and sea bass are also lean and affordable choices. Occasional servings of darker-fleshed fish, like salmon and tuna, provide valuable omega-3 fatty acids, which can help lower blood cholesterol.

MEDITERRANEAN BAKED FISH

Flavorings from the coast of southern France permeate this easy baked fish, making it a great recipe for less expensive items like cod, haddock, and other white-fleshed fish.

Per serving
Calories 168
Total fat 3.6 g.
Saturated fat 0.4 g.
Cholesterol 49 mg.
Sodium 234 mg.
Fiber 1.6 g.

Cost per serving

$1.21

¼ cup white wine or water
1 teaspoon olive oil
3 cloves garlic, minced
1¼ cups fish stock or defatted chicken stock
1 cup chopped tomatoes
½ cup chopped onions
⅓ cup chopped green or sweet red peppers
½ teaspoon dried thyme
⅛ teaspoon dried sage
2 bay leaves
5 small black olives, pitted and chopped
4 cod or haddock fillets (4 ounces each)
¼ teaspoon salt
¼ teaspoon ground black pepper

❁ Preheat the oven to 400°F. Coat a Dutch oven with no-stick spray; set it over medium-high heat. When the Dutch oven is hot, add the wine or water, oil, and garlic; cook and stir for 2 minutes. Add the stock, tomatoes, onions, peppers, thyme, sage, bay leaves, and olives; bring to a boil. Lay the fish over the vegetables; cover and bake for 10 minutes, or until the fish is opaque in the center. Check by inserting the tip of a sharp knife in the center of 1 fillet. Remove and discard the bay leaves. Add the salt and pepper.

SALMON BURGERS

Canned salmon is a convenient and cheap way to get good fish protein into your menus. It makes delicious burgers with this lemon-ginger seasoning.

  1 can (16 ounces) salmon, flaked
 ½ cup reduced-sodium dry bread crumbs
  3 scallions, chopped
  2 eggs, lightly beaten
  1 teaspoon minced fresh ginger
  1 teaspoon lemon juice
 ⅛ teaspoon paprika
 ½ teaspoon ground black pepper
  2 tablespoons nonfat plain yogurt
  1 tablespoon nonfat mayonnaise
 ½ teaspoon honey
  1 teaspoon Dijon mustard

❁ In a medium bowl, combine the salmon, bread crumbs, scallions, eggs, ginger, lemon juice, and paprika. Form into 4 burgers; sprinkle with the pepper. Cover and refrigerate for 10 minutes.

❁ Coat a 10″ no-stick skillet with no-stick spray; set it over medium-high heat. When the skillet is hot, add the burgers. Cook for 5 minutes; turn and cook for 3 minutes more, or until the burgers are firm and golden brown.

❁ In a small bowl, combine the yogurt, mayonnaise, honey, and mustard; spread on the burgers.

Makes 4 servings

Per serving
Calories 262
Total fat 11.9 g.
Saturated fat 2.9 g.
Cholesterol 133 mg.
Sodium 759 mg.
Fiber 0.3 g.

Cost per serving

73¢

KITCHEN TIP

You can serve the burgers on reduced-sodium sesame buns.

Per serving
Calories 168
Total fat 2.2 g.
Saturated fat 0.3 g.
Cholesterol 27 mg.
Sodium 53 mg.
Fiber 1.3 g.

Cost per serving

$1.99

HALIBUT WITH TROPICAL SALSA

This fruit salsa is delicious on any type of fish. It's made from canned pineapple and mandarin oranges, which are often on sale at the supermarket.

1 can (8 ounces) unsweetened crushed pineapple (with juice)
1 can (8 ounces) mandarin oranges, drained
½ cup minced green peppers
¼ cup minced red onions
¼ cup lime juice
2 tablespoons minced fresh parsley or cilantro
2 cloves garlic, minced
1 teaspoon ground cumin
4 halibut steaks (3 ounces each)

❋ Preheat the grill or broiler. In a medium bowl, combine the pineapple (with juice), oranges, peppers, onions, lime juice, parsley or cilantro, garlic, and cumin; stir well. Cover; let stand at room temperature for 10 minutes.

❋ Coat the halibut with no-stick spray; grill or broil 4″ from the heat for 5 minutes. Turn and grill or broil for 5 to 7 minutes, or until the fish is opaque in the center. Check by inserting the tip of a sharp knife in the center of 1 steak. Top with the salsa.

CHOOSE YOUR COOKING METHOD

The darker the flesh, the drier the heat, say cooking experts about cooking fish. Many white-fleshed fish are delicate and tend to dry out faster, so they are best cooked by poaching, steaming, baking in a liquid, or cooking in parchment or foil. Firmer-fleshed fish, such as salmon and catfish, are perfect for grilling and broiling.

OVEN-BAKED FISH AND CHIPS

This leaner oven-baked version of British street fare uses catfish instead of cod, a less expensive but more flavorful choice.

 2 large baking potatoes, cut into ¼" lengthwise slices
½ teaspoon paprika
¼ cup fine dry bread crumbs
½ teaspoon baking powder
¼ teaspoon dried thyme
¼ teaspoon dried basil
¼ teaspoon ground black pepper
⅛ teaspoon ground red pepper
⅛ teaspoon salt
¼ cup skim milk
 1 egg, lightly beaten
 4 catfish fillets (4 ounces each)

❀ Preheat the oven to 350°F. Coat a baking sheet with no-stick spray. Arrange the potatoes on the baking sheet; coat lightly with no-stick spray. Sprinkle them with the paprika. Toss to combine. Bake for 30 minutes, or until tender but not browned. Remove from the oven. Move the potatoes so they cover one half of the baking sheet.

❀ In a medium bowl, combine the bread crumbs, baking powder, thyme, basil, black pepper, red pepper, and salt. Add the milk and egg; mix well. Pat the catfish dry with paper towels. Dip the fish into the batter; place it next to the potatoes on the baking sheet. Bake for 20 minutes, or until the potatoes are crisp and golden brown and the fish is opaque in the center. Check by inserting the tip of a sharp knife into 1 fillet.

Makes 4 servings

Per serving
Calories 313
Total fat 5.9 g.
Saturated fat 1.6 g.
Cholesterol 157 mg.
Sodium 269 mg.
Fiber 2.6 g.

Cost per serving

$1.15

Orange Roughy
with Rosemary and Lemon

Makes 4 servings

Per serving
Calories 107
Total fat 1 g.
Saturated fat 0 g.
Cholesterol 22 mg.
Sodium 72 mg.
Fiber 1.2 g.

Cost per serving

51¢

Although orange roughy gives a rich flavor, you can use any regional white-fleshed fish for this easy oven-baked recipe.

4 orange roughy fillets (4 ounces each)
1 cup minced onions
½ cup minced green or sweet red peppers
   Juice of 1 small lemon
2 teaspoons minced garlic
½ teaspoon paprika
½ teaspoon dried rosemary, crushed
¼ teaspoon ground cumin

● Coat a 13" × 9" glass baking dish with no-stick spray; arrange the fish in the baking dish and top with the onions and peppers.

● In a small bowl, combine the lemon juice, garlic, paprika, rosemary, and cumin; pour over the fish. Cover and refrigerate for 1 hour.

● Preheat the oven to 300°F. Bake the fish in the marinade for 1 hour, or until the fish is opaque in the center. Check by inserting the tip of a sharp knife in the center of 1 fillet.

Instant Fish Toppers

Try this tasty quick topping to dress up leftover cooked seafood. In a blender, combine equal amounts of nonfat plain yogurt and low-fat cottage cheese; puree. Season with lemon juice, minced garlic, prepared horseradish, Dijon mustard, or minced fresh herbs. Spoon over the seafood.

TERIYAKI FISH WITH VEGETABLES

Classic Japanese teriyaki sauce couldn't be simpler to make at home, and you save 45¢ a serving over the bottled variety. In this recipe, it's both marinade and topping for broiled fish and vegetables.

1½ cups fish stock or defatted chicken stock
⅓ cup sugar or honey
¼ cup reduced-sodium soy sauce
2 onions, thickly sliced
2 carrots, diagonally sliced
1 medium zucchini, diagonally sliced
1 cup brown rice
4 red snapper fillets (4 ounces each)

❀ In a medium saucepan, combine the stock, sugar or honey, and soy sauce; bring to a boil over medium-high heat. Cook and stir for 5 minutes. Pour the sauce into a shallow baking dish. Arrange the onions, carrots, and zucchini in the baking dish; cover and refrigerate for 1 hour, turning occasionally.

❀ Cook the rice according to the package directions; cover to keep warm.

❀ Meanwhile, preheat the broiler. Coat a broiler pan with no-stick spray. Remove the vegetables from the sauce and place on the broiler pan. Broil 4″ from the heat for 5 minutes, turning frequently, or until they are lightly browned and tender. Place the vegetables on a plate; cover to keep warm.

❀ Coat the fish with no-stick spray; brush with the sauce. Place the fish on the broiler pan. Place the remaining sauce in a small saucepan. Bring to a boil over medium-high heat. Reduce the heat to low; keep warm.

❀ Broil the fish for 3 minutes; turn and cook for 3 minutes more, or until the fish is opaque in the center. Check by inserting the tip of a sharp knife in the center of 1 fillet.

❀ Place the rice on a platter. Arrange the vegetables on the rice; place the fish on top. Serve with the sauce.

Makes 4 servings

Per serving
Calories 412
Total fat 3.2 g.
Saturated fat 0.6 g.
Cholesterol 42 mg.
Sodium 598 mg.
Fiber 5.2 g.

Cost per serving

$1.67

Per serving
Calories 135
Total fat 1 g.
Saturated fat 0.2 g.
Cholesterol 49 mg.
Sodium 90 mg.
Fiber 1.5 g.

Cost per serving

$1.07

SPICY FISH WITH PEPPERS

This Jamaican recipe calls for a variety of sweet and hot peppers. It's most economical to make in late summer, when peppers are on sale or ripe from your garden.

1 green pepper, chopped
1 sweet red pepper, chopped
¼ cup chopped fresh parsley
1 small jalapeño pepper, seeded and chopped
    (wear plastic gloves when handling)
    Juice of 1 lime
2 tablespoons cider vinegar
4 cloves garlic, minced
2 teaspoons packed brown sugar
4 cod fillets (4 ounces each)

✴ In a small bowl, combine the green peppers, red peppers, parsley, jalapeño peppers, lime juice, vinegar, garlic, and brown sugar; stir well. Let stand at room temperature for 15 minutes.

✴ Preheat the oven to 400°F. Coat a 13" × 9" glass baking dish with no-stick spray; arrange the fish in the baking dish. Top with the sauce.

✴ Bake for 15 minutes, or until the fish is opaque in the center. Check by inserting the tip of a sharp knife in the center of 1 fillet.

SEAFOOD SAFETY TIPS

Seafood is particularly perishable, so it's good to know a few safety guidelines for storage and preparation.

✴ Keep seafood refrigerated until you're ready to cook it.

✴ Use fresh seafood within 24 hours.

✴ Wash your hands thoroughly in hot soapy water before and after you handle seafood.

✴ Marinate seafood in the refrigerator.

✴ Cut fish on a plate or cutting board and wash the plate or board thoroughly after using it.

SEAFOOD CREOLE

We trimmed down the cost—but kept the zesty appeal—of this traditional New Orleans one-pot meal by using cod along with the shrimp. Serve it with cooked rice.

 2 teaspoons olive oil
 4 cups chopped reduced-sodium canned tomatoes (with juice)
 2 cups chopped onions
 1 cup chopped green peppers
 1 cup chopped celery
 2 teaspoons minced garlic
¼ cup white wine (optional)
 1 cup fish stock or defatted chicken stock
 1 tablespoon paprika
 1 teaspoon ground red pepper
 2 bay leaves
 8 ounces cod fillets, cut into 1" cubes
 4 ounces peeled and deveined uncooked medium
      shrimp
 1 tablespoon cornstarch
¼ cup water
¼ teaspoon salt
¼ teaspoon ground black pepper

✹ Coat a Dutch oven with no-stick spray; add the oil. Set the Dutch oven over medium-high heat. When the oil is hot, add the tomatoes (with juice), onions, green peppers, celery, and garlic; cook and stir for 5 minutes, or until the onions are soft. Add the stock, wine (if using), paprika, red pepper, and bay leaves; bring to a boil. Cook and stir for 5 minutes. Add the fish; cover and cook for 3 to 5 minutes, or until the fish is opaque in the center. Check by inserting the tip of a sharp knife in the center of 1 cube of fish. Add the shrimp; cover and cook for 1 minute, or until the shrimp turns pink.

✹ In a small bowl, combine the cornstarch and water; add to the Dutch oven. Cook and stir for 1 minute, or until the sauce thickens slightly. Add the salt and pepper. Remove and discard the bay leaves.

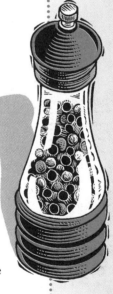

Makes 4 servings

Per serving
Calories 209
Total fat 4 g.
Saturated fat 0.6 g.
Cholesterol 68 mg.
Sodium 280 mg.
Fiber 4.6 g.

Cost per serving

$1.13

Per serving
Calories 160
Total fat 0.9 g.
Saturated fat 0.2 g.
Cholesterol 49 mg.
Sodium 239 mg.
Fiber 2.7 g.

Cost per serving

$1.32

SKILLET FISH WITH TOMATO-ONION SAUCE

On a rushed night, this recipe saves you time and money. Just layer your supermarket's catch of the day in a skillet, cover the fillets with a simple tomato sauce, and cook for 10 minutes—that's it!

    1 can (16 ounces) reduced-sodium tomato sauce
    1 large onion, chopped
    1 green pepper, chopped
    4 cod or orange roughy fillets (4 ounces each)
    ¼ teaspoon salt
    ¼ teaspoon ground black pepper
    ¼ cup chopped fresh parsley

⚜ In a medium bowl, combine the tomato sauce, onions, and peppers. Set aside.

⚜ Coat a 10″ no-stick skillet with no-stick spray; set it over medium heat. When the pan is hot, add the fish. Top with the sauce. Cover and cook for 10 minutes, or until the fish is opaque in the center. Check by inserting the tip of a sharp knife in the center of 1 fillet. Add the salt and pepper. Sprinkle with the parsley.

GLAZED FISH KABOBS

Makes 4 servings

Per serving
Calories 148
Total fat 1.7 g.
Saturated fat 0.3 g.
Cholesterol 32 mg.
Sodium 375 mg.
Fiber 2.5 g.

Cost per serving

92¢

Smart cooks make meat or fish more affordable by grilling it with plenty of vegetables on skewers. This recipe uses an easy glaze made with mustard and vinegar to keep the fish moist.

    1 can (8 ounces) unsweetened pineapple chunks (with juice)
    ¼ cup stone-ground mustard
    1 tablespoon reduced-sodium soy sauce
    1 tablespoon honey
    1 tablespoon frozen apple juice concentrate
    1 teaspoon vinegar
    6 ounces pollack fillets, cut into 2″ cubes
    1 green pepper, cut into 1″ pieces
    1 sweet red pepper, cut into 1″ pieces
    8 mushrooms
    1 medium onion, cut into 1″ pieces

- Drain the pineapple. Place the juice in a shallow nonmetal dish. Add the mustard, soy sauce, honey, apple juice concentrate, and vinegar; mix well. Add the fish; toss to coat. Cover and refrigerate for 1 hour, stirring occasionally.

- Preheat the grill or broiler. Thread the fish onto skewers, alternating with the green and red peppers, mushrooms, onions, and pineapple. Brush with the marinade. Grill or broil 4″ from the heat, turning frequently and brushing with the marinade, for 5 minutes, or until the fish is opaque in the center and the vegetables are lightly browned. Check by inserting the tip of a sharp knife in the center of 1 piece of fish.

TROUT WITH GREEK-STYLE BULGUR

If you live in an area that regularly receives fresh trout, grill it and offer it along with this delicious mint- and lemon-flavored bulgur.

½ cup shredded carrots
¼ cup minced red onions
¼ cup minced green or sweet red peppers
2 cloves garlic, minced
2 teaspoons minced fresh mint
1 cup defatted chicken stock or fish stock
2 teaspoons lemon juice
½ cup medium bulgur
2 whole trout (8 ounces each)

- Coat a 10″ no-stick skillet with no-stick spray; set it over medium-high heat. Add the carrots, onions, peppers, garlic, and mint; cook and stir for 2 minutes. Add the stock and lemon juice; bring to a boil. Add the bulgur; cook for 10 minutes. Remove the skillet from the heat. Cover and let stand for 10 minutes, or until the bulgur is tender and the liquid is absorbed.

- Meanwhile, preheat the grill or broiler. Coat the trout with no-stick spray. Grill or broil 4″ from the heat for 5 minutes; turn and cook for 5 to 7 minutes more, or until the fish is opaque in the center. Check by inserting the tip of a sharp knife in the center of 1 trout. Divide into 4 servings. Serve with the bulgur.

Makes 4 servings

Per serving
Calories 215
Total fat 4.2 g.
Saturated fat 0.8 g.
Cholesterol 66 mg.
Sodium 40 mg.
Fiber 4.9 g.

Cost per serving

$1.51

Makes 4 servings

Per serving
Calories 187
Total fat 5.2 g.
Saturated fat 0.8 g.
Cholesterol 22 mg.
Sodium 190 mg.
Fiber 2.2 g.

Cost per serving

99¢

CHILLED POACHED FISH SALAD

Only 6 ounces of salmon serve 4 people with this delicious cold plate—ideal in the summer when vegetables are abundant.

 1 salmon fillet (6 ounces)
½ medium onion, sliced
½ cup white wine or fish stock
¼ cup balsamic vinegar
 2 tablespoons lime juice or lemon juice
 2 tablespoons nonfat plain yogurt
 1 tablespoon olive oil
 2 teaspoons sugar or honey
 4 cups torn leaf lettuce
 1 cup shredded carrots
 1 cucumber, peeled, seeded and sliced
 1 can (8 ounces) mandarin oranges, drained
¼ teaspoon salt
¼ teaspoon ground black pepper

❉ In a small no-stick skillet, combine the fish, onions, and wine or stock; bring to a boil over medium-high heat. Cover and cook for 6 minutes, or until the fish is opaque in the center. Check by inserting the tip of a sharp knife in the center of the fillet. Transfer the fish to a plate; cover and refrigerate for 1 hour, or until chilled.

❉ Strain the onions from the stock; reserve the stock for another use. Place the onions in a blender or food processor. Add the vinegar, lime juice or lemon juice, yogurt, oil, and sugar or honey; puree.

❉ In a large salad bowl, combine the lettuce, carrots, cucumbers, and oranges; add three-fourths of the dressing. Toss well. Divide among serving plates. Flake the salmon and divide it among the plates; drizzle with the remaining dressing. Sprinkle with the salt and pepper.

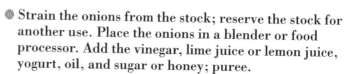

SESAME FISH WITH VEGETABLES

Makes 4 servings

Per serving
Calories 182
Total fat 3.3 g.
Saturated fat 0.6 g.
Cholesterol 47 mg.
Sodium 187 mg.
Fiber 3.2 g.

Cost per serving

$1.76

Marinated fish is sautéed, then served over a bed of vegetable couscous—a satisfying yet economical summer entrée for only $1.76 a serving.

4 red snapper fillets (4 ounces each)
2 scallions, chopped
1 tablespoon frozen orange juice concentrate
2 teaspoons reduced-sodium soy sauce
2 teaspoons cornstarch
1 teaspoon grated fresh ginger
1 teaspoon minced garlic
1 teaspoon dark sesame oil
2 cups chopped broccoli
1 cup shredded carrots
2 cups chopped spinach

❋ In a shallow nonmetal dish, combine the fish, scallions, orange juice concentrate, soy sauce, cornstarch, ginger, garlic, and oil; cover and refrigerate for 1 hour, turning occasionally.

❋ Coat a 10″ no-stick skillet with no-stick spray; set it over medium-high heat. When the pan is hot, add the broccoli and carrots; cook and stir for 2 minutes, or until the vegetables are bright in color. Add the spinach, fish, and marinade. Cover and cook for 4 to 6 minutes, or until the fish is opaque in the center. Check by inserting the tip of a sharp knife in the center of 1 fillet.

Per serving
Calories 479
Total fat 9.5 g.
Saturated fat 1.6 g.
Cholesterol 89 mg.
Sodium 420 mg.
Fiber 1.7 g.

Cost per serving

$1.57

SHRIMP AND ORZO SALAD

Orzo is an inexpensive rice-shaped pasta that is easily found in supermarkets. If using less expensive bulk orzo, measure 3 cups (uncooked) for this recipe.

    1 package (16 ounces) orzo
    8 ounces peeled and deveined uncooked medium shrimp
    1 cup chopped reduced-sodium canned tomatoes, drained
    1 cup shredded carrots
    1 cup peeled, seeded, and sliced cucumbers
   ½ cup chopped scallions
   ¼ cup lemon juice
    2 tablespoons olive oil
    2 tablespoons nonfat plain yogurt
    1 tablespoon grated Parmesan cheese
    1 teaspoon grated lemon rind
    1 teaspoon minced garlic
   ½ teaspoon salt
   ½ teaspoon ground black pepper

❀ Bring a large pot of water to a boil over medium-high heat. Add the orzo; cook for 6 minutes. Add the shrimp; cook for 2 minutes, or until the shrimp turns pink and the orzo is tender. Drain well.

❀ In a large salad bowl, combine the orzo, shrimp, tomatoes, carrots, cucumbers, scallions, lemon juice, oil, yogurt, Parmesan, lemon rind, garlic, salt, and pepper; toss to combine.

SHRIMP RAVIOLI WITH HERBED TOMATO SAUCE

Wonton skins make this shrimp-cheese ravioli elegant and easy, and you can buy them for less than the cost of fresh ravioli pasta in the supermarket.

Makes 4 servings

Per serving
Calories 232
Total fat 3.3 g.
Saturated fat 1.6 g.
Cholesterol 43 mg.
Sodium 557 mg.
Fiber 2.4 g.

Cost per serving

76¢

- 1 cup minced onions
- 2 cans (14 ounces each) reduced-sodium tomatoes, chopped (with juice)
- 1 teaspoon dried oregano
- 1 teaspoon dried basil
- 2 cloves garlic, minced
- ¼ teaspoon salt
- ¼ teaspoon ground black pepper
- 3 ounces peeled and deveined cooked medium shrimp
- ½ cup nonfat ricotta cheese
- ¼ cup shredded low-fat mozzarella cheese
- 2 tablespoons grated Parmesan cheese
- 2 tablespoons minced fresh parsley
- 16 wonton skins

❋ Coat a 10″ no-stick skillet with no-stick spray; set it over medium-high heat. When the skillet is hot, add the onions; cook and stir for 3 minutes. Add the tomatoes (with juice), oregano, basil, and garlic; bring to a boil. Reduce the heat to medium; cook, stirring occasionally, for 20 minutes, or until the sauce is thick. Add the salt and pepper.

❋ Meanwhile, in a food processor or blender, combine the shrimp, ricotta, mozzarella, and Parmesan; puree. Transfer to a medium bowl. Stir in the parsley. Spoon 1 tablespoon of the shrimp mixture into the center of each wonton skin; lightly brush the edges with water. Fold in a triangle shape and press to seal.

❋ Bring a large pot of water to a boil. Cook the ravioli, stirring occasionally, for 2 minutes, or until tender. Drain well. Top with the tomato sauce.

TIPS FOR TOP-NOTCH FISH MENUS

Selecting Fish

❋ Shop for warehouse store bulk buys on flash-frozen seafood and fillets; compare the cost per pound with supermarket sales. Loose packs allow you to keep the fish frozen, taking out just the amount you need for a recipe.

❋ Fish, such as whitefish or small salmon, plummets in cost when you buy it whole. It's often fresher, too. Look for firm flesh, clear eyes, shiny scales, and deep red color under the gills—a sure sign that the fish was just caught. Cut steaks and fillets should be moist and firm. Give fish the "smell test." Fresh fish should never smell strong or unpleasant. If it does, pass it by.

❋ Refrigerate or freeze all fish in its original wrappings. Avoid letting frozen fish thaw even partially until you're ready to cook it. Keep fish refrigerated until cooking time.

Storing Fish

❋ Try a fisherman's technique: Fillets and whole fish you will be storing for more than 2 weeks will stay freshest frozen in water. Place your fresh fish in a plastic bag; seal well. Place the bag in an empty milk carton. Fill the carton with water; freeze. The liquid protects the fish from freezer odors and burn. You'll be amazed at how fresh it tastes when you cook it.

❋ Be sure to use fresh or thawed fish sooner than 3 days of refrigerating it.

❋ For best results, store your fish in the coldest part of the refrigerator (often on the back of the top shelf).

Cooking Fish

❋ Let frozen fish thaw in the refrigerator overnight—not on your kitchen counter or in the sink.

❋ Rinse and pat dry all fish before cooking to remove any odors or bacteria.

(continued)

- Allow 8 to 10 minutes of cooking time per inch of thickness for most fish. The exception: Fish cooks slightly faster in foil or parchment because of the intense steam heat inside the wrapping.

- Delicate fish like cod, sole, and flounder dry out quickly and are best cooked in moist heat (such as steaming, braising, or cooking in foil or parchment). Firmer fish like salmon, tuna, orange roughy, and halibut do fine on the grill or under the broiler.

- Test for doneness by inserting the tip of a sharp knife in the center of the fish.

SALMON AND POTATO HASH

Despite its pricey reputation, salmon is often on sale for as little as $4.99 a pound. This easy recipe can be doubled and frozen. It makes a great brunch or light supper. Leftover potatoes work well for this dish.

Makes 4 servings

Per serving
Calories 318
Total fat 3.8 g.
Saturated fat 0.4 g.
Cholesterol 21 mg.
Sodium 54 mg.
Fiber 6.1 g.

Cost per serving

$1.25

- 1 teaspoon olive oil
- 4 cups diced potatoes
- 1½ cups diced onions
- 1 cup diced green or sweet red peppers
- 1 teaspoon minced garlic
- 4 ounces salmon fillet, finely chopped
- 1 tablespoon minced fresh parsley
- 2 teaspoons lemon juice
- ½ teaspoon prepared horseradish
- ⅓ cup low-fat sour cream
- 2 tablespoons chopped scallions

- Cook the potatoes in boiling water for 12 to 15 minutes, or until soft but not mushy. Drain and cool.

- Coat a 10″ no-stick skillet with no-stick spray; set it over medium-high heat. When the skillet is hot, add the oil, potatoes, onions, peppers, and garlic; cook and stir for 5 minutes, or until golden brown. Add the salmon, parsley, lemon juice, and horseradish; cook and stir for 5 minutes, or until the mixture is hot. Top with the sour cream and scallions.

SHRIMP, TOMATO, AND SPINACH SAUTÉ OVER NOODLES

Buy frozen shrimp in bulk at your warehouse store for this Greek-inspired dish of feta cheese, fresh spinach, and tomatoes.

8 ounces yolk-free egg noodles
½ cup minced onions
¼ cup defatted chicken stock
½ teaspoon olive oil
2 cloves garlic, minced
4 cups chopped fresh spinach
2 cups chopped fresh tomatoes
8 ounces peeled and deveined uncooked shrimp
⅓ cup nonfat sour cream
¼ cup crumbled feta cheese

❋ Cook the noodles according to the package directions; drain well.

❋ Meanwhile, in a 10″ no-stick skillet, combine the onions, chicken stock, oil, and garlic; bring to a boil over medium-high heat. Cook and stir for 5 minutes, or until the liquid evaporates. Add the spinach, tomatoes, and shrimp; cover and cook for 3 minutes, or until the shrimp turn pink. Add the noodles; cover and cook for 1 minute. Add the sour cream and feta cheese; remove the skillet from the heat. Stir well.

BULK BUYS ON SEAFOOD

Warehouse store bargains include plenty of seafood buys—often loose-packed in bulk bags in the frozen food section. You can pick up cooked, peeled shrimp for as little as $4.99 a pound, making them as affordable as fin fish. Just scoop out as much as you need for each recipe and keep the rest frozen for up to 2 months.

Basque Seafood Paella

Seafood lovers will flip over this hearty one-pot meal. It features two kinds of shellfish but costs only $1.90 a serving due to the high percentage of vegetables and rice.

2   teaspoons olive oil
2   teaspoons minced garlic
2   cups sliced onions
2   cups long-grain white rice
1   cup chopped sweet red or green peppers
1   package (10 ounces) frozen artichoke hearts, thawed
      and chopped
1   cup whole kernel corn
¼   cup white wine or apple juice
4   cups defatted chicken stock
2   cups diced reduced-sodium canned tomatoes
      (with juice)
2   drops hot-pepper sauce
1   cup frozen peas
6   ounces peeled and deveined uncooked medium
      shrimp
4   sea scallops, quartered
½   teaspoon ground black pepper
¼   teaspoon salt
¼   cup chopped fresh parsley

❋ Preheat the oven to 350°F. Coat a Dutch oven with no-stick spray; set it over medium-high heat. When the Dutch oven is hot, add the oil, garlic and onions; cook and stir for 5 minutes. Add the rice, peppers, artichoke hearts, corn, and wine or apple juice; cook and stir for 2 minutes. Add the chicken stock, tomatoes (with juice), and hot-pepper sauce; bring to a boil.

❋ Cover and bake for 35 minutes, or until the liquid is absorbed. Arrange the peas, shrimp, and scallops on top of the rice. Cover and bake for 5 minutes, or until the shrimp is bright pink. Add the pepper and salt; sprinkle with the parsley.

Makes 4 servings

Per serving
Calories 608
Total fat 4.7 g.
Saturated fat 0.8 g.
Cholesterol 78 mg.
Sodium 373 mg.
Fiber 9.1 g.

Cost per serving

$1.90

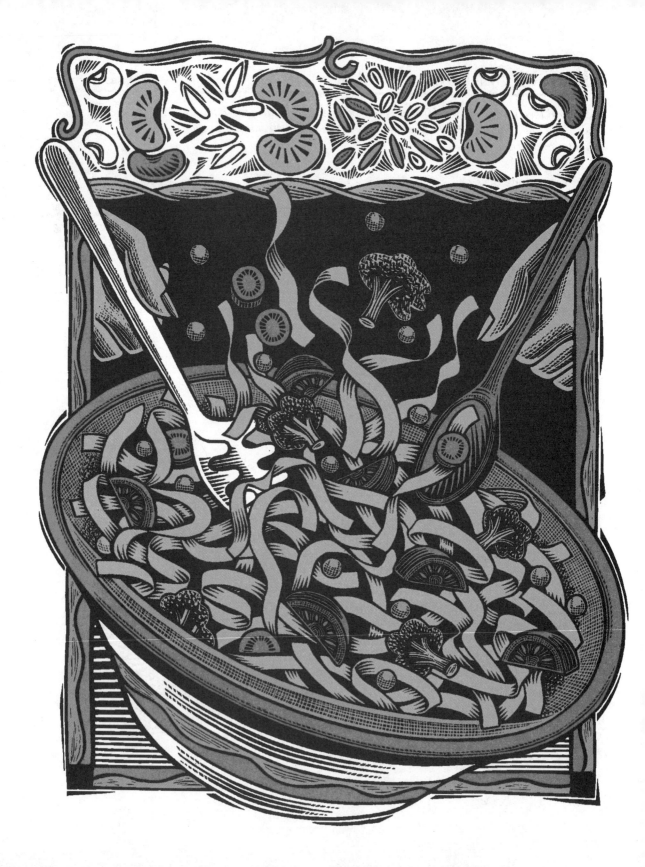

CHAPTER 8

PASTA AND GRAIN MAIN DISHES

W hat's basic to every culture's daily fare? Whole grains, beans, and pasta—the literal staff of life. They come in so many shapes, sizes, and flavors that you can eat a different kind every day for weeks and never have the same one twice. Not only that, grains, beans, and pasta can be the best bargain ever to hit your dinner table. For pennies a serving, you get plenty of complex carbohydrates, fiber, vitamins, and minerals with virtually no fat.

Economy experts like Amy Dacyczyn, author of *The Tightwad Gazette* books, and Jonni McCoy, author of *Miserly Moms*, sing the praises of whole grains and beans. These foods give you many times more lean protein than comparable amounts of meat or poultry. That's why healthwise budget-watchers serve fiber-filled whole grains and beans to stretch the protein dollar.

Per serving
Calories 279
Total fat 4.7 g.
Saturated fat 1.5 g.
Cholesterol 20 mg.
Sodium 469 mg.
Fiber 5.7 g.

Cost per serving

$1.20

CHICKEN LASAGNA

Layering sautéed strips of chicken breast with the vegetables makes this lasagna different and delicious.

12 lasagna noodles
 1 cup chopped onions
 2 chicken breast halves, skinned, boned, and cut into ¼" strips
⅓ cup apple juice
 2 cloves garlic, minced
 2 cups thinly sliced mushrooms
 1 cup diced green peppers
 1 cup shredded carrots
½ teaspoon salt
½ teaspoon ground black pepper
 1 cup nonfat cottage cheese
½ cup low-fat ricotta cheese
¼ cup grated Parmesan cheese
 2 cans (14 ounces each) reduced-sodium tomato sauce
¼ cup shredded low-fat mozzarella cheese

✺ Cook the noodles according to the package directions. Drain well; rinse under cold water.

✺ Meanwhile, in a 10" no-stick skillet, combine the onions, chicken, apple juice, and garlic; cook and stir over medium-high heat for 5 minutes, or until the onions soften. Add the mushrooms, green peppers, and carrots; cook and stir for 2 minutes. Remove from the heat; add the salt and pepper.

✺ In a blender or food processor, combine the cottage cheese, ricotta, and Parmesan; puree.

✺ Preheat the oven to 350°F. Coat a 13" × 9" baking pan with no-stick spray. Spread one-third of the chicken mixture in the pan. Top with 3 noodles and one-third of the cheese mixture and one-third of the tomato sauce. Repeat two times. Top with the remaining 3 noodles and the mozzarella.

✺ Cover and bake for 45 minutes. Uncover and bake for 10 to 15 minutes, or until the lasagna is bubbling and golden brown.

Spaghetti with Eggplant-Tomato Sauce

Eggplant replaces ground beef in this rich spaghetti sauce. You save dramatically on fat and cost.

1 teaspoon olive oil
1 cup chopped onions
2 cloves garlic, minced
3 cups chopped reduced-sodium canned tomatoes
   (with juice)
2 cups cubed peeled eggplant
½ cup chopped green or sweet red peppers
¼ cup balsamic vinegar
2 tablespoons tomato paste
1 teaspoon dried basil
½ teaspoon dried oregano
¼ teaspoon salt
¼ teaspoon ground black pepper
8 ounces spaghetti
1 tablespoon grated Parmesan cheese

❋ Coat a large saucepan with no-stick spray; set it over medium-high heat. When the pan is hot, add the oil, onions and garlic; cook and stir for 5 minutes, or until the onions are golden brown. Add the tomatoes, eggplant, peppers, vinegar, tomato paste, basil, and oregano; bring to a boil. Reduce the heat to medium; cook, stirring occasionally, for 20 minutes. Add the salt and pepper.

❋ Meanwhile, cook the spaghetti according to the package directions; drain well. Toss with the pasta sauce. Sprinkle with the Parmesan.

Makes 4 servings

Per serving
Calories 362
Total fat 3.5 g.
Saturated fat 0.7 g.
Cholesterol 1 mg.
Sodium 257 mg.
Fiber 2.8 g.

Cost per serving

60¢

Cheese Ends Can Be Big Bargains

Check with the deli counter in your supermarket for the price for the end of a loaf of low-fat or nonfat cheese (the part that can't be reached by the deli slicer). You can often save per pound because delis can't sell these ends. But always compare the price per pound to bulk prices, such as five-pound loaves at the warehouse store.

Mediterranean Baked Pasta with Cheese

Olives and Mediterranean herbs give this pasta dish a uniquely French flavor.

Makes 4 servings

Per serving
Calories 362
Total fat 5.9 g.
Saturated fat 2 g.
Cholesterol 8 mg.
Sodium 278 mg.
Fiber 2.9 g.

Cost per serving

70¢

8 ounces penne
½ defatted chicken stock
½ cup chopped onions
1 teaspoon olive oil
4 cloves garlic, chopped
2 cans (28 ounces each) reduced-sodium canned
    tomatoes (with juice), chopped
2 tablespoons tomato paste
1 tablespoon chopped black olives
1 teaspoon sugar
2 tablespoons chopped fresh parsley
½ teaspoon dried thyme
½ teaspoon dried basil
½ cup shredded low-fat mozzarella cheese

✤ Preheat the oven to 350°F. Coat a 3-quart casserole dish with no-stick spray. Cook the penne according to the package directions; drain well. Place in the casserole dish.

✤ Meanwhile, in a 10″ no-stick skillet, combine the chicken stock, onions, oil, and garlic. Bring to a boil over medium-high heat. Cook and stir for 2 minutes. Add the tomatoes (with juice), tomato paste, olives, and sugar. Cook and stir for 5 minutes, or until the tomatoes soften. Remove from the heat. Add the parsley, thyme, and basil. Pour over the penne; top with the mozzarella.

✤ Bake for 15 minutes, or until the sauce is thick and the cheese has melted.

Linguine with Chicken in Cream Sauce

Skim milk and low-fat ricotta cheese make this quick pasta dish a low-cost substitute for fettuccine Alfredo.

Makes 4 servings

Per serving
Calories 353
Total fat 5.9 g.
Saturated fat 1 g.
Cholesterol 82 mg.
Sodium 609 mg.
Fiber 3.7 g.

Cost per serving

95¢

- 1 cup chopped onions
- ½ cup apple juice
- 1 tablespoon minced garlic
- 1 chicken breast half, boned, skinned, and cut into 1" cubes
- ½ cup defatted chicken stock
- 1 green pepper, chopped
- 1 sweet red pepper, chopped
- ½ small jalapeño pepper, seeded and chopped (wear plastic gloves when handling)
- ½ teaspoon dried thyme
- 8 ounces linguine
- 1 cup skim milk
- 1 cup low-fat ricotta cheese
- ½ teaspoon salt
- ½ teaspoon ground black pepper

✱ In a 10" no-stick skillet, combine the onions, apple juice, and garlic; cook and stir over medium-high heat for 3 minutes. Add the chicken; cook and stir for 5 minutes, or until lightly browned. Add the chicken stock. Bring to a boil, scraping to loosen any browned bits. Add the green peppers, red peppers, jalapeño peppers, and thyme. Cook and stir for 10 minutes. Meanwhile, cook the linguine according to the package directions; drain well. In a blender or food processor, combine the milk, ricotta, salt, and pepper; puree. Add the pasta and cheese mixture to the skillet; toss well.

Extend Dairy Bargains

Amy Dacyczyn, author of *The Tightwad Gazette* books, gives the following tip on how to extend the "use by" date of container-packed dairy products such as cottage cheese and sour cream. Store the opened or unopened container upside down in the refrigerator. This seals off the mixture from bacteria and can extend the shelf life up to 2 weeks.

Per serving
Calories 334
Total fat 5.9 g.
Saturated fat 0.4 g.
Cholesterol 15 mg.
Sodium 320 mg.
Fiber 2.5 g.

Cost per serving

63¢

CHINESE-STYLE NOODLES WITH VEGETABLES

This Asian-style pasta dish contains a gingery stir-fry. Dark sesame oil and peanuts contribute exotic flavor for only pennies.

12 ounces fettuccine
¼ cup dry sherry or apple juice
1 teaspoon olive oil
½ cup chopped onions
2 teaspoons minced garlic
2 cups shredded green or napa cabbage
½ cup shredded carrots
½ teaspoon seeded and chopped jalapeño peppers
      (wear plastic gloves when handling)
½ cup frozen peas, thawed
2 tablespoons reduced-sodium soy sauce
1 tablespoon minced fresh ginger
1 teaspoon dark sesame oil
1 teaspoon chopped raw peanuts

✤ Cook the fettuccine according to the package directions; drain well.

✤ Meanwhile, in a 10" no-stick skillet, combine the sherry or apple juice and olive oil; bring to a boil over medium-high heat. Add the onions and garlic; cook and stir for 3 minutes. Add the cabbage, carrots, and peppers; cook and stir for 5 to 7 minutes, or until the vegetables are crisp-tender. Remove from the heat; add the peas, soy sauce, ginger, sesame oil, and fettuccine; toss well. Sprinkle with the peanuts.

PESTO CALZONES

Calzones are simply folded pizzas. Since they are less messy to transport, leftovers make great lunchbox fare. Try this summertime recipe when fresh herbs are plentiful.

Makes 6 servings

Per serving
Calories 319
Total fat 8.6 g.
Saturated fat 2.9 g.
Cholesterol 12 mg.
Sodium 279 mg.
Fiber 1.4 g.

Cost per serving

69¢

1	cup water, warmed to about 115°F
1	tablespoon active dry yeast
1	tablespoon sugar
2½	cups all-purpose flour
½	cup yellow cornmeal
2	tablespoons canola oil
¼	teaspoon salt
2	cups chopped fresh basil
1	cup chopped fresh parsley
3	cloves garlic, minced
2	tablespoons grated Parmesan cheese
1	tablespoon defatted chicken stock
1	cup shredded low-fat mozzarella cheese
1	egg white, lightly beaten

❋ In a large bowl, combine the water, yeast, and sugar; stir well. Let stand for 5 minutes in a warm place, or until foamy. Gradually add the flour, cornmeal, salt, and 1 tablespoon of the oil to make a kneadable dough.

❋ Turn the dough out onto a lightly floured surface. Knead, adding more flour as necessary, for about 10 minutes, or until smooth and elastic. Coat a large bowl with no-stick spray. Add the dough and turn to coat all sides. Cover and set in a warm place for 15 minutes.

❋ Preheat the oven to 450°F. Coat a large baking sheet with no-stick spray.

❋ Divide the dough in half; roll each half into a 12″ circle. Brush the surface of each circle with the remaining 1 tablespoon oil.

❋ In a blender or food processor, combine the basil, parsley, garlic, Parmesan, and stock; process until smooth. Spread over the dough. Top with the mozzarella. Fold each circle in half, pinching to seal. Cut two slits in the top of each calzone; brush with the egg white. Place on the baking sheet.

❋ Bake for 20 to 30 minutes, or until the crusts are golden brown. Cut each calzone into 3 pieces.

Per serving
Calories 323
Total fat 5.3 g.
Saturated fat 1.6 g.
Cholesterol 61 mg.
Sodium 325 mg.
Fiber 9.6 g.

Cost per serving

$1.32

FETTUCCINE WITH CHUNKY VEGETABLE SAUCE

When you clean out your vegetable drawer before the weekly shopping trip, make enough of this delicious pasta sauce to freeze.

    1 teaspoon olive oil
    1 cup chopped onions
    3 cloves garlic, minced
    2 cups chopped broccoli
    1 package (10 ounces) frozen artichoke hearts, thawed and
         chopped
    1 cup shredded carrots
    2 cups chopped tomatoes
    1 cup reduced-sodium tomato puree
   ⅛ teaspoon crushed red-pepper flakes
   ¼ teaspoon salt
   ¼ teaspoon ground black pepper
    8 ounces fettuccine
    2 tablespoons grated Parmesan cheese

❋ Coat a large saucepan with no-stick spray; set it over medium-high heat. When the pan is hot, add the oil, onions, and garlic. Cook and stir for 5 minutes, or until the onions are golden brown. Add the broccoli, artichoke hearts, and carrots. Cook and stir for 3 minutes. Add the tomatoes and tomato puree; bring to a boil. Lower the heat to medium. Cover and cook for 20 minutes, or until the sauce is thick. Add the red-pepper flakes, salt, and pepper.

❋ Meanwhile, cook the fettuccine according to the package directions; drain well. Return to the pot. Add the sauce and toss well. Sprinkle with the Parmesan.

ROTELLE WITH SWEET PEPPER SAUCE

Colored sweet peppers all seem to ripen at once—as gardeners know. At peak season, you can snap up bargain buys on sweet red and yellow peppers, sometimes for as little as 25¢ apiece. That's the time to make just the sauce portion of this recipe. Freeze extra for up to 4 months.

Makes 4 servings

Per serving
Calories 366
Total fat 5.1 g.
Saturated fat 1.5 g.
Cholesterol 5 mg.
Sodium 258 mg.
Fiber 5.6 g.

Cost per serving

$1.03

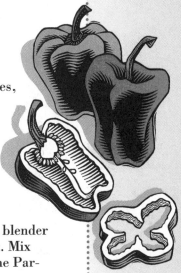

 1 teaspoon olive oil
 1 cup chopped onions
 4 cloves garlic, minced
 ¼ cup defatted chicken stock
 4 cups chopped sweet red or yellow peppers
 1 cup chopped fresh tomatoes
 ½ teaspoon dried basil
 ¼ teaspoon salt
 8 ounces rotelle
 ¼ cup grated Parmesan cheese

✽ In a 10″ no-stick skillet, combine the oil, onions, and garlic; cook and stir over medium-high heat for 5 minutes, or until the onions are golden brown. Add the chicken stock; bring to a boil. Add the peppers. Cook and stir for 5 minutes. Add the tomatoes and basil. Cover and cook, stirring occasionally, for 20 minutes, or until the peppers are very soft.

✽ Meanwhile, cook the rotelle according to the package directions; drain well. Return to the pot.

✽ Add the salt to the sauce. Pour 1 cup of the sauce into a blender or food processor; puree. Return the puree to the skillet. Mix well. Pour over the pasta and toss well. Sprinkle with the Parmesan; toss well.

BAG BIGGER BARGAINS

Thrifty shoppers always keep an eye out for
bargains in the day-old bakery, sale produce
carts, or dented-package bins. As long as cans are
not bulging and packages are unopened, they're safe to
use. You can use most bakery products for 5 days and
dairy products for 3 days after the pull date. Taste how good
savings can be with these ideas.

❋ *Apples and Pears.* Slice, cover with water, and simmer
  until tender. Puree then season with ground cinnamon and
  ground nutmeg to taste. Freeze in airtight containers.

❋ *Bananas.* Peel, cut into chunks, and freeze. Puree in a
  blender or food processor for instant creamy banana sorbet.

❋ *Bread* (day-old). (1) Cut into cubes and toast at 300°F for
  25 minutes, or until golden brown and crisp. Store in an
  airtight container and use for croutons. (2) Freeze slices for
  French toast. (3) Grind in a blender to make fine crumbs.
  Spread on a baking sheet. Toast at 300°F for 25 minutes, or
  until golden brown and crisp. Crumbs are delicious in place
  of Parmesan cheese to top casseroles, pasta, or soups.

❋ *Cottage cheese.* Puree in a blender or food processor with
  2 tablespoons buttermilk and 1 teaspoon lemon juice for
  every cup of cottage cheese. Use in place of sour cream.
  Keeps for 3 days refrigerated.

❋ *Fruit.* Slice and place in a single layer on a baking sheet;
  freeze. Transfer to airtight freezer containers. Chop and
  add the frozen fruit to pancake or waffle batter. Berries,
  peaches, plums, nectarines, and apples work best.

❋ *Fruit juices.* Add sweetener to taste. Pour into a pan and
  freeze. When frozen, cut into chunks; puree in a blender or
  food processor for sorbet.

❋ *Milk.* Use in creamy soups like potato-leek. Or make pudding or homemade yogurt. Or make homemade buttermilk
  (add 1 tablespoon lemon juice or white vinegar to each cup
  of milk; let stand at room temperature for 10 minutes). Use
  in baking.

(*continued*)

- *Mushrooms.* Cook equal amounts of chopped mushrooms and onions in a small amount of oil until the mushrooms exude moisture. Freeze in small containers to add to sauces and soups.

- *Rolls* (day-old). Sprinkle with water. Wrap in foil and bake at 350°F until soft.

- *Tomatoes.* Freeze whole (unpeeled) in a plastic bag. Run under hot water while frozen to remove the skin. Add to spaghetti sauce or soup.

- *Vegetables.* Collect in a freezer container for soup stock.

ROTELLE WITH GREEN TOMATO SAUCE

This bright green sauce from New Mexican cuisine is equally good on enchiladas. We recommend it as a great way to use up green garden tomatoes before the first frost.

¼ cup balsamic vinegar
2 tablespoons minced garlic
1 cup chopped onions
½ cup chopped celery
3 cups chopped green tomatoes
¼ cup chopped fresh parsley
½ small jalapeño pepper, seeded and chopped
    (wear plastic gloves when handling)
1 tablespoon minced fresh cilantro
1 teaspoon sugar
½ teaspoon salt
8 ounces rotelle

- In a 10″ no-stick skillet, combine the vinegar and garlic. Cook and stir over medium-high heat for 3 minutes. Add the onions and celery. Cook and stir for 5 minutes, or until the onions soften. Add the tomatoes, parsley, peppers, cilantro, sugar, and salt; cook and stir for 15 minutes, or until the tomatoes are very soft. Pour into a blender or food processor; puree.

- Meanwhile, cook the rotelle according to the package directions; drain well. Return to the pot. Add the sauce and toss well.

Makes 4 servings

Per serving
Calories 301
Total fat 1.4 g.
Saturated fat 0.2 g.
Cholesterol 0 mg.
Sodium 313 mg.
Fiber 1.8 g.

Cost per serving

83¢

*Pasta and Grain
Main Dishes*

Pita Pockets
with Vegetable-Cheese Spread

Makes 4 servings

Per serving
Calories 270
Total fat 2.2 g.
Saturated fat 0.9 g.
Cholesterol 5 mg.
Sodium 706 mg.
Fiber 2.2 g.

Cost per serving

78¢

At only 36¢ a serving, cottage cheese is a great source of low-fat calcium. It also makes a delicious sandwich filler—especially when combined with minced vegetables and curry powder.

- 2 cups low-fat cottage cheese
- 2 scallions, thinly sliced
- ⅔ cup minced green peppers
- ⅔ cup minced sweet red peppers
- 1 tablespoon seeded and minced jalapeño peppers
  (wear plastic gloves when handling)
- 1 tablespoon minced fresh basil
- 2 teaspoons cider vinegar
- 1 teaspoon dried dillweed
- 1 teaspoon curry powder
- 1 teaspoon minced garlic
- ¼ teaspoon ground black pepper
- 4 lettuce leaves
- 4 reduced-sodium pita bread rounds (6" diameter), halved

✳ In a medium bowl, combine the cottage cheese, scallions, green peppers, red peppers, jalapeño peppers, basil, vinegar, dill, curry powder, garlic, and black pepper; mix well. Place the lettuce leaves in the pita bread halves; add the cheese mixture.

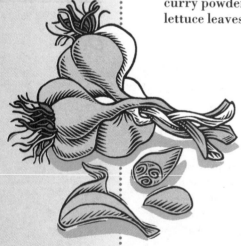

Garlic and Tomato Risotto

Risotto, the comfort food of Italy, is easy to make. Here, flavor comes from plenty of garlic and ripe tomatoes rather than costly cheeses. Italian Arborio rice is easy to find in supermarkets. It gives the perfect creamy texture for this dish.

     1 medium onion, diced
     2 cups chopped spinach
     1 cup chopped fresh tomatoes
     1 sweet red or green pepper, diced
     3 tablespoons minced garlic
     1 tablespoon chopped sun-dried tomatoes (without oil)
     2 cups Arborio rice
   4–5 cups defatted chicken stock, heated
     1 tablespoon grated Parmesan cheese
    ¼ teaspoon salt
    ¼ teaspoon ground black pepper

❊ Coat a Dutch oven with no-stick spray. Set it over medium-high heat. When the pan is hot, add the onions. Cook and stir for 5 minutes, or until the onions are golden brown. Add the spinach, fresh tomatoes, peppers, garlic, and sun-dried tomatoes; cook and stir for 5 minutes.

❊ Add the rice. Cook and stir for 1 minute. Add ½ cup of the chicken stock. Stirring continuously, cook until the liquid has completely evaporated. Add another ½ cup of the stock; cook and stir until the liquid has completely evaporated. Continue adding stock and continuously stirring for 25 minutes, or until the rice is creamy and just tender; add more stock only after each previous addition has been absorbed.

❊ Remove from the heat. Add the Parmesan, salt, and pepper.

Makes 4 servings

Per serving
Calories 512
Total fat 1.5 g.
Saturated fat 0.5 g.
Cholesterol 7 mg.
Sodium 216 mg.
Fiber 5.3 g.

Cost per serving

$1.12

Make Your Own Dried Tomatoes

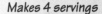

Sun-dried tomatoes lend intense tomato flavor to any dish. In summer when tomatoes are plentiful, you can make your own version. Thickly slice fresh Italian tomatoes; place on no-stick baking sheets. Bake in a 200°F oven for 5 to 8 hours, or until the slices bend like leather but are not brittle. Cool, then store in airtight containers.

*Pasta and Grain
Main Dishes*

Per serving
Calories 334
Total fat 4.1 g.
Saturated fat 0.4 g.
Cholesterol 4 mg.
Sodium 171 mg.
Fiber 6.4 g.

Cost per serving

57¢

CURRIED MUSHROOMS ON INDIAN RICE AND BARLEY

Basmati rice is a quick-cooking Indian rice with a nutty flavor. It's easily found in most supermarkets. You can also use long-grain white rice in this colorful dish.

  1 cup basmati rice
 ½ cup pearl barley
 ¼ cup defatted chicken stock
  2 teaspoons olive oil
  1 cup sliced onions
  2 cloves garlic, minced
 ¾ teaspoon curry powder
 ½ teaspoon minced fresh ginger
 ¼ teaspoon caraway seeds
  2 cups sliced mushrooms
  1 cup diced peeled eggplant
  1 cup diced sweet red peppers
 ¾ cup apple juice
 ¼ teaspoon salt
 ¼ teaspoon ground black pepper

❀ Cook the rice and barley separately according to the package directions.

❀ Meanwhile, in a 10″ no-stick skillet, combine the chicken stock and oil. Bring to a boil over medium-high heat. Add the onions; cook and stir for 3 minutes. Add the garlic, curry powder, ginger, and caraway seeds. Cook and stir for 2 minutes. Add the mushrooms, eggplant, peppers, and apple juice. Cook and stir for 8 to 10 minutes, or until the vegetables are very soft. Add the rice and barley. Cover and cook for 2 minutes, or until the rice is hot. Add the salt and pepper.

Sweet Potato and Quinoa Casserole

Quinoa, a delicious nutty grain from South America, has an impressive amount of protein per serving. Always rinse the quinoa in a strainer before cooking to remove its naturally bitter coating. You can also use long-grain white rice if you can't find quinoa in your supermarket.

- 2 cups quinoa, rinsed well
- 4 cups defatted chicken stock
- 1 teaspoon olive oil
- 1 large sweet potato, peeled and cubed
- ¼ cup chopped onions
- ¼ cup chopped sweet red or green peppers
- 6 large cloves garlic, minced
- 4 cups chopped fresh spinach
- 1 cup soft bread crumbs
- ¼ cup grated Parmesan cheese
- ½ teaspoon ground black pepper
- ¼ teaspoon salt
- ¼ cup white wine or apple juice

❁ In a medium saucepan, combine the quinoa and 3½ cups of the chicken stock. Bring to a boil over medium-high heat. Reduce the heat to medium; cover and cook for 15 minutes, or until all the stock is absorbed.

❁ Meanwhile, in a 10″ no-stick skillet, combine the oil, sweet potatoes, onions, peppers, and remaining ½ cup of stock. Cook and stir over medium-high heat for 5 minutes, or until the vegetables soften. Add the spinach. Cover and cook for 2 to 3 minutes, or until the spinach wilts.

❁ Preheat the oven to 350°F. Coat a 2-quart shallow baking dish with no-stick spray. Spread the quinoa in the baking dish. Top with the vegetables, bread crumbs, Parmesan, pepper, and salt. Pour the wine or apple juice over the mixture.

❁ Bake for 30 minutes, or until hot and bubbly.

Makes 4 servings

Per serving
Calories 545
Total fat 10 g.
Saturated fat 2.3 g.
Cholesterol 11 mg.
Sodium 555 mg.
Fiber 7.4 g.

Cost per serving

$1.05

Hot and Spicy Fried Rice with Vegetables

When you have a craving for fried rice, trim your budget by eating in instead of ordering in. This stir-fried rice will hit the spot and save you over $3 a serving.

Makes 4 servings

Per serving
Calories 437
Total fat 4.2 g.
Saturated fat 0.7 g.
Cholesterol 0 mg.
Sodium 290 mg.
Fiber 3 g.

Cost per serving

47¢

2 cups long-grain white rice
¼ cup dry sherry or defatted chicken stock
1 teaspoon canola oil
1 cup thinly sliced carrots
1 cup thinly sliced broccoli stems
2 tablespoons minced fresh ginger
2 cloves garlic, minced
1 cup thinly sliced green cabbage
2 scallions, diagonally sliced
¼ cup water
1 tablespoon honey
2 teaspoons dark sesame oil
½ teaspoon ground red pepper
1 teaspoon hoisin sauce (optional)
2 tablespoons reduced-sodium soy sauce

❀ Cook the rice according to the package directions.

❀ Meanwhile, in a 10″ no-stick skillet, combine the sherry or stock and canola oil; bring to a boil over medium-high heat. Add the carrots, broccoli, ginger, and garlic. Cook and stir for 5 minutes, or until the carrots soften slightly. Add the cabbage and scallions. Cover and cook for 3 minutes. Transfer the vegetables to a plate; cover to keep warm.

❀ Add the water, honey, sesame oil, red pepper, and hoisin sauce (if using) to the skillet. Bring to a boil. Add the rice. Cook and stir for 3 minutes, or until hot. Add the vegetables. Cook and stir for 1 minute. Add the soy sauce.

Vegetable Kabobs over Rice

Serve this summer main dish with a leafy salad, sliced tomatoes, and whole-grain bread. For the best flavor, marinate the vegetables overnight.

- 2 teaspoons olive oil
- ¼ cup orange juice
- ¼ cup white wine or apple juice
- 4 cloves garlic, minced
- 1 tablespoon minced fresh basil
- 1 teaspoon dried oregano
- ½ small eggplant, cut into 2" cubes
- 12 mushrooms
- 1 green pepper, cut into 12 pieces
- 1 medium red onion, cut into 2" cubes
- 2 cups long-grain white rice
- ¼ cup minced fresh parsley

❋ In a large shallow nonmetal dish, combine the oil, orange juice, wine or apple juice, garlic, basil, and oregano; stir well. Add the eggplant, mushrooms, peppers, and onions. Cover and refrigerate for 24 hours, stirring occasionally.

❋ Cook the rice according to the package directions.

❋ Meanwhile, preheat the grill or broiler. Thread the eggplant, mushrooms, peppers, and onions onto skewers. Grill or broil 4" from the heat for 5 to 8 minutes, or until the vegetables are golden brown, turning frequently and basting with the marinade. Serve over the rice. Top with the parsley.

Makes 4 servings

Per serving
Calories 422
Total fat 3.3 g.
Saturated fat 0.5 g.
Cholesterol 0 mg.
Sodium 12 mg.
Fiber 2.7 g.

Cost per serving

55¢

Cooking Grains

Most grains are a bargain to cook at home. Regular brown rice costs only 14¢ a cup cooked, compared with 70¢ for the instant variety. Take a little time and put money in your pocket.

Whole grains – 1 cup dry	Water	Time	Yield
Basmati rice	2 cups	20 minutes	3 cups
Brown rice	2 cups	1 hour	3 cups
Bulgur	2 cups	20 minutes	2½ cups
Long-grain white rice	2 cups	20 minutes	3 cups
Millet	3 cups	45 minutes	3½ cups
Pearl barley	3 cups	1¼ hours	3½ cups
Quinoa	2 cups	30 minutes	3 cups
Wild rice	3 cups	1 hour	4 cups

CAJUN DIRTY RICE

Makes 4 servings

Per serving
Calories 682
Total fat 2.8 g.
Saturated fat 0.6 g.
Cholesterol 6 mg.
Sodium 312 mg.
Fiber 6.2 g.

Cost per serving

49¢

This Louisiana version of rice pilaf gets its name from the onions and other sautéed ingredients that give it its distinctive flavor and color. We've replaced the traditional chicken livers with plenty of fresh vegetables, making this a nutritious one-dish meal.

1 teaspoon olive oil
1 tablespoon all-purpose flour
3 large onions, chopped
¼ cup dry sherry or apple juice
1 sweet potato, peeled and diced
2 stalks celery, chopped
1 carrot, diced
1 cup whole kernel corn
4 large cloves garlic, minced
3 cups long-grain white rice
4 cups defatted chicken stock
½ teaspoon salt
½ teaspoon ground red pepper
½ teaspoon ground black pepper

✻ In a 10″ no-stick skillet, combine the oil and flour. Cook and stir over medium heat for 2 minutes without browning to cook off any flour taste. Add the onions and sherry or apple juice; cook and stir for 10 minutes, or until the onions are very soft and brown.

✻ Add the sweet potatoes, celery, carrots, corn, and garlic. Cook and stir for 3 minutes. Add the rice. Cook and stir for 1 minute. Add the chicken stock; bring to a boil. Cover and cook for 20 to 25 minutes, or until all the liquid is absorbed and the rice is tender. Add the salt, red pepper, and black pepper.

BARLEY AND VEGETABLE BAKE

Barley is loaded with fiber. In only one cup cooked barley, you get 8 grams, about the equivalent in 3 cups cooked brown rice. A truly underrated whole grain, barley also has a nutty, delicious flavor that pairs well with vegetables and cheese.

Makes 4 servings

Per serving
Calories 366
Total fat 6.7 g.
Saturated fat 1.9 g.
Cholesterol 24 mg.
Sodium 345 mg.
Fiber 11.2 g.

Cost per serving

62¢

  1 teaspoon olive oil
½ cup chopped onions
  3 cloves garlic, minced
  2 cups chopped green cabbage
  1 cup shredded carrots
  1 cup whole kernel corn
½ cup chopped sweet red or green peppers
¼ cup sliced scallions
  3 cups defatted chicken stock
  1 cup pearl barley
½ cup shredded nonfat Swiss cheese
½ cup shredded low-fat Monterey Jack cheese
½ cup low-fat sour cream

❈ Preheat the oven to 400°F. Coat a Dutch oven with no-stick spray; set it over medium-high heat. When the Dutch oven is hot, add the oil, onions, and garlic. Cook and stir for 2 minutes. Add the cabbage, carrots, corn, peppers, and scallions; cook and stir for 3 minutes. Add the chicken stock and barley; bring to a boil. Cover and bake for 30 minutes.

❈ In a medium bowl, combine the Swiss cheese, Monterey Jack, and sour cream. Dollop spoonfuls onto the casserole; cover and bake for 10 minutes, or until the cheese has melted and the barley is tender.

Per serving
Calories 394
Total fat 6 g.
Saturated fat 1.5 g.
Cholesterol 107 mg.
Sodium 525 mg.
Fiber 8.7 g.

Cost per serving

31¢

LENTIL BEAN BURGERS

These vegetable burgers cook up moist and satisfy the heartiest appetite, but they cost 40¢ less per serving than hamburgers. And they contain a mere one-quarter as much fat as the leanest beef burger.

```
  1 cup cooked lentils (page 199)
  2 cups cooked navy beans (page 199)
 ¼ teaspoon salt
 ¼ teaspoon ground black pepper
  1 cup grated onions
  1 teaspoon olive oil
 ½ cup minced fresh parsley
 ½ cup shredded nonfat mozzarella cheese
 ⅓ cup minced scallions
 ⅓ cup shredded carrots
  2 eggs, lightly beaten
½–1 cup dry bread crumbs
  1 teaspoon honey
  1 teaspoon Dijon mustard
```

❋ Preheat the oven to 400°F. In a medium bowl, mash the lentils and beans. Add the salt and pepper; stir to combine. Set aside.

❋ In a 10″ no-stick skillet, combine the onions and oil. Cook and stir over medium-high heat for 3 minutes, or until the onions are golden brown. Add to the lentil mixture. Add the parsley, mozzarella, scallions, carrots, eggs, and ½ cup of the bread crumbs; mix well. Form into 4 burgers, adding up to ½ cup more bread crumbs if the mixture is too wet. Place on a baking sheet; brush with the honey and mustard.

❋ Bake for 20 minutes, or until firm and lightly browned.

Vegetarian Enchiladas

Reduced-fat tofu replaces the ground beef in this enchilada entrée, saving 10¢ per serving and cutting the fat by more than one-third.

4	ounces reduced-fat extra-firm tofu
½	cup medium-hot salsa
⅓	cup shredded low-fat Monterey Jack cheese
¼	cup chopped mild green chili peppers, such as Anaheim
¼	cup shredded carrots
2	scallions, minced
4	flour tortillas (8" diameter)
1½	cups reduced-sodium tomato puree
1	teaspoon chili powder
¼	teaspoon ground cumin
¼	cup shredded nonfat mozzarella cheese
¼	cup nonfat sour cream
½	cup chopped fresh cilantro

❋ Preheat the oven to 425°F. Coat a 13" × 9" baking dish with no-stick spray.

❋ In a medium bowl, mash the tofu and salsa. Add the Monterey Jack, chili peppers, carrots, and scallions. Spoon onto the tortillas; roll up. Place seam side down in the baking dish.

❋ In a small bowl, combine the tomato puree, chili powder, and cumin. Spoon over the enchiladas. Top with the mozzarella and sour cream.

❋ Bake for 20 to 25 minutes, or until browned and bubbly. Top with the cilantro.

Makes 4 servings

Per serving
Calories 219
Total fat 4 g.
Saturated fat 1.3 g.
Cholesterol 7 mg.
Sodium 420 mg.
Fiber 3.7 g.

Cost per serving

75¢

Tortilla Tips

Extra tortillas can be baked into delicious chips that save you bundles over purchased snacks. Using kitchen scissors, cut the tortillas into wedges; place on a baking sheet in a single layer. Coat with no-stick spray and sprinkle with salt, ground cumin, and ground black pepper— or with Southwestern spice mix (page 103). Bake at 300°F for 20 minutes, or until brown and crisp. Cool, then store in an airtight container.

*Pasta and Grain
Main Dishes*

Couscous with Chick-Peas and Tomatoes

Makes 4 servings

Per serving
Calories 603
Total fat 5.8 g.
Saturated fat 0.8 g.
Cholesterol 5 mg.
Sodium 361 mg.
Fiber 11.5 g.

Cost per serving

$1.05

Couscous is a quick-cooking semolina pasta. It's also the national dish of Morocco, Tunisia, and Algeria. Serve this slightly spicy entrée with pita bread and a dish of cooling nonfat yogurt on the side.

2 teaspoons olive oil
1 onion, thinly sliced
2 carrots, diagonally sliced
1 cup chopped reduced-sodium canned tomatoes (with juice)
1 cup frozen peas
2 tablespoons raisins
¾ teaspoon curry powder
¼ teaspoon ground cinnamon
2 cups cooked chick-peas (page 199)
2 cups couscous
2 scallions, sliced
1 teaspoon seeded and chopped jalapeño peppers
    (wear plastic gloves when handling)
3 cups defatted chicken stock
¼ cup chopped fresh parsley
½ teaspoon salt
½ teaspoon ground black pepper

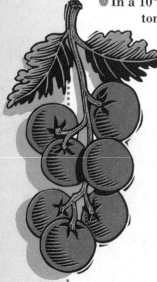

❀ In a 10" no-stick skillet, combine the oil, onions, carrots and tomatoes (with juice). Cook and stir over medium-high heat for 5 minutes. Add the peas, raisins, curry powder, and cinnamon. Cook and stir for 1 minute. Add the chick-peas, couscous, scallions, and peppers. Cook and stir for 1 minute. Add the chicken stock; bring to a boil.

❀ Remove the skillet from the heat; cover and let stand for 5 minutes, or until the liquid has been absorbed. Add the parsley, salt, and pepper. Toss with a fork to combine.

BEAN BARGAINS

Cooking up a pot of your own beans instead of relying on canned cooked varieties saves you $1 every time. We compared the price of canned pinto or kidney beans ($1.20 for 40 ounces) and the price of the same amount of home-cooked dried beans (25¢).

To save time, use the quick soak method for beans. (Lentils and split peas don't require soaking.) Place the beans in a Dutch oven with water to cover. Bring to a boil. Remove from the heat. Cover and set aside for 1 hour.

Drain and rinse. Add fresh water to cover by 2″. Simmer over medium heat until tender. Drain. Do not add salt or acidic foods, like tomatoes, before the beans are cooked—it interferes with the softening process.

The cooking times below are approximate.

BEANS

1 cup dried	Water	Time	Yield
Black beans	4 cups	1½ hours	2 cups
Chick-peas	4 cups	2–3 hours	2 cups
Kidney beans	3 cups	1½ hours	2 cups
Lentils	3 cups	1 hour	2 cups
Lima beans	2 cups	1½ hours	1½ cups
Navy beans	3 cups	1½ hours	2 cups
Pinto beans	3 cups	2½ hours	2 cups
Split peas	3 cups	1 hour	2 cups

Per serving
Calories 581
Total fat 6.8 g.
Saturated fat 1.2 g.
Cholesterol 4 mg.
Sodium 679 mg.
Fiber 14.9 g.

Cost per serving

93¢

SPICY BEAN AND BISCUIT POT PIE

The ultimate comfort food, pot pies are Mom's favorite way to fill up the family without busting the weekly food budget. Both fat and cost are trimmed even more in this southwestern-inspired dish. Instead of beef, spicy beans and vegetables are topped with flaky lean biscuits. Serve with a simple green salad.

Filling

1½	cups defatted chicken stock
1	tablespoon honey
2	cups chopped onions
2	cups diced tomatoes
1	cup sliced mushrooms
1	cup diced green peppers
2	tablespoons minced garlic
2	tablespoons canned diced mild green chili peppers
2	cups cooked pinto beans (page 199)
1	cup cooked chick-peas (page 199)
⅓	cup whole kernel corn
1	tablespoon chili powder
1½	teaspoons ground cumin
2	tablespoons tomato paste
2	tablespoons reduced-sodium soy sauce

Biscuit Crust

1¾	cups all-purpose flour
2	teaspoons baking powder
2	tablespoons reduced-calorie butter or margarine
¾–1	cup low-fat buttermilk
2	teaspoons honey

To make the filling

❋ Preheat the oven to 350°F. Coat a large casserole dish with no-stick spray.

❋ In a Dutch oven, combine the chicken stock and honey. Bring to a boil. Add the onions. Cook and stir for 3 minutes. Add the tomatoes, mushrooms, peppers, garlic, and chili peppers. Cook and stir for 5 minutes. Add the beans, chick-peas, corn, chili powder, and cumin. Cook and stir for 5 minutes. Remove from the heat.

❋ Pour ¼ cup of the cooking liquid into a small bowl. Add the tomato paste and soy sauce. Stir until the tomato paste dissolves. Add to the vegetables. Pour into the casserole dish.

To make the biscuit crust

❁ Sift the flour and baking powder into a large mixing bowl. Using a pastry blender or fork, cut the butter or margarine into the flour mixture until it resembles coarse meal.

❁ In a measuring cup, combine the honey and ¾ cup of the buttermilk. Add to the flour mixture; stir with a fork. Add up to ¼ cup more buttermilk if needed to form a stiff dough. Knead lightly in the bowl for 3 minutes, or until the dough is no longer sticky. Turn onto a lightly floured surface. Roll out and cut into biscuits. Place the biscuits on top of the filling; do not seal the edges.

❁ Bake uncovered for 30 minutes. Cover and bake for 10 minutes more. Let the pot pie cool for 5 minutes before serving.

TERIYAKI TOFU AND GRILLED VEGETABLES

Tofu is an inexpensive soy protein that has the talent of absorbing flavors—as in this teriyaki dish.

```
 3  tablespoons reduced-sodium soy sauce
 2  tablespoons packed brown sugar
 1  tablespoon apple juice
12  ounces reduced-fat extra-firm tofu, thickly sliced
 2  cups brown rice
 1  green pepper, quartered
 1  medium onion, thickly sliced
½  large sweet potato, thinly sliced
 2  ears corn, cut in half
```

❁ In a 13" × 9" glass dish, combine the soy sauce, brown sugar, and apple juice; mix well. Add the tofu in a single layer. Refrigerate for 1 hour, turning frequently.

❁ Cook the rice according to the package directions.

❁ Meanwhile, preheat the grill or broiler. Place the tofu in the center of a large piece of foil. Drizzle with 2 tablespoons of the marinade. Seal the foil tightly. Place the tofu on a grill rack or broiler pan. Surround with the peppers, onions, sweet potatoes, and corn. Grill or broil 4" from the heat, brushing the vegetables frequently with the marinade, for 8 to 10 minutes, or until the tofu is hot and the sweet potatoes are browned and tender.

❁ Serve with the rice.

Makes 4 servings

Per serving
Calories 485
Total fat 4.8 g.
Saturated fat 0.6 g.
Cholesterol 0 mg.
Sodium 494 mg.
Fiber 7.4 g.

Cost per serving

54¢

CHAPTER 9

MAIN-COURSE AND SIDE-DISH SALADS

Fresh vegetables, ripe for the picking, are a gardener's joy. But you don't have to sow with the seasons to see that rotating your vegetable choices makes them an affordable part of the healthy food budget.

In spring, lettuces and other greens, radishes, and scallions are plentiful in both the garden and the market. In the summer and early fall, cucumbers, tomatoes, sweet peppers, and zucchini are abundant. Late fall offers good values in cold-weather vegetables like onions, hard-shelled squash, pumpkin, cauliflower, broccoli, sweet potatoes, and carrots.

In the winter, build salads around inexpensive frozen vegetables—often the best choice in a lot of areas. Eating seasonally gives you a wide variety of the nutrients so important to robust health.

We've chosen delicious main-course and side-dish salads that will provide affordable eating all year round. With these recipes, you can have your lettuce and eat it too—in season.

203

Per side-dish serving
Calories 75
Total fat 2.5 g.
Saturated fat 0.3 g.
Cholesterol 0 mg.
Sodium 90 mg.
Fiber 2.2 g.

Cost per serving

40¢

ASIAN COLESLAW

A small amount of fresh cilantro and dark sesame oil creates extraordinary flavor for this winter-vegetable salad.

    6 cups thinly sliced green cabbage
    1 can (8 ounces) mandarin oranges, drained
  1/4 cup minced onions
  1/4 cup minced fresh cilantro
  1/4 cup cider vinegar
    1 teaspoon dark sesame oil
    1 teaspoon canola oil
    1 teaspoon sugar
  1/8 teaspoon crushed red-pepper flakes
  1/8 teaspoon salt
  1/8 teaspoon ground black pepper

✲ In a large bowl, combine the cabbage, oranges, onions, and cilantro; toss well. In a small bowl, combine the vinegar, sesame oil, canola oil, sugar and red-pepper flakes; pour over the cabbage. Toss well. Add the salt and pepper.

Per main-dish serving
Calories 293
Total fat 3.3 g.
Saturated fat 0.5 g.
Cholesterol 12 mg.
Sodium 308 mg.
Fiber 6.9 g.

Cost per serving

61¢

MEDITERRANEAN TUNA AND POTATO SALAD

Salade Niçoise costs $9.95 in French restaurants, but this home-style variation combines fresh vegetables with marinated tuna for an easy meal at less than 75¢ a serving.

    2 cups diced unpeeled red potatoes
    1 cup cooked navy beans (page 199)
  1/4 cup balsamic vinegar
    1 tablespoon minced garlic
    2 teaspoons olive oil
  1/4 teaspoon salt
    4 cups torn romaine lettuce
    1 can (6 ounces) water-packed tuna, drained
    2 tomatoes, chopped
    1 cup shredded carrots

* Place the potatoes in a medium saucepan and cover with water; boil for 15 minutes, or until they are tender but not mushy. Check by inserting the tip of a sharp knife in a piece of potato. Drain.

* In a medium bowl, combine the potatoes, beans, vinegar, garlic, oil, and salt; toss well. Let stand at room temperature for 1 hour, stirring occasionally.

* Line salad plates with the lettuce; arrange rows of the tuna, tomatoes and carrots over the lettuce. Strain the potatoes and beans, reserving the marinade. Add the potatoes and beans to the salads. Drizzle with the marinade.

SAVE PENNIES WITH HOMEMADE SALAD DRESSINGS

Most commercial low-fat and fat-free salad dressings are high in salt to make up for lack of flavor. Making your own at home adds money to your pocket as well as flavor to your salad. Some tips:

* Experiment with flavored vinegars, such as raspberry, balsamic, and herb vinegars.

* Substitute low-fat soft cheeses, such as ricotta or cottage cheese, for oil. Puree them in the blender or food processor.

* Add more spices and seasonings to low-fat salad dressings. Best choices are garlic, onions, citrus juice and rind, reduced-sodium tomato juice, Dijon mustard, and herbs.

Per main-dish serving
Calories 375
Total fat 3.3 g.
Saturated fat 1.5 g.
Cholesterol 11 mg.
Sodium 287 mg.
Fiber 2 g.

Cost per serving

42¢

KITCHEN TIP

Freeze the
leftover stock to
add to soup for
extra flavor.

WARM LENTIL SALAD WITH TOMATOES

You save about $3.50 a serving over the restaurant version of this traditional Mediterranean salad. The lentils are cooked with onions and stock to give them a hearty flavor.

  4 cups defatted chicken stock
  2 cups lentils
  1 medium onion, diced
  ½ cup balsamic vinegar
  3 tablespoons sugar or honey
  2 tablespoons minced garlic
  ½ cup diced sweet red peppers
  ½ cup diced fresh tomatoes
  ½ cup diced celery
  ½ cup chopped fresh parsley
  ¼ cup grated Parmesan cheese
  ¼ teaspoon salt
  ¼ teaspoon ground black pepper

✤ In a medium saucepan, combine the chicken stock, lentils, and onions; bring to a boil over medium-high heat. Cook, stirring occasionally, for 20 minutes, or until the lentils are tender but not mushy. Drain the lentils and onions; reserve the stock for another use.

✤ In a large bowl, combine the vinegar, sugar or honey, garlic, lentils, and onions; toss well. Let stand at room temperature for 30 minutes, stirring occasionally.

✤ Add the red peppers, tomatoes, celery, parsley, Parmesan, salt, and pepper; toss well.

Gazpacho Salad

We turned a favorite chilled summer soup into a salad—with lots more fresh vegetables and spicy flavor.

2½ cups chopped fresh tomatoes
  1 cup chopped sweet red or yellow peppers
  1 cup chopped green peppers
  1 cup peeled, seeded, and chopped cucumbers
  ½ cup chopped onions
  2 scallions, chopped
  ⅓ cup chopped fresh parsley
  ¼ cup chopped fresh basil
  ¼ cup lime juice or lemon juice
  ¼ teaspoon dried tarragon
  2 tablespoons balsamic vinegar
  1 tablespoon honey or sugar
  3 cloves garlic, minced
  3 cups torn leaf lettuce
  ¼ teaspoon salt
  ¼ teaspoon ground black pepper

❁ In a large bowl, combine the tomatoes, red or yellow peppers, green peppers, cucumbers, onions, scallions, parsley, and basil; toss well.

❁ In a small bowl, combine the lime juice or lemon juice, tarragon, vinegar, honey or sugar, and garlic; pour over the vegetables. Cover and refrigerate for 1 hour, stirring frequently.

❁ Add the lettuce, salt, and pepper; toss well.

Makes 4 servings

Per main-dish serving
Calories 117
Total fat 1 g.
Saturated fat 0.1 g.
Cholesterol 0 mg.
Sodium 157 mg.
Fiber 4.7 g.

Cost per serving

79¢

Tips on Storing Salad Vegetables

Most salad vegetables keep 7 to 10 days if stored in the moist coolness of your refrigerator's vegetable drawer. Greens and lettuce keep longer if washed and dried, then stored wrapped in paper towels or in a salad spinner with the water drained out. The main exception is mushrooms—refrigerate them unwashed in a brown paper bag for the longest shelf life.

Onions, garlic, sweet potatoes, potatoes, and winter squash keep best in a cool, dry place, such as a basket or bin in a cupboard, rather than in the refrigerator.

Per main-dish serving
Calories 347
Total fat 5.2 g.
Saturated fat 0.8 g.
Cholesterol 6 mg.
Sodium 169 mg.
Fiber 17.6 g.

Cost per serving

67¢

GINGERED WHEAT BERRY SALAD

Wheat berries, ground fine, make flour. In this delicious dish they're cooked whole in a gingery broth, then chilled and tossed with a Chinese dressing for an unusual spring salad. You can buy them in bulk at supermarkets, natural foods stores, and co-ops.

- 4 cups defatted chicken stock
- 2 cups wheat berries
- ¼ cup chopped fresh ginger
- ¼ cup balsamic vinegar
- 1 tablespoon reduced-sodium soy sauce
- 1 tablespoon honey
- 2 cloves garlic, minced
- 2 teaspoons canola oil
- 1 teaspoon dark sesame oil
- 1½ cups peeled, seeded, and sliced cucumbers
- 4 scallions, diagonally sliced
- 1 cup sliced radishes
- 4 cups torn leaf lettuce

✴ In a large saucepan, combine the chicken stock, wheat berries, and ginger; bring to a boil over medium-high heat. Reduce the heat to medium; cook, stirring occasionally, for 1 hour, or until the wheat berries are tender. Drain the wheat berries; reserve the stock for another use.

✴ In a large bowl, combine the vinegar, soy sauce, honey, garlic, canola oil, and sesame oil; mix well. Add the cucumbers, scallions, radishes, and wheat berries; toss well. Serve on the lettuce leaves.

STUFFED TOMATOES WITH CORN SALAD

If you're over the top with too many tomatoes, this recipe will help. It also uses late-summer garden corn and green peppers. Save the tomato pulp for soup—it will make the salad too watery.

   4 large tomatoes
   2 cups shredded green cabbage
  ½ cup peeled and minced apples
  ½ cup whole kernel corn
  ½ green pepper, minced
   2 tablespoons minced red onions
   2 tablespoons cider vinegar
   2 tablespoons nonfat mayonnaise
   1 tablespoon balsamic vinegar
   1 tablespoon honey
  ¼ teaspoon celery seeds
  ¼ teaspoon dry mustard
  ¼ teaspoon ground black pepper
  ⅛ teaspoon salt

✸ Slice the tops off the tomatoes; scoop out the tomato pulp and reserve for another use. Place the tomatoes on a platter.

✸ In a large bowl, combine the cabbage, apples, corn, green peppers, onions, cider vinegar, mayonnaise, balsamic vinegar, honey, celery seeds, dry mustard, pepper, and salt; toss well. Spoon into the tomatoes.

Makes 8 servings

Per main-dish serving
Calories 95
Total fat 0.7 g.
Saturated fat 0.1 g.
Cholesterol 0 mg.
Sodium 160 mg.
Fiber 3.3 g.

Cost per serving

54¢

KITCHEN TIP

Since tomatoes vary in size, there may be more corn salad than will fit into the tomato shells. The extra salad can be served alongside or stored for up to 4 days in the refrigerator.

Main-Course and Side-Dish Salads

Per main-dish serving
Calories 206
Total fat 4.7 g.
Saturated fat 0.5 g.
Cholesterol 0 mg.
Sodium 147 mg.
Fiber 4.7 g.

Cost per serving

33¢

MARINATED CHICK-PEA SALAD

This brightly colored salad keeps well for up to 5 days and tastes better the longer it's allowed to marinate. Adjust the amount of garlic to your taste.

2	cups cooked chick-peas (page 199)
1	cup minced red onions
½	cup chopped fresh or canned tomatoes
½	cup chopped green peppers
3	tablespoons cider vinegar
3	tablespoons minced garlic
2	tablespoons lemon juice
2	tablespoons chopped fresh parsley
2	teaspoons olive oil
¼	teaspoon salt
¼	teaspoon ground black pepper

❋ In a large bowl, combine the chick-peas, onions, tomatoes, green peppers, vinegar, garlic, lemon juice, parsley, and oil; toss well. Cover and refrigerate overnight, stirring occasionally. Add the salt and pepper.

Per side-dish serving
Calories 120
Total fat 1.7 g.
Saturated fat 0.2 g.
Cholesterol 0 mg.
Sodium 6 mg.
Fiber 4.8 g.

Cost per serving

63¢

SUMMER FRUIT SALAD

Berries taste great in this marinated salad—the honey and orange juice make them sweeter. This salad is perfect for June when strawberries are only 99¢ a pint at the supermarket—and even less at your local U-Pick.

2	cups sliced fresh strawberries
2	cups chopped oranges
⅓	cup chopped scallions
1	tablespoon honey
1	teaspoon canola oil
¼	teaspoon ground cinnamon
4	cups torn romaine lettuce

❋ In a large bowl, combine the strawberries, oranges, scallions, honey, oil, and cinnamon; toss gently. Let stand at room temperature for 30 minutes, stirring occasionally.

❋ Arrange the lettuce on salad plates; divide the fruit among them, reserving the marinade. Drizzle the marinade over the salads.

What's in Season?
What's on Sale?

Keep this chart handy to follow the peak seasons for most produce to keep your budget healthy. Take advantage of supermarket sales for holidays and back-to-school days.

January
Grapefruit
Greens
Lemons
Limes
Oranges

February
Grapefruit
Grapes
Lemons
Limes
Oranges

March
Cabbage
   (St. Patrick's
   Day sales)
Grapefruit
Grapes
Lemons
Limes
Oranges

April
Asparagus
Artichokes
Lettuces

May
Asparagus
Lettuces
Radishes
Scallions
Strawberries

June
Nectarines
Onions
Peaches
Plums
Strawberries

July
Cherries
Corn
Cucumbers
Grapes
Green beans
Melons
Peppers
Strawberries
Tomatoes
Zucchini

August
Corn
Eggplant
Grapes
Green beans
Melons
Nectarines
Peaches
Peppers
Plums
Tomatoes
Zucchini

September
Apples
Bananas (back-
   to-school lunch
   box sales)
Corn
Pears
Winter squash

October
Apples
Broccoli
Brussels sprouts
Cabbage
Greens
Potatoes
Pumpkins
Sweet potatoes
Winter squash

November
Cranberries
   (Thanksgiving
   sales)
Grapefruit
Oranges

December
Bananas
Grapefruit
Greens
Mushrooms
Onions
Oranges
Sweet potatoes

SPICY RICE SALAD WITH CHICKEN

Makes 6 servings

Per main-dish serving
Calories 365
Total fat 7.4 g.
Saturated fat 1 g.
Cholesterol 28 mg.
Sodium 163 mg.
Fiber 1.9 g.

Cost per serving

98¢

Spanish cuisine influences this warm rice salad, elegant enough to serve company but less than $1 a serving. Use leftover roast chicken for this recipe, if you wish.

2 chicken breast halves, skinned, boned, and cut into 1" pieces
1 small onion, finely chopped
2 tablespoons minced garlic
¼ teaspoon mild curry powder
4 cups defatted chicken stock
2 cups basmati rice
½ small jalapeño pepper, minced
   (wear plastic gloves when handling)
¼ cup chopped fresh cilantro
⅓ cup lemon juice
2 tablespoons olive oil
2 tablespoons honey or sugar
1 tablespoon balsamic vinegar
1 cup chopped sweet red peppers
1 cup chopped green peppers
1 cup peeled and chopped cucumbers
¼ teaspoon salt
¼ teaspoon ground black pepper

❀ Coat a Dutch oven with no-stick spray; set it over medium-high heat. When the Dutch oven is hot, add the chicken, onions, garlic, and curry powder; cook and stir for 5 minutes, or until the onions are golden brown. Add the chicken stock, rice, and jalapeño peppers; bring to a boil. Reduce the heat to low; cover and cook for 20 minutes, or until the rice is tender and the liquid has been absorbed.

❀ Meanwhile, in a large bowl combine the cilantro, lemon juice, oil, honey or sugar, and vinegar; stir well. Add the red peppers, green peppers, cucumbers, and rice mixture; toss well. Let stand at room temperature for 15 minutes, stirring occasionally. Add the salt and pepper.

SPICY LEMON LENTIL SALAD

Lentils are a real deal at only 11¢ a cup uncooked. Serve this salad with broiled chicken or fish.

    3 cups defatted chicken stock
    2 cups lentils
 1½ cups minced scallions
    1 cup shredded carrots
    1 cup chopped fresh tomatoes or canned reduced-
         sodium tomatoes
    1 cup whole kernel corn
    3 tablespoons lemon juice
    2 tablespoons minced fresh parsley
    2 tablespoons canola oil
    1 tablespoon chopped garlic
    1 teaspoon dried basil
  ½ teaspoon minced jalapeño peppers
         (wear plastic gloves when handling)
  ¼ teaspoon salt
  ¼ teaspoon ground black pepper

✸ In a medium saucepan, combine the chicken stock and lentils; bring to a boil over medium-high heat. Reduce the heat to medium; cook for 20 minutes, or until the lentils are tender but not mushy. Drain well; reserve the stock for another use.

✸ In a large bowl, combine the scallions, carrots, tomatoes, corn, lemon juice, parsley, oil, garlic, basil, peppers, and lentils; toss well. Let stand for 20 minutes at room temperature, stirring occasionally. Add the salt and pepper.

Makes 4 servings

Per main-dish serving
Calories 370
Total fat 8.2 g.
Saturated fat 1.1 g.
Cholesterol 5 mg.
Sodium 170 mg.
Fiber 3.4 g.

Cost per serving

50¢

KITCHEN TIP

Freeze the leftover stock to add to your next soup. The lentils give it delicious flavor.

Per side-dish serving
Calories 161
Total fat 3 g.
Saturated fat 0.5 g.
Cholesterol 0 mg.
Sodium 300 mg.
Fiber 4.9 g.

Cost per serving

56¢

Green and White Summer Bean Salad

Blanching brings out the vivid color in green beans but leaves them with a crisp texture that contrasts nicely with the cooked white beans in this marinated salad.

    3 cups diagonally sliced green beans
    1 cup cooked navy beans (page 199)
    ⅓ cup balsamic vinegar
    ¼ cup minced fresh parsley
    ¼ cup minced fresh basil
    ¼ onion, minced
    2 teaspoons olive oil
    1 teaspoon honey
    1 teaspoon Dijon mustard
    2 large tomatoes, thickly sliced
    ½ teaspoon salt
    ½ teaspoon ground black pepper

❀ Bring a medium saucepan of water to a boil over medium-high heat; add the green beans. Cook for 30 seconds; drain and rinse under cold water. Drain well; pat dry.

❀ In a large bowl, combine the green beans, navy beans, vinegar, parsley, basil, onions, oil, honey, and mustard; toss well. Let stand at room temperature for 20 minutes, stirring occasionally.

❀ Arrange the tomatoes around the edge of a salad platter; mound the bean salad in the center. Sprinkle with the salt and pepper.

Cool Beans to Cut the Salt

Beans right out of the cooking pot will absorb more flavor from the dressing than cooled beans, so the salad may taste like it needs more salt. Cool the beans to room temperature before mixing them with the dressing to cut back on the salt you need.

MELON SALAD

August is the most economical time to make this chilled fruit salad, and it goes down easy in the heat. You can use several types of melon if you have them on hand. Serve it with lean beef or pasta.

6 cups cubed melon
¼ cup chopped fresh cilantro
¼ cup lime juice
3 black olives, minced
1 tablespoon honey
⅛ teaspoon salt

❋ In a large bowl, combine the melon, cilantro, lime juice, olives, honey, and salt; stir well. Cover and refrigerate, stirring occasionally, for 1 hour, or until the flavors blend.

Makes 4 servings

Per side-dish serving
Calories 109
Total fat 1.2 g.
Saturated fat 0.1 g.
Cholesterol 0 mg.
Sodium 104 mg.
Fiber 1.7 g.

Cost per serving

21¢

CARROT SALAD

A wonderful staple in winter meals, carrots cost less than 29¢ a pound but they give plenty of valuable vitamin A. They're jazzed up in this recipe with chopped apples and raisins.

3 tablespoons cider vinegar
3 tablespoons frozen apple juice concentrate, thawed
1 tablespoon canola oil
1 tablespoon lemon juice
3 cups shredded carrots
1 tart apple, peeled and shredded
½ cup raisins
3 tablespoons chopped fresh parsley
¼ teaspoon salt
¼ teaspoon ground black pepper

❋ In a large bowl, combine the vinegar, apple juice concentrate, oil, and lemon juice; stir well. Add the carrots, apples, raisins, and parsley; toss well. Add the salt and pepper.

Makes 4 servings

Per main-dish serving
Calories 160
Total fat 3.8 g.
Saturated fat 0.5 g.
Cholesterol 0 mg.
Sodium 169 mg.
Fiber 4 g.

Cost per serving

40¢

Red Cabbage and Beet Salad

A bright winter salad for a potluck or party, this slaw is even better if made ahead. And you don't have to peel or cook the beets. Just scrub them thoroughly. Shredded raw, they taste as sweet as carrots.

¼ large red cabbage, shredded
1 cup shredded carrots
½ cup shredded beets
1 large apple, shredded
½ cup orange juice
¼ cup raisins
2 tablespoons minced fresh parsley
4 teaspoons lemon juice or lime juice
4 teaspoons cider vinegar
4 teaspoons frozen apple juice concentrate, thawed
¼ teaspoon ground black pepper
¼ teaspoon celery seeds
⅛ teaspoon dry mustard
⅛ teaspoon salt

✺ In a large bowl, combine the cabbage, carrots, beets, apples, orange juice, raisins, parsley, lemon or lime juice, vinegar, apple juice concentrate, pepper, celery seeds, mustard, and salt; toss well. Let stand at room temperature for 30 minutes, or until the flavors blend, stirring occasionally.

Per side-dish serving
Calories 118
Total fat 0.6 g.
Saturated fat 0.1 g.
Cholesterol 0 mg.
Sodium 111 mg.
Fiber 4.7 g.

Cost per serving

46¢

Kitchen Tip

For less mess, shred the beets in a food processor. Be careful of staining your hands or clothes.

Cucumber Salad with Dill

Cucumbers all seem to ripen at once, so there are plenty of summer sales. This salad takes advantage of summer cucumber prices, which sometimes dip as low as 15¢ per cucumber. Add chopped fresh mint, if desired.

   2 large cucumbers, peeled and sliced
 1/3 cup nonfat sour cream
 1/3 cup nonfat plain yogurt
 1/3 cup peeled and diced tart apples
 1/4 cup thinly sliced radishes
   2 tablespoons minced onions
   2 large cloves garlic, minced
   1 teaspoon chopped fresh dill
 1/2 teaspoon salt
 1/2 teaspoon ground black pepper

❋ In a large bowl, combine the cucumbers, sour cream, yogurt, apples, radishes, onions, garlic, and dill; toss well. Cover and refrigerate overnight, or until the flavors blend. Add the salt and pepper.

What to Do with Leftover Onions?

Some recipes use only a smidgen of onion. You can keep the rest of the onion in the refrigerator for up to 6 days without loss of flavor. Or you can chop and freeze the remainder for up to 3 months. Chopped onions freeze loose, so it's easy to measure out small quantities as you need them.

Makes 4 servings

Per side-dish serving
Calories 55
Total fat 0.4 g.
Saturated fat 0.1 g.
Cholesterol 0 mg.
Sodium 300 mg.
Fiber 0.7 g.

Cost per serving

29¢

Main-Course and Side-Dish Salads

Per main-dish serving
Calories 285
Total fat 2.2 g.
Saturated fat 0.3 g.
Cholesterol 0 mg.
Sodium 474 mg.
Fiber 1.7 g.

Cost per serving

44¢

ASIAN PASTA SALAD

*Flat noodles, especially yolk-free egg noodles, are great for this slightly spicy
Asian salad. You can make it heartier by adding cooked seafood or chicken.*

8	ounces yolk-free egg noodles
¼	cup chopped fresh cilantro
3	tablespoons reduced-sodium soy sauce
2	tablespoons sugar
2	tablespoons lemon juice or lime juice
1	tablespoon minced garlic
1	teaspoon minced fresh ginger
⅛	teaspoon crushed red-pepper flakes
1	teaspoon peanut butter
1	teaspoon dark sesame oil
1	cup sliced snow peas
1	cup peeled, seeded, and sliced cucumbers
½	cup diced sweet red peppers
⅛	teaspoon salt
⅛	teaspoon ground black pepper

❋ Cook the noodles according to the package directions; drain well.

❋ In a large bowl, combine the cilantro, soy sauce, sugar, lemon
juice or lime juice, garlic, ginger, red-pepper flakes, peanut
butter, and oil; stir well. Add the noodles, snow peas, cucumbers, and red peppers; toss well. Let stand at room
temperature for 1 hour, stirring occasionally.
Add the salt and pepper.

VEGETABLES DO DELICIOUS DOUBLE DUTY

Use leftover vegetables or cook extra just to have on hand for these tasty dishes.

❋ *Chinese Tacos*. Pack leftover cooked Chinese vegetables and tofu into taco shells. Add chopped lettuce, shredded carrots, shredded cucumbers, and a drizzle of hoisin sauce.

❋ *It's a Wrap*. Slice leftover grilled vegetables and wrap them in warm tortillas. Top with tomato sauce and cheese.

❋ *Meat and Greens Salad*. Arrange leftover salad greens on a platter. Top with chopped cooked beef or chicken and sliced tomatoes. Drizzle with curry-spiked nonfat plain yogurt or with lemon juice and olive oil for a main-course summer salad.

❋ *Pan Bagna*. Pack leftover marinated tomatoes and cucumbers into a hollowed-out round loaf of Italian bread. Add drained, flaked water-packed tuna and chopped cabbage. Wrap tightly and refrigerate for 1 hour, then slice into wedges.

❋ *Perfect Pickles*. Save the brine from your next jar of pickles. Add sliced cucumbers to it. Refrigerate for 3 days to make homemade pickles. The brine can be reused twice.

❋ *Summer Pasta Plate*. Toss cooked noodles with leftover marinated salad vegetables. Add nonfat plain yogurt, caraway seeds, minced scallions, chopped pimentos, salt, and ground black pepper.

❋ *Supper Sub*. Sandwich leftover cabbage slaw between slices of rye bread. Add thinly sliced cooked chicken, tomatoes, and low-fat mozzarella cheese.

❋ *Texas Pizza*. Top a homemade pizza shell with leftover cooked chili and chopped vegetables. Sprinkle with shredded low-fat cheese before baking.

Per side-dish serving
Calories 255
Total fat 0.9 g.
Saturated fat 0.5 g.
Cholesterol 2 mg.
Sodium 455 mg.
Fiber 4.7 g.

Cost per serving

27¢

KITCHEN TIP

Freeze leftover blue cheese in small containers. It will keep its flavor for 4 months.

DILLY POTATO SALAD

Buttermilk and nonfat mayonnaise make a delightful dressing for this easy summer salad. And potatoes—always a superb bulk buy (page 5)—keep the price way down. Leftover cooked potatoes work great in this salad.

4 cups cubed unpeeled red potatoes
1 cup diced celery
½ cup nonfat mayonnaise
¼ cup chopped scallions
3 tablespoons low-fat buttermilk
2 tablespoons vinegar
1 tablespoon chopped fresh dill
1 tablespoon crumbed blue cheese
½ teaspoon ground black pepper

❋ Place the potatoes in a large saucepan; cover with water and boil for 15 minutes, or until they are soft but not mushy. Check by inserting the tip of a sharp knife into one cube. Drain and cool.

❋ In a large bowl, combine the potatoes, celery, mayonnaise, scallions, buttermilk, vinegar, and dill; toss well. Cover and refrigerate, stirring occasionally, for 1 hour, or until the flavors blend. Add the blue cheese and pepper.

HAWAIIAN MELON AND PINEAPPLE SALAD

Late summer's the perfect time for this tasty melon salad, when melons are dirt cheap. It makes a lovely, light lunch with chilled cooked chicken or turkey breasts.

1 large orange
8 cups cubed melon
1 can (8 ounces) unsweetened pineapple chunks (with juice)
¼ cup chopped fresh mint
2 tablespoons honey or packed brown sugar

❋ Grate 2 teaspoons of orange rind; peel and chop the orange. In a large bowl, combine the orange rind, oranges, melon, pineapple (with juice), mint, and honey or brown sugar; toss well. Cover and refrigerate for 15 minutes, or until the flavors blend.

Makes 4 servings

Per side-dish serving
Calories 195
Total fat 1 g.
Saturated fat 0 g.
Cholesterol 0 mg.
Sodium 31 mg.
Fiber 3.4 g.

Cost per serving

49¢

Summer Tomato Salad

Try a variety of red, yellow, plum, cherry, and beefsteak tomatoes in this easy summertime dish. The salad tastes best if served within 4 hours of preparation.

2½ pounds tomatoes, thickly sliced
2 tablespoons minced fresh basil
2 tablespoons balsamic vinegar
2 teaspoons cider vinegar
1 teaspoon sugar
1 teaspoon Dijon mustard
¼ teaspoon salt
¼ teaspoon ground black pepper

❋ Arrange the tomatoes in a 13″ × 9″ nonmetal dish. In a small bowl, combine the basil, balsamic vinegar, cider vinegar, sugar, mustard, salt, and pepper; stir well. Pour over the tomatoes. Cover and let stand at room temperature for 30 minutes, or until the flavors blend.

Makes 4 servings

Per side-dish serving
Calories 73
Total fat 1 g.
Saturated fat 0.1 g.
Cholesterol 0 mg.
Sodium 177 mg.
Fiber 3.4 g.

Cost per serving

34¢

Great Greens to Grow

It's easy to start a back porch or window-sill garden of fresh greens—they grow like weeds and are ready for harvesting in three or four weeks, at a savings of 99¢ a pound over store-bought. Start with a good soil mix (check with your local gardening store) and a shallow pot with good drainage. Experiment with a variety of lettuces and greens, such as chicory, curly endive, escarole, oak leaf lettuce, romaine, and others. Keep the soil moist but not soaking wet; provide plenty of southern exposure. Thin the greens by using them in salads.

VEGETABLE SIDE DISHES

Vegetables rank high on the USDA's Food Guide Pyramid as sources of fiber, vitamins, minerals, and complex carbohydrates. They're linked with cancer prevention and help us combat a host of other diseases. In the low-cost kitchen, vegetables provide solid nutrition for the dinner plate at affordable prices. Have a look at our Best Bulk Buys chart on page 5 to see how many vegetables take starring roles as best foods for the money.

Vegetables also offer limitless variations for the cook to explore. Taste, texture, color, and aroma all enchant. You can eat vegetables raw, cooked, hot, chilled, grilled—there's never a dull moment with vegetables if they're treated right. So venture into some of the wonderful recipes in this chapter and reintroduce yourself to world of vegetables. Mom will be proud—and your budget and your health will be glad you did.

Per serving
Calories 129
Total fat 2.6 g.
Saturated fat 0.4 g.
Cholesterol 0 mg.
Sodium 279 mg.
Fiber 0.3 g.

Cost per serving

15¢

SPICY SPANISH POTATOES

In this wintertime favorite, sliced oven-baked potatoes are topped with a spicy tomato sauce. Its robust flavor makes it perfect for supper alongside an omelet or frittata.

- 1 pound small red potatoes, thinly sliced
- ¼ cup chopped fresh parsley
- 1 tablespoon chopped onions
- 2 teaspoons olive oil
- 1 clove garlic, chopped
- 1 teaspoon all-purpose flour
- 1 teaspoon ground red pepper
- ½ cup chopped reduced-sodium canned tomatoes, drained
- 1 teaspoon honey
- ½ teaspoon salt
- 1 bay leaf
- ¼ cup defatted chicken stock

✸ Preheat the oven to 400°F. Place the potato slices on a no-stick baking sheet in an even layer. Coat them with no-stick spray. Bake for 20 minutes, or until golden and tender. Check by inserting the tip of a sharp knife into 1 potato slice.

✸ Meanwhile, in a 10″ no-stick skillet, combine the parsley, onions, oil, and garlic; cook and stir over medium-high heat for 5 minutes, or until the onions are soft but not browned. Add the flour and red pepper; stir well. Add the tomatoes, honey, salt, and bay leaf. Reduce the heat to low; cook and stir for 10 minutes. Add the chicken stock; cook and stir for 5 minutes. Remove and discard the bay leaf. Spoon the sauce over the potatoes.

MAKE POTATO CHIPS
FOR PEANUTS

You can save fat, sodium, and calories—not to mention plenty of pennies—when you make your own oven-baked chips at home. Thinly slice raw unpeeled baking potatoes or sweet potatoes, place on a baking sheet, coat with no-stick spray, and toss. Arrange on the baking sheet in a single layer. Bake at 350°F for 35 to 40 minutes, or until golden brown and crisp. Season to taste with salt and ground black pepper.

BAKED SWEET AND RED POTATOES

Makes 6 servings

Per serving
Calories 223
Total fat 1.7 g.
Saturated fat 0.3 g.
Cholesterol 0 mg.
Sodium 195 mg.
Fiber 1.8 g.

Cost per serving

24¢

Two types of potatoes make a satisfying side to keep the holiday table lean yet festive. Warming the olive oil for 30 seconds in the microwave oven makes it easier to use and lets you use less.

3 large sweet potatoes, cut into ½" slices
8 small red potatoes, halved
2 teaspoons olive oil, warmed
1 teaspoon ground black pepper
½ teaspoon salt

✽ Preheat the oven to 400°F. Arrange the sweet potatoes and red potatoes on a no-stick baking sheet. Brush with the olive oil. Sprinkle with the pepper and salt.

✽ Bake for 40 minutes, or until the potatoes are soft and golden brown. Check by inserting the tip of a sharp knife into 1 slice.

PERFECT POTATO PARTNERS

If you buy them in bags of 10 pounds or more, potatoes can cost you as little as 5¢ apiece. Create a balanced, speedy supper with a baked spud and one of these toppings or stuffings.

✽ Grilled sliced onions and mushrooms, seasoned with dried thyme to taste.

✽ Leftover chili and shredded low-fat Monterey Jack cheese.

✽ Nonfat cottage cheese and a dab of pesto.

✽ Nonfat plain yogurt, chopped scallions, and ground black pepper.

✽ Salsa and chopped fresh chives.

✽ Spaghetti sauce and grated Parmesan cheese.

✽ Steamed broccoli and grated Parmesan cheese.

✽ Stir-fried chicken and vegetables, splashed with reduced-sodium soy sauce.

CARROT-POTATO PANCAKES

Makes 4 servings

Per serving
Calories 171
Total fat 1.5 g.
Saturated fat 0.4 g.
Cholesterol 53 mg.
Sodium 165 mg.
Fiber 4 g.

Cost per serving

16¢

Carrots and potatoes are best buys for both nutritional value and cost. They also look good together in these warming root-vegetable pancakes. Serve them as a meal with a green salad or as an easy side dish for roast chicken or turkey.

    2   large baking potatoes, peeled and shredded
    1   carrot, shredded
    1   large egg
    1   tablespoon all-purpose flour
    1   teaspoon dried thyme
    ¼   teaspoon salt
    ¼   teaspoon ground black pepper
    1   cup unsweetened applesauce

❊ In a large bowl, combine the potatoes, carrots, egg, flour, thyme, salt, and pepper; mix well.

❊ Coat a 10″ no-stick skillet or griddle with no-stick spray; set it over medium-high heat. For each pancake, ladle ¼ cup of the batter onto the skillet, spreading with a spoon if necessary. Cook for 3 minutes; turn and cook for 3 minutes more, or until golden brown. Cook in 2 batches, if necessary, coating the skillet or griddle lightly with no-stick spray between batches. You should have 8 pancakes. Drain the pancakes on paper towels. Serve with the applesauce.

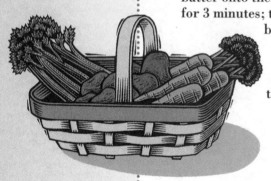

PESTO MASHED POTATOES

Make this side dish in early fall, when fresh basil is abundant and cheap. Or use frozen homemade pesto.

6 medium baking potatoes, peeled and cubed
2 tablespoons instant nonfat dry milk
½ cup chopped fresh basil
1 tablespoon olive oil
1 tablespoon grated Parmesan cheese
2 cloves garlic, chopped
¼ teaspoon ground black pepper

❋ Place the potatoes in a large saucepan; cover with water and boil for 20 minutes, or until the potatoes are soft. Check by inserting the tip of a sharp knife in 1 cube. Drain; reserve the cooking water for another use.

❋ Place the potatoes in a large bowl; sprinkle with the dry milk. With an electric beater or potato masher, whip the potatoes until they are light and fluffy.

❋ In a blender or food processor, combine the basil, oil, Parmesan and garlic; puree. Stir into the potatoes. Add the pepper.

STOCK UP ON HOMEMADE PESTO

When basil's bursting in your garden, harvest it and stock up on homemade pesto. It freezes beautifully. For each cup of basil, add ½ cup dry bread crumbs, ¼ cup grated Parmesan cheese, 2 cloves garlic, and 1 tablespoon olive oil. Puree in a blender or food processor. Pack into ice cube trays coated lightly with no-stick spray, pour a thin layer of olive oil on top of each compartment to prevent browning. Freeze until solid, then transfer to airtight freezer containers. Simply thaw one or two cubes as needed for soups or pastas.

Makes 4 servings

Per serving
Calories 266
Total fat 4.1 g.
Saturated fat 0.8 g.
Cholesterol 2 mg.
Sodium 53 mg.
Fiber 5.7 g.

Cost per serving

26¢

KITCHEN TIP

Use the cooled potato water when making bread instead of plain water. The potato starch will give the bread a chewy texture and rich flavor.

Per serving
Calories 259
Total fat 1.6 g.
Saturated fat .1 g.
Cholesterol 4 mg.
Sodium 111 mg.
Fiber 5.1 g.

Cost per serving

32¢

KITCHEN TIP

The leftover potato tops can be coated with no-stick spray, sprinkled with ground black pepper, and baked at 375°F until crisp for a fast low-fat snack.

STUFFED BAKED POTATOES

Make extra stuffed potatoes for lunch later in the week. They are convenient and delicious reheated. They keep about 4 days in the refrigerator.

- 6 large baking potatoes
- 1 cup nonfat plain yogurt
- ¼ cup crumbled blue cheese
- 4 scallions, chopped
- ⅛ teaspoon paprika

❋ Preheat the oven to 425°F. Pierce the potatoes with a fork; place on the oven rack. Bake for 1 hour, or until very soft. Check by inserting the tip of a sharp knife into 1 potato.

❋ Preheat the broiler.

❋ Slice off the top third of each potato; reserve for another use. Remove enough of the potato pulp to leave ½" shells. In a medium bowl, combine the potato pulp, yogurt, blue cheese, and scallions; mash well. Spoon into the potato shells; sprinkle with the paprika. Broil for 5 minutes, or until the tops are lightly browned.

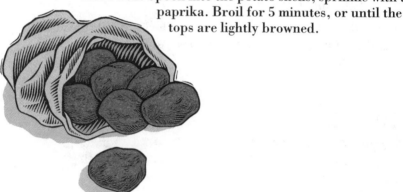

GRILLED SUMMER PEPPERS

When the garden's overflowing with colorful peppers, fire up the grill. Grilling brings out the sweetness of peppers like no other cooking method. The peppers can also be broiled.

¼ cup red wine vinegar
2 tablespoons minced onions
1 tablespoon Dijon mustard
4 cloves garlic, minced
¼ teaspoon ground black pepper
1 large sweet red pepper, quartered
1 large sweet yellow pepper, quartered
2 large green peppers, quartered

❀ Preheat the grill. In a small bowl, combine the vinegar, onions, mustard, garlic, and pepper.

❀ Place the red, yellow, and green peppers on the grill; lightly brush with the vinegar mixture. Cook for 3 minutes, or until the peppers are lightly browned; turn and brush the other side. Cook for 2 minutes, or until the peppers are softened and browned. Drizzle with the remaining vinegar.

Makes 4 servings

Per serving
Calories 54
Total fat 0.6 g.
Saturated fat 0.1 g.
Cholesterol 0 mg.
Sodium 53 mg.
Fiber 1.9 g.

Cost per serving

46¢

GRILLING TIPS FOR SUMMER VEGETABLES

Grilling can be an economical, hassle-free way to cook in the heat of summer, especially if you have a gas grill and can avoid charcoal expense. Most vegetables love the grill. The intense heat sweetens them as they cook. Try grilling sliced eggplant, mushrooms, sliced onions, quartered sweet red peppers or sweet yellow peppers, sliced yellow summer squash, sliced zucchini, or whole green beans. Scout yard sales for grilling baskets, which allow you to cook smaller vegetables without having them fall through the grate.

To prepare vegetables for grilling, marinate them for 30 minutes in balsamic vinegar and herbs. Use the marinade to baste the vegetables as they cook to prevent drying out. The sugar in the balsamic vinegar will caramelize and flavor the grilled vegetables.

Per serving
Calories 33
Total fat 0.7 g.
Saturated fat 0.1 g.
Cholesterol 0 mg.
Sodium 80 mg.
Fiber 0.0 g.

Cost per serving

9¢

Green Beans with Basil

Stir-fried and subtly seasoned, these nutritious green beans take only 10 minutes from garden to table.

 1 **pound whole fresh green beans, trimmed**
½ **teaspoon dark sesame oil**
 1 **clove garlic, minced**
 2 **teaspoons minced fresh basil**
⅛ **teaspoon salt**
⅛ **teaspoon ground black pepper**

❋ Coat a 10″ no-stick skillet with no-stick spray; set it over medium-high heat. When the skillet is hot, add the beans, oil, and garlic; cook and stir for 5 to 8 minutes, or until the beans are tender and browned. Add the basil, salt, and pepper; toss well.

Exploring Winter Squash

Winter squash is a nutritional bargain. It provides plenty of beta-carotene and other nutrients and keeps up to two months when stored in a cool, dry place. Introduce your family to some of these winter squash as they appear in your supermarket:

❋ *Acorn:* acorn-shaped with ridges; dark green or orange rind; sweet orange flesh.

❋ *Buttercup:* flat, turban-shape; dark green or orange rind; sweet orange flesh.

❋ *Butternut:* torpedo-shaped, wider at the base; tan rind; extra-sweet orange interior.

❋ *Delicata:* small torpedo-shaped cream-colored rind with green stripes; sweet creamy yellow flesh.

❋ *Kabocha:* turban-shaped; dark green rind; very sweet pale orange flesh.

❋ *Spaghetti:* torpedo-shaped; pale yellow rind; interior breaks into crunchy strands that resemble spaghetti when cooked.

STUFFED PUMPKINS

During pumpkin harvest, you can pick up a bagful of miniature pumpkins at less than 35¢ apiece. Also called Jack-Be-Littles, they're great stuffed with herbs and bread crumbs for a festive side dish for Thanksgiving or holiday parties.

8 miniature pumpkins
½ cup defatted chicken stock
½ cup minced onions
1 cup soft whole-wheat bread crumbs
2 cloves garlic, minced
½ teaspoon dried sage
½ teaspoon dried thyme
½ cup shredded nonfat mozzarella cheese
⅓ cup chopped celery
¼ cup chopped dried apricots
2 teaspoons toasted chopped walnuts
⅛ teaspoon salt

❋ Preheat the oven to 350°F. Slice the top ½" off each pumpkin; scoop out the seeds. Place the pumpkins in a 13" × 9" baking dish; bake for 15 minutes.

❋ Meanwhile, in a 10" no-stick skillet, combine the chicken stock and onions; cook and stir over medium-high heat for 8 minutes, or until the onions are golden brown. Add the bread crumbs, garlic, sage, and thyme; cook and stir for 1 minute. Add the mozzarella, celery, apricots, walnuts, and salt; remove from the heat.

❋ Spoon the stuffing into the pumpkins; spoon any remaining stuffing around the pumpkins. Bake for 15 minutes, or until the stuffing is golden brown.

Makes 8 servings

Per serving
Calories 115
Total fat 1.3 g.
Saturated fat 0.3 g.
Cholesterol 0 mg.
Sodium 206 mg.
Fiber 2.6 g.

Cost per serving

35¢

KITCHEN TIP

Be careful not to overbake the pumpkins or they will split.

Makes 4 servings

Per serving
Calories 67
Total fat 0.6 g.
Saturated fat 0.3 g.
Cholesterol 1 mg.
Sodium 26 mg.
Fiber 1.9 g.

Cost per serving

12¢

GLAZED CARROTS

This colorful dish is super easy, packed with vitamin A, and a big hit with kids who love carrots.

- 2 cups sliced carrots
- ¾ cup apple juice
- 1 tablespoon honey
- ½ teaspoon butter
- 1 teaspoon grated orange rind
- 1 teaspoon grated lemon rind

❋ In a medium saucepan, combine the carrots and apple juice; cover and cook over medium-high heat for 10 minutes, or until the carrots are soft. Check by inserting the tip of a sharp knife into 1 slice. Add the honey, butter, orange rind, and lemon rind; cook and stir for 3 to 5 minutes, or until the sauce is thick.

Makes 4 servings

Per serving
Calories 120
Total fat 1.3 g.
Saturated fat 0.2 g.
Cholesterol 0 mg.
Sodium 167 mg.
Fiber 3.6 g.

Cost per serving

23¢

ROOT-VEGETABLE MEDLEY

The quick cooking of the grill or broiler allows these root vegetables to stay crisp-tender inside and golden brown on the outside. Don't bother peeling the vegetables. Just scrub them well.

- 1 large sweet potato, thickly sliced
- 1 turnip, halved and sliced into thick strips
- 2 red potatoes, thickly sliced
- 1 carrot, halved and sliced into thick strips
  Juice of ½ lemon
- 2 cloves garlic, minced
- 1 teaspoon olive oil
- ½ teaspoon ground black pepper
- ¼ teaspoon salt

* In a shallow nonmetal dish, combine the sweet potatoes, turnips, red potatoes, carrots, lemon juice, garlic, and oil; toss well. Let stand for 15 minutes at room temperature, stirring occasionally.

* Preheat the grill or broiler. Drain the vegetables and place them in a grill basket or on a broiler pan; reserve the marinade. Grill or broil the vegetables 4″ from the heat, turning frequently and basting with the marinade, for 15 minutes, or until they are crisp-tender and golden brown. Check by inserting the tip of a sharp knife into 1 piece. Sprinkle with the pepper and salt.

BAKED FENNEL WITH CHEESE

Fennel is easy to grow in the garden and is often a bargain at farmstands during the summer months. Its delicious licorice flavor sweetens as it bakes.

```
2   medium fennel bulbs, trimmed, peeled, and julienned
3   cloves garlic, thinly sliced
½   teaspoon dried thyme
1   cup defatted chicken stock
2   teaspoons Dijon mustard
½   teaspoon ground nutmeg
1   cup toasted fine bread crumbs
2   tablespoons grated Parmesan cheese
```

* Preheat the oven to 400°F. Coat a 1½-quart shallow casserole dish with no-stick spray. Spread the fennel and garlic in the dish; sprinkle with the thyme.

* In a small bowl, combine the chicken stock, mustard, and nutmeg; pour over the fennel. Top with the bread crumbs and Parmesan.

* Cover and bake for 20 minutes; uncover and bake for 20 minutes more, or until golden brown.

Makes 4 servings

Per serving
Calories 145
Total fat 2.9 g.
Saturated fat 1 g.
Cholesterol 4 mg.
Sodium 349 mg.
Fiber 0.1 g.

Cost per serving

61¢

KITCHEN TIP

Trim the fennel bulb by peeling away any tough outer layer and cutting the feathery tips—which can be saved to add to soup stock or chopped for salads.

CAJUN CORN ON THE COB

No costly ingredients are needed to make this authentic Cajun dish—just a combination of supermarket seasonings.

½ teaspoon olive oil
1 small clove garlic, minced
½ teaspoon paprika
1 drop hot-pepper sauce
¼ teaspoon salt
4 large ears corn

❁ Preheat the grill or broiler. In a small bowl, combine the oil, garlic, paprika, hot-pepper sauce, and salt. Brush on the corn.

❁ Grill or broil 4" from the heat, turning frequently and brushing with the seasoning mixture, for 3 to 5 minutes, or until lightly browned.

Makes 4 servings

Per serving
Calories 124
Total fat 1.5 g.
Saturated fat 0.2 g.
Cholesterol 0 mg.
Sodium 139 mg.
Fiber 2.7 g.

Cost per serving

17¢

SOUTHERN-STYLE GREENS AND BEANS

The bacon fat traditionally used in this dish is replaced with orange juice and vinegar for a delicious sweet-and-sour flavor. Collard greens, spinach, Swiss chard, and kale all work well in this recipe.

½ cup defatted chicken stock
1 teaspoon olive oil
2 cups sliced green beans
1 cup sliced mushrooms
3 cups chopped greens
¼ cup orange juice
1 tablespoon balsamic vinegar
½ teaspoon packed brown sugar
¼ teaspoon salt
¼ teaspoon ground black pepper

❁ In a 10" no-stick skillet, combine the stock and oil; bring to a boil over medium-high heat. Add the beans and mushrooms; cook and stir for 5 minutes. Add the greens, orange juice, vinegar, and brown sugar; cover and cook for 5 minutes, or until the beans are tender. Add the salt and pepper. Stir to combine.

Makes 4 servings

Per serving
Calories 70
Total fat 1.8 g.
Saturated fat 0.3 g.
Cholesterol 1 mg.
Sodium 169 mg.
Fiber 3 g.

Cost per serving

48¢

Caraway Cabbage Sauté

Caraway seeds turn sweet when sautéed. This German-style dish is great paired with pork.

  3 tablespoons chopped onions
  1 teaspoon olive oil
  ¼ teaspoon caraway seeds
  4 cups sliced red cabbage
  ⅓ cup defatted chicken stock
  2 teaspoons lemon juice
  ¼ teaspoon ground black pepper

✢ In a 10″ no-stick skillet, combine the onions, oil, and caraway seeds; cook and stir over medium-high heat for 1 minute. Add the cabbage; cook and stir for 1 minute. Add the chicken stock. Reduce the heat to low; cover and cook for 7 to 10 minutes, or until the cabbage is tender. Add the lemon juice and pepper; stir well.

Makes 4 servings

Per serving
Calories 34
Total fat 1.4 g.
Saturated fat 0.2 g.
Cholesterol 1 mg.
Sodium 8 mg.
Fiber 1.6 g.

Cost per serving

20¢

Storing Fresh Greens

Greens can age quickly in the refrigerator. To get your money's worth and help fresh greens last at least a week, follow these storage tips: As soon as you get them home, wash the greens and dry them in a salad spinner or between clean kitchen towels. Pack them into perforated plastic bread bags lined with paper towels to absorb excess moisture. Store the greens in the vegetable drawer of your refrigerator.

WILTED GERMAN CABBAGE AND CHARD

Cabbage is a best buy in produce year-round. This recipe works well with either green or red cabbage. You can use collard greens, kale, or spinach in place of the Swiss chard.

1 medium onion, thinly sliced
½ cup defatted chicken stock
2 tablespoons minced garlic
4 cups sliced cabbage
2 cups chopped Swiss chard
¼ cup cider vinegar
2 tablespoons packed brown sugar
1 tablespoon molasses

❋ In a 10″ no-stick skillet, combine the onions, chicken stock, and garlic; bring to a boil over medium-high heat. Cover and cook for 3 minutes. Reduce the heat to medium; add the cabbage, chard, vinegar, and brown sugar; cover and cook for 12 to 15 minutes, or until the liquid has evaporated. Add the molasses; cook and stir for 3 minutes, or until hot.

ZUCCHINI WITH FRESH HERBS

This Italian-style tomato and zucchini medley is a colorful sidebar to grilled fish. For variety, try yellow summer squash instead of zucchini. You can substitute dried oregano and basil for the fresh, but use half as much.

⅓ cup minced scallions
¼ cup defatted chicken stock
3 cloves garlic, minced
2 cups diced tomatoes
2 cups sliced zucchini
1 teaspoon minced fresh oregano
1 tablespoon minced fresh basil
1 tablespoon minced fresh parsley

❋ In a 10″ no-stick skillet, combine the scallions, stock, and garlic; cook and stir over medium-high heat for 3 minutes. Add the tomatoes, zucchini, and oregano; cook and stir for 3 minutes. Cover and cook for 2 minutes more, or until the zucchini is tender. Check by inserting the tip of a sharp knife into 1 piece. Stir in the basil and parsley.

Hot and Spicy Indian Cauliflower

Makes 4 servings

Per serving
Calories 76
Total fat 1.9 g.
Saturated fat 0.2 g.
Cholesterol 0 mg.
Sodium 92 mg.
Fiber 6.8 g.

Cost per serving

58¢

Cauliflower provides plenty of flavor for only 30¢ a serving. It takes on a golden color in this lively Indian side dish.

¼ cup apple juice
1 teaspoon olive oil
1 medium onion, sliced
1 small jalapeño pepper, seeded and minced
    (wear plastic gloves when handling)
1 teaspoon minced fresh ginger
1 teaspoon curry powder
½ teaspoon dry mustard
1 large head cauliflower, broken into florets
2 tablespoons lemon juice
2 tablespoons chopped fresh cilantro or parsley

✺ In a Dutch oven, combine the apple juice and oil; bring to a boil over medium-high heat. Add the onions, peppers, ginger, curry powder, and dry mustard; cook and stir for 3 minutes, or until the onions are soft.

✺ Reduce the heat to low. Add the cauliflower; cover and cook for 12 to 15 minutes, or until just tender. Check by inserting the tip of a sharp knife into 1 floret. Add the lemon juice and cilantro or parsley; toss well.

Minted Broccoli

Makes 4 servings

Per serving
Calories 49
Total fat 0.9 g.
Saturated fat 0.1 g.
Cholesterol 0 mg.
Sodium 161 mg.
Fiber 3 g.

Cost per serving

36¢

Broccoli is a year-round health bargain at only 22¢ a cup. It's full of anti-oxidants believed to help prevent certain cancers. It takes on a light minty flavor in this delicious side dish, which will win over the whole family.

4 cups chopped broccoli
¼ cup balsamic vinegar
¼ cup chopped fresh mint
2 cloves garlic, finely minced
½ teaspoon olive oil
¼ teaspoon salt
¼ teaspoon ground black pepper

✺ In a large saucepan over medium-high heat, cook the broccoli in boiling water for 4 minutes; drain well. In a large bowl, combine the broccoli, vinegar, mint, garlic, oil, salt, and pepper; toss well. Let stand at room temperature, tossing frequently, for 10 minutes, or until the flavors blend.

BREADS AND OTHER BAKED GOODS

The aroma and flavor of fresh-baked bread are incomparable. Luckily, bread is an indispensable staple for the lean lifestyle. Breads, pizzas, and sandwiches are all complex carbohydrates, and you're healthiest eating 6 to 11 servings of grain-based foods a day. Making your own saves you plenty, since one nutritious whole-grain loaf from your own kitchen costs only 25 cents, at least 75 cents less than most bakery or even supermarket brands.

If you're concerned about time, relax. Breads are easy—and faster to prepare at home than you might imagine. Even rustic country-style yeast breads take only 30 minutes of hands-on work. The rest is rising and baking time. And quick breads live up to their name. A speedy assembly and baking makes our muffins and coffee cakes ready in time for a weekend breakfast. Wake up to the pleasure of fresh breads piping hot from the oven!

Orange Muffins with Dates

Makes 12

Per muffin
Calories 130
Total fat 3 g.
Saturated fat 0.5 g.
Cholesterol 18 mg.
Sodium 150 mg.
Fiber 1.4 g.

Cost per serving

17¢

Orange pulp and rind give these breakfast muffins a refreshing citrus flavor. Applesauce replaces 6 tablespoons of the butter (and eliminates over 28 grams of fat in the recipe!) to keep them light and lean.

1	large navel orange
½	cup pitted dates
½	cup low-fat buttermilk
1	egg
3	tablespoons packed brown sugar
2	tablespoons unsweetened applesauce
2	tablespoons canola oil
1½	cups all-purpose flour
1	teaspoon baking powder
1	teaspoon baking soda

❋ Preheat the oven to 400°F. Coat a 12-cup no-stick muffin tin with no-stick spray.

❋ Grate the rind from the orange and set aside. Peel the orange and chop the pulp. In a food processor or blender, combine the orange pulp, dates, and orange rind; chop coarsely. Add the buttermilk, egg, brown sugar, applesauce, and oil; puree.

❋ In a large bowl, combine the flour, baking powder, and baking soda; add the orange mixture. Stir until just blended. Pour into the muffin tin, filling the cups three-fourths full.

❋ Bake for 12 to 15 minutes, or until a toothpick inserted in the center of a muffin comes out clean.

CHOCOLATE MUFFINS WITH RAISINS

Serve these chocolate muffins to kids on winter mornings. You'll save money over boxed cold cereal, and kids love the taste of these homemade low-fat treats.

Makes 12

Per muffin
Calories 177
Total fat 5.6 g.
Saturated fat 0.8 g.
Cholesterol 18 mg.
Sodium 140 mg.
Fiber 1.2 g.

Cost per serving

14¢

¾ cup rolled oats
1¼ cups all-purpose flour
2 tablespoons cocoa powder
1 teaspoon ground cinnamon
1 teaspoon baking powder
½ teaspoon baking soda
¼ teaspoon salt
¾ cup raisins
¾ cup skim milk
⅓ cup honey
¼ cup canola oil
1 egg

❋ Preheat the oven to 400°F. Coat a 12-cup no-stick muffin tin with no-stick spray.

❋ In a blender or food processor, grind the oats to a coarse powder. In a large bowl, combine the oats, flour, cocoa, cinnamon, baking powder, baking soda, and salt; mix well. Add the raisins; stir well.

❋ In a medium bowl, combine the milk, honey, oil, and egg; add to the flour mixture. Stir until just blended. Pour into the muffin tin, filling the cups three-fourths full.

❋ Bake for 12 to 15 minutes, or until a toothpick inserted in the center of a muffin comes out clean.

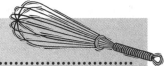

MUFFIN SUCCESS

❋ Always preheat the oven. Muffins bake quickly and need a hot oven to rise properly.

❋ Keep the wet and dry ingredients separate until just before baking. Combining them too early creates tough muffins.

❋ Add hot water to any unfilled muffin cups to keep the heat even in the pan.

CREATE A BREAKFAST MUFFIN

With a little improvising, you can make and serve scrumptious low-fat muffins in a variety of flavors to make use of (and use up) ingredients you might have on hand at home. (You'll save about $1 apiece, too.) Use this basic muffin recipe and its options to get started.

ORANGE MUFFINS

Makes 12

Per muffin
Calories 92
Total fat 1.8 g.
Saturated fat 0.4 g.
Cholesterol 18 mg.
Sodium 171 mg.
Fiber 2.1 g.

Cost per serving

7¢

1½ cups whole-wheat flour
 1 teaspoon baking powder
 1 teaspoon baking soda
½ cup low-fat buttermilk
 1 egg
 3 tablespoons honey
 2 tablespoons reduced-calorie butter
 2 tablespoons applesauce
½ cup chopped oranges

❋ Preheat the oven to 400°F. Lightly coat a 12-cup no-stick muffin tin with no-stick spray.

❋ In a large bowl, combine the flour, baking powder, and baking soda; mix well.

❋ In a medium bowl, combine the buttermilk, egg, honey, butter, and applesauce; mix well. Stir the wet ingredients into the flour mixture; add the oranges. Pour into the muffin cups, filling about three-fourths full.

❋ Bake for 12 to 15 minutes, or until a toothpick inserted in the center of a muffin comes out clean.

Make-Your-Own-Muffin Options

* *Flour.* Use a combination of flours, such as whole-wheat flour, all-purpose flour, or cornmeal. You can also substitute up to ½ cup cooked rice or bran cereal for an equal amount of flour.

* *Milk or Juice.* Use low-fat buttermilk, soy milk, nonfat sour cream, skim milk, nonfat plain yogurt, orange juice, or apple juice.

* *Sweetener.* Use honey, maple syrup, granulated sugar, brown sugar, molasses, or frozen apple juice concentrate.

* *Oil.* Use oil, melted butter, or margarine.

* *Applesauce.* Use any pureed fruit (such as baby food prunes) or nonfat plain yogurt.

* *Flavoring.* Use chopped oranges, apples, mashed bananas, dates, drained and chopped canned fruits, blueberries, raspberries, cranberries, raisins, pumpkin puree, mashed cooked sweet potatoes, shredded carrots or zucchini, nuts, or shredded low-fat cheeses. As long as you stay under ½ cup, the wetter ingredients won't throw off the wet-dry balance of the recipe.

Freezing Muffins

Save yourself time and make double or triple batches of your favorite muffins to freeze and reheat later. Bake and cool the muffins, freeze them on a baking sheet, then transfer them to tightly sealed plastic bags (this is a good use for old bread wrappers). They'll keep frozen for up to 2 months without losing flavor. Thaw muffins in the refrigerator overnight, then reheat individually in the microwave on high power for 1 minute, or until steaming hot.

Per muffin
Calories 134
Total fat 3 g.
Saturated fat 0.5 g.
Cholesterol 18 mg.
Sodium 120 mg.
Fiber 1.3 g.

Cost per serving

17¢

SWEET-TART CRANBERRY MUFFINS

Holiday flavors permeate these jewel-like muffins. Make them in the late fall when cranberries are on sale. Buy a few extra bags and freeze them.

½ cup coarsely chopped fresh or frozen cranberries
½ cup coarsely chopped pitted dates
½ cup low-fat buttermilk
1 egg
⅓ cup maple syrup or packed brown sugar
2 tablespoons unsweetened applesauce
2 tablespoons canola oil
1½ cups all-purpose flour
1 teaspoon baking powder
1 teaspoon ground cinnamon
¾ teaspoon ground nutmeg
½ teaspoon baking soda
⅛ teaspoon salt

❋ Preheat the oven to 400°F. Coat a 12-cup no-stick muffin tin with no-stick spray.

❋ In a medium bowl, combine the cranberries, dates, buttermilk, egg, maple syrup or brown sugar, applesauce, and oil; stir well.

❋ In a large bowl, combine the flour, baking powder, cinnamon, nutmeg, baking soda, and salt; add the cranberry mixture. Stir until just blended. Pour into the muffin tin, filling the cups three-fourths full.

❋ Bake for 12 to 15 minutes, or until a toothpick inserted in the center of a muffin comes out clean.

SPICED BREAKFAST BREAD

You save 10¢ a slice making this delicious bread at home rather than buying a comparable loaf of breakfast bread in the market. You can substitute a combination of ½ teaspoon ground cinnamon, ½ teaspoon ground nutmeg, and ¼ teaspoon ground cloves for the pumpkin pie spice.

1 cup whole-wheat flour
⅔ cup all-purpose flour
1¼ teaspoons baking powder
1 teaspoon baking soda
1 teaspoon pumpkin pie spice
¼ teaspoon salt
⅓ cup rolled oats
1 cup low-fat buttermilk
⅓ cup honey
2 tablespoons canola oil
1 tablespoon grated orange rind
1 egg

❁ Preheat the oven to 400°F. Coat a 9″ × 5″ loaf pan with no-stick spray.

❁ In a large bowl, combine the whole-wheat flour, all-purpose flour, baking powder, baking soda, pumpkin pie spice, and salt. Add the oats; stir well.

❁ In a medium bowl, combine the buttermilk, honey, oil, orange rind, and egg; mix well. Add to the flour mixture; stir until just blended. Pour into the pan.

❁ Bake for 45 minutes, or until a toothpick inserted in the center of the loaf comes out clean. Cool before slicing.

Makes 12 slices

Per slice
Calories 133
Total fat 3.3 g.
Saturated fat 0.6 g.
Cholesterol 19 mg.
Sodium 212 mg.
Fiber 1.7 g.

Cost per serving

13¢

Per scone
Calories 53
Total fat 1.6 g.
Saturated fat 0.3 g.
Cholesterol 1 mg.
Sodium 144 mg.
Fiber 0.2 g.

Cost per serving

6¢

CHEDDAR-CHUTNEY SCONES

Scones are traditional British tea-time fare and are usually high in fat and calories. These are trimmed down but still richly flavored—with low-fat extra-sharp Cheddar cheese and chutney.

- ¾ cup all-purpose flour
- 1 teaspoon baking powder
- 1 teaspoon sugar
- ¼ teaspoon baking soda
- ¼ teaspoon salt
- ¼ cup nonfat cottage cheese
- 1 tablespoon canola oil
- 1 tablespoon mango or other fruit chutney
- ¼ cup shredded low-fat extra-sharp Cheddar cheese
- 1–2 tablespoons low-fat buttermilk

❀ Preheat the oven to 425°F. Coat a large baking sheet with no-stick spray.

❀ In a medium bowl, combine the flour, baking powder, sugar, baking soda, and salt; stir well.

❀ In a large bowl, mash together the cottage cheese, oil, and chutney; add the Cheddar and 1 tablespoon of the buttermilk. Add the flour mixture; stir briefly until just blended. Turn the mixture out onto a lightly floured surface. Knead 5 times, or until the dough is soft and satiny, adding the remaining tablespoon buttermilk if needed.

❀ On a lightly floured surface, roll the dough into a large rectangle. With a 2" round cookie cutter, cut into 12 rounds, rerolling and cutting the scraps as needed. Place the rounds on the baking sheet.

❀ Bake for 7 to 10 minutes, or until just golden brown.

BLUEBERRY-BUTTERMILK COFFEECAKE

A great coffee-klatch or potluck dish, this coffeecake is studded with fruit and is moist from the secret ingredient of mashed bananas. It travels well and makes a good dessert for lunchboxes.

Makes 12 servings

Per serving
Calories 250
Total fat 5.9 g.
Saturated fat 0.9 g.
Cholesterol 18 mg.
Sodium 306 mg.
Fiber 2.7 g.

Cost per serving

39¢

1 cup whole-wheat flour
1 cup all-purpose flour
2 teaspoons baking powder
2 teaspoons baking soda
2 cups fresh or frozen blueberries
¾ cup honey
1 egg
3 egg whites
¾ cup low-fat buttermilk
½ cup mashed bananas
⅓ cup prune puree
¼ cup canola oil
1 tablespoon chopped walnuts
⅓ cup packed brown sugar

❋ Preheat the oven to 350°F. Coat a 13″ × 9″ baking pan with no-stick spray.

❋ In a large bowl, combine the whole-wheat flour, all-purpose flour, baking powder, and baking soda; fold in the blueberries.

❋ In a medium bowl, combine the honey, egg, egg whites, buttermilk, bananas, prune puree, and oil; add to the flour mixture. Stir until just blended.

❋ Pour the batter into the baking pan; smooth the top with a spatula. Sprinkle with the walnuts and brown sugar.

❋ Bake for 40 to 45 minutes, or until a toothpick inserted in the center comes out clean. Cool before cutting.

BARGAIN BANANAS FOR BAKING

Save those over-the-hill bananas for baking. They can replace up to half the oil in your muffin and quick bread recipes. To store, peel and mash the bananas. Pack them into ½-cup freezer containers. Freeze for up to 2 months.

Breads and Other
Baked Goods

WHOLE-WHEAT APPLE BREAD

Per slice
Calories 131
Total fat 4 g.
Saturated fat 0.6 g.
Cholesterol 1 mg.
Sodium 153 mg.
Fiber 2.6 g.

Cost per serving

19¢

Apple chunks flavor this robust quick bread. It freezes well and leftover slices make great French toast.

1¼ cups whole-wheat flour
 2 teaspoons ground cinnamon
 1 teaspoon ground nutmeg
 1 teaspoon ground allspice
 1 teaspoon baking powder
 ½ teaspoon baking soda
 ¼ teaspoon salt
1½ cups peeled and chopped tart apples
 ½ cup chopped pitted dates
 ¾ cup low-fat buttermilk
 ½ cup unsweetened applesauce
 ⅓ cup frozen apple juice concentrate, thawed
 3 tablespoons canola oil
 2 egg whites, lightly beaten

❁ Preheat the oven to 400°F. Coat a 9″ × 5″ loaf pan with no-stick spray; dust the pan with flour, shaking out the excess.

❁ In a large bowl, combine the flour, cinnamon, nutmeg, allspice, baking powder, baking soda, and salt. Add the apples and dates; toss well.

❁ In a medium bowl, combine the buttermilk, applesauce, apple juice concentrate, oil, and egg whites; add to the flour mixture. Stir until just blended; pour into the loaf pan.

❁ Bake for 25 minutes. Reduce the heat to 300°F; bake for 15 minutes more, or until a toothpick inserted in the center of the loaf comes out clean. Cool before slicing.

TIPS TO SAVE TIME AND DOUGH

❋ Make pizza crusts six at a time (just increase the recipe) and bake at 400°F for 8 minutes. Cool, stack, and wrap well. Keep them frozen until ready to use.

❋ When slicing homemade bread, slice the entire loaf at once. Collect all the crumbs into a plastic bag and freeze for bread crumbs.

❋ Use leftover bread dough to make homemade pretzels. Roll into ropes, twist, and place on baking sheets. Brush with beaten egg white and sprinkle lightly with salt. Bake at 425°F for 15 minutes, or until golden.

❋ Most muffins are sweet enough to enjoy for dessert—and much less expensive to make than a cake or pie. Just mix a double batch of muffin batter and bake in a 13″ × 9″ pan. Bake at 400°F for 25 to 30 minutes. Cut into squares for an inexpensive cake or coffee cake.

Per serving
Calories 260
Total fat 7.5 g.
Saturated fat 1.1 g.
Cholesterol 27 mg.
Sodium 305 mg.
Fiber 7.2 g.

Cost per serving

7¢

KITCHEN TIP

You can let the cornmeal, sugar, salt, oil, and water stand at room temperature for 40 minutes before baking to soften the cornmeal and lighten the batter even more. For a crunchy crust, preheat the baking pan for 5 minutes before adding the batter.

BASIL CORNBREAD

Cornbread has long been a bargain and a favorite at Southern suppers. This one has an herbal twist with chopped fresh basil stirred into the batter. You can use 2 teaspoons of dried basil if fresh isn't available.

3 cups yellow cornmeal
¼ cup sugar
½ teaspoon salt
3 tablespoons canola oil
2 cups boiling water
1 cup skim milk
1 egg, lightly beaten
¼ cup chopped fresh basil
¼ cup chopped sweet red peppers
1 tablespoon baking powder
1 teaspoon minced jalapeño peppers
    (wear plastic gloves when handling)

❋ In a large bowl, combine the cornmeal, sugar, and salt; stir well. Add the oil and water; stir well.

❋ Preheat the oven to 400°F. Coat a 13" × 9" baking pan with no-stick spray.

❋ Add the milk and egg to the cornmeal mixture; stir well. Add the basil, red peppers, baking powder, and jalapeño peppers; stir well. Pour into the pan. Bake for 40 minutes, or until a toothpick inserted in the center of the cornbread comes out clean. Cool before cutting.

Honey-Raisin Bagels

You may have crossed bagels off your make-at-home list, but they are super easy. Any yeast bread dough can be rolled into bagel rings. Just boil the rings briefly to get the bagel's chewy texture, then bake them to lightly brown them. You'll save yourself 45¢ each over the store-bought kind.

¾ cup skim milk
½ cup water
½ cup honey
1 tablespoon or 1 package active dry yeast
½ cup raisins
5–6 cups all-purpose flour
2 eggs, lightly beaten
2 tablespoons canola oil
1 egg white, lightly beaten

❋ Combine the milk and water in a large bowl. Microwave on high for 30 seconds, or until warmed to about 115°F.

❋ Add the honey and yeast; stir well. Let stand for 5 minutes in a warm place, or until foamy. Add the raisins and 3 cups of the flour; stir well. Cover and set in a warm place for 30 minutes, or until doubled in size.

❋ Stir in the eggs, oil, and about 2 cups of the remaining flour to make a kneadable dough.

❋ Turn the dough out onto a lightly floured surface. Knead, adding more flour as necessary, for about 10 minutes, or until smooth and elastic. Coat a large bowl with no-stick spray. Add the dough and turn to coat all sides. Cover and set in a warm place for 1 hour, or until doubled in size.

❋ Divide the dough into 15 fist-sized balls. Roll each to make a rope 1″ in diameter and 6″ long. Form rings by pinching the ends of the ropes firmly together. Place the bagels on 2 no-stick baking sheets; let them rise in a warm place for 10 minutes.

❋ Preheat the oven to 350°F.

❋ Bring a large pot of water to a boil over high heat. Add the bagels to the water 2 or 3 at a time; when the bagels rise to the surface, cook them for 5 minutes, or until firm. Drain well; place on the baking sheets. Continue until all the bagels are boiled.

❋ Brush the tops with the egg white. Bake for 25 to 30 minutes, or until golden brown.

Makes 15

Per bagel
Calories 234
Total fat 2.9 g.
Saturated fat 0.5 g.
Cholesterol 29 mg.
Sodium 21 mg.
Fiber 1.5 g.

Cost per serving

15¢

CINNAMON-RAISIN ROLLS

If the aroma of sweet rolls at the mall has you swooning, don't spend $1 or more. Make your own at home for pennies. These are stuffed with raisins and sprinkled with cinnamon—and they have a wonderful maple flavor.

Makes 9

Per roll
Calories 242
Total fat 2.6 g.
Saturated fat 0.4 g.
Cholesterol 0 mg.
Sodium 46 mg.
Fiber 1.8 g.

Cost per serving

35¢

 ¾ cup skim milk, warmed to about 115°F
 2 tablespoons packed brown sugar
 1 tablespoon or 1 package active dry yeast
1¾ cups all-purpose flour
 1 large orange
 ¾ cup maple syrup
 1 tablespoon ground cinnamon
 ½ teaspoon ground cardamom
 ¾ cup raisins
 2 tablespoons finely chopped walnuts
 2 tablespoons reduced-calorie butter, melted

❀ In a large bowl, combine the milk, brown sugar, and yeast; stir well. Let stand for 5 minutes in a warm place, or until foamy. Add 1 cup of the flour; stir well. Cover and set in a warm place for 30 minutes, or until doubled in size. Stir in the remaining ¾ cup flour to make a kneadable dough.

❀ Turn the dough out onto a lightly floured surface. Knead, adding more flour as necessary, for about 10 minutes, or until smooth and elastic. Coat a large bowl with no-stick spray. Add the dough and turn to coat all sides. Cover and set in a warm place for 1 hour, or until doubled in size.

❀ Coat a 9″ × 9″ baking pan with no-stick spray. Grate 1 teaspoon orange rind and set aside. Juice the orange. In a medium bowl, combine the orange rind, orange juice, cinnamon, cardamom, and ½ cup of the maple syrup; mix well. Pour into the baking pan, tilting to evenly coat the bottom.

* On a lightly floured surface, roll the dough into a 12″ × 10″ rectangle; sprinkle with the raisins and walnuts. Roll the dough from the longer side into a cylinder; cut into 9 sections. Arrange the rolls cut sides down in the baking pan with the sides touching; cover and set in a warm place for 30 minutes.

* Preheat the oven to 350°F. In a small saucepan, combine the butter and the remaining ¼ cup maple syrup; place over low heat for 1 minute. Pour over the rolls. Bake for 25 to 30 minutes, or until golden brown. Let cool; invert over a plate and separate the rolls.

BOOST BREADS' NUTRIENTS

Add whole-wheat flour to your bread recipes to boost the fiber, vitamin, and mineral content and give breads a chewy texture and nutty flavor. You can substitute whole-wheat flour for up to one-half the total amount of flour without changing the recipe's lightness. Whole-wheat flour adds more gluten, so the bread will be denser if you add more than half.

Other whole-grain flours to experiment with in yeasted breads are rye, light rye, triticale, pumpernickel, and cornmeal. With these heavier flours, use up to one-fourth the total amount of flour without changing the bread's density.

PARMESAN-GARLIC BREADSTICKS

Serve these Italian breadsticks at your next dinner party to truly impress your guests. They are a breeze to make, and they freeze well, so bake extra.

³/₄ cup water, warmed to about 115°F
¼ cup honey
1 tablespoon or 1 package active dry yeast
2–2½ cups all-purpose flour
1 tablespoon canola oil
¼ cup grated Parmesan cheese
2 tablespoons minced garlic
½ teaspoon ground red pepper
1 egg white, lightly beaten

❀ In a large bowl, combine the water, honey, and yeast; stir well. Let stand for 5 minutes in a warm place, or until foamy. Add 1½ cups of the flour; stir well. Cover and set in a warm place for 30 minutes, or until doubled in size. Stir in the oil and about ½ cup of the remaining flour to make a kneadable dough.

❀ Turn the dough out onto a lightly floured surface. Knead, adding up to ½ cup of the remaining flour as necessary, for about 10 minutes, or until smooth and elastic. Coat a large bowl with no-stick spray. Add the dough and turn to coat all sides. Cover and set in a warm place for 1 hour, or until doubled in size.

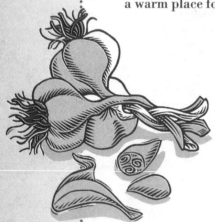

❀ Preheat the oven to 450°F. Place the dough on a lightly floured surface. Knead the Parmesan, garlic and red pepper into the dough. Form into 24 small balls. Roll each ball into a 14″ bread-stick. Arrange the breadsticks on 2 no-stick baking sheets; brush with the egg white.

❀ Bake for 12 to 15 minutes, or until the breadsticks are golden brown.

BAKERS' TIPS FOR MAKING BREADS AHEAD

Most yeast breads, bagels, and rolls can be made ahead to save time if you plan to serve them for a week-end brunch. Prepare the recipe through the first rising. Place the dough in a large bowl to allow it plenty of space to grow. Cover the bowl with plastic wrap and refrigerate up to 10 hours (even overnight). Bring the dough to room temperature by setting the bowl on a counter for about 2 hours. Press the air out and continue with the recipe where you left off.

You can also form the dough into rolls or loaves and freeze them right in the loaf pans or on a baking sheet. Let them thaw in the refrigerator and complete the second rising, then bake them as instructed in the recipe.

Per twist
Calories 163
Total fat 3 g.
Saturated fat 0.5 g.
Cholesterol 1 mg.
Sodium 46 mg.
Fiber 1.7 g.

Cost per serving

10¢

MUSTARDY CORN TWISTS

A Midwestern favorite, these harvest rolls taste great with a big bowl of chili.

1¼ cups low-fat buttermilk, warmed to about 115°F
 3 tablespoons honey
 1 tablespoon or 1 package active dry yeast
 4 cups all-purpose flour
¾ cup yellow cornmeal
 3 tablespoons canola oil
 2 tablespoons whole kernel corn
 2 tablespoons minced sweet red peppers
 2 tablespoons Dijon mustard
 1 egg white, lightly beaten

❋ In a large bowl, combine the buttermilk, honey, and yeast; stir
well. Let stand for 5 minutes in a warm place, or until foamy.
Add 2 cups of the flour; stir well. Cover and set in a warm place
for 30 minutes, or until doubled in size. Stir in the cornmeal, oil,
corn, peppers, mustard, and about 2 cups of the remaining flour
to make a kneadable dough.

❋ Turn the dough out onto a lightly floured surface. Knead, adding
more flour as necessary, for about 10 minutes, or until smooth
and elastic. Coat a large bowl with no-stick spray. Add the dough
and turn to coat all sides. Cover and set in a warm place for
1 hour, or until doubled in size.

❋ Coat a large baking sheet with no-stick spray. Divide the dough
into 18 balls; roll each ball into a 6″ rope. Twist the ropes by
rolling each end in the opposite direction; pinch the
ends together, forming a circle. Place the twists on
the baking sheet; cover and set in a warm place for
10 minutes.

❋ Preheat the oven to 375°F. Brush the twists
with the egg white. Bake for 15 to 20 minutes, or until the twists are golden brown.

RUSSIAN SAUERKRAUT BREAD

This unusual melt-in-your-mouth bread, filled with cooked sauerkraut and grated carrots, is surprisingly sweet; it makes a good supper alongside chicken soup. Cover and refrigerate leftovers; they'll keep for about a week.

Makes 12 servings

Per serving
Calories 241
Total fat 0.6 g.
Saturated fat 0.1 g.
Cholesterol 1 mg.
Sodium 207 mg.
Fiber 3.2 g.

Cost per serving

17¢

- 1½ cups skim milk
- ½ cup water
- ½ cup honey
- 1 tablespoon or 1 package active dry yeast
- 4–5 cups all-purpose flour
- 1 cup whole-wheat flour
- 2 cups reduced-sodium sauerkraut, rinsed and drained
- 1 large carrot, shredded
- 1 tablespoon sugar
- 2 bay leaves
- 1 egg white, lightly beaten

✸ Combine the milk and water in a large bowl. Microwave on high for 30 seconds, or until warmed to about 115°F.

✸ Add the honey and yeast; stir well. Let stand for 5 minutes in a warm place, or until foamy. Add 3 cups of the all-purpose flour; stir well. Cover and set in a warm place for 30 minutes, or until doubled in size. Stir in the whole-wheat flour and about ½ cup all-purpose flour to make a kneadable dough.

✸ Turn the dough out onto a lightly floured surface. Knead, adding more all-purpose flour as necessary, for about 10 minutes, or until smooth and elastic. Coat a large bowl with no-stick spray. Add the dough and turn to coat all sides. Cover and set in a warm place for 1 hour, or until doubled in size.

✸ Meanwhile, in a medium saucepan, combine the sauerkraut, carrots, sugar, and bay leaves; cook and stir over low heat for 10 minutes, or until the liquid has evaporated. Remove and discard the bay leaves.

✸ Preheat the oven to 350°F. Coat a 13″ × 9″ baking pan with no-stick spray. Divide the dough in half; roll each half into a 13″ × 10″ rectangle. Place one half in the baking pan, letting the edges overlap the sides. Spoon the sauerkraut mixture on top of the dough; top with the remaining half of the dough. Pinch the edges of the two pieces of dough together, forming a seal. With a sharp knife, cut three slits in the top of the loaf. Brush with the egg white.

✸ Bake for 50 minutes, or until golden brown. Cool before cutting.

HERBED FOCACCIA

Focaccia is a simple Italian yeast flatbread often flavored with herbs or cheese. If desired, you can sprinkle the top of this focaccia with coarse salt, grated Parmesan, or chopped herbs before baking it. Use whatever herbs are fresh and readily available—rosemary, parsley, and basil work well.

¾ cup water, warmed to about 115°F
1 tablespoon or 1 package active dry yeast
½ teaspoon sugar
2 cups all-purpose flour
¼ teaspoon salt
1 teaspoon canola oil
2 teaspoons chopped fresh herbs

❋ In a large bowl, combine the water, yeast, and sugar; stir well. Let stand for 5 minutes in a warm place, or until foamy. Gradually add the flour, salt, oil, and herbs to make a kneadable dough.

❋ Turn the dough out onto a lightly floured surface. Knead, adding more flour as necessary, for about 10 minutes, or until smooth and elastic. Coat a large bowl with no-stick spray. Add the dough and turn to coat all sides. Cover and set in a warm place for 15 minutes, or until risen slightly.

❋ Coat a large baking sheet with no-stick spray. Roll the dough into a 12" × 9" rectangle; place on the baking sheet. Cover and set in a warm place for 30 minutes, or until doubled in size. With fingertips, press ¼" deep indentations into the surface of the dough.

❋ Preheat the oven to 400°F. Bake for 20 minutes, or until golden brown.

Pizza Margherita

Make extra pizza shells to freeze and use for impromptu suppers on busy nights. This famous pizza echoes the colors of the Italian flag and was created in 1889 in honor of Queen Margherita.

- 1 cup water, warmed to about 115°F
- 1 tablespoon or 1 package active dry yeast
- 1 tablespoon sugar
- 2½ cups all-purpose flour
- ½ cup yellow cornmeal
- ¼ teaspoon salt
- 2 tablespoons canola oil
- 4 medium tomatoes, sliced
- ½ cup chopped fresh basil
- 1 cup shredded low-fat mozzarella cheese

✤ In a large bowl, combine the water, yeast, and sugar; stir well. Let stand for 5 minutes in a warm place, or until foamy. Gradually add the flour, cornmeal, salt, and 1 tablespoon of the oil to make a kneadable dough.

✤ Turn the dough out onto a lightly floured surface. Knead, adding more flour as necessary, for about 10 minutes, or until smooth and elastic. Coat a large bowl with no-stick spray. Add the dough and turn to coat all sides. Cover and set in a warm place for 15 minutes.

✤ Preheat the oven to 450°F. Coat two 12″ pizza pans or large baking sheets with no-stick spray. Divide the dough in half; roll each half into a 12″ circle. Place the circles on the pizza pans or baking sheets. Brush the surface of each pizza with the remaining 1 tablespoon oil. Top with the tomatoes, basil, and mozzarella.

✤ Bake for 20 minutes, or until the crusts are golden brown and the cheese is bubbling.

Makes 8 servings

Per serving
Calories 274
Total fat 6.5 g.
Saturated fat 2.1 g.
Cholesterol 8 mg.
Sodium 182 mg.
Fiber 3.9 g.

Cost per serving

36¢

SAUCES, RELISHES, AND DRESSINGS

Our thrifty grandparents made salsas, chutneys, and relishes to take advantage of bountiful produce harvests. Seasoned carefully with garlic, ginger, spices, and sugar, these side dishes transformed ordinary fare into something special. Following in their footsteps, we've created scrumptious sides and sauces for your entrées, pastas, and salads.

We've kept the zest but made these condiments healthier. They have much less sugar, salt, and fat than traditional versions because they take advantage of the naturally intense flavor of seasonal fruits and vegetables. Make double or triple the recipe if you get a windfall of produce. Most of the recipes in this chapter freeze well for two months or more.

Select recipes that fit what you can buy on sale and in season, and you'll save over store-bought versions every time you make your own.

261

SALSA VERDE

Makes 2 cups

Per ¼ cup
Calories 41
Total fat 2.1 g.
Saturated fat 0.2 g.
Cholesterol 0 mg.
Sodium 2 mg.
Fiber 0.6 g.

Cost per serving

17¢

This Mexican green salsa can be made with tomatillos—the Southwestern fruit that looks like a tomato—or green tomatoes from your fall garden. Leftover refrigerated salsa keeps for two weeks.

2 cups chopped tomatillos or green tomatoes
1 cup chopped onions
½ cup diced canned mild green chili peppers
3 cloves garlic, chopped
2 tablespoons orange juice
1 tablespoon olive oil
1 tablespoon chopped fresh cilantro
1 teaspoon ground red pepper

❊ In a medium saucepan, combine the tomatillos or green tomatoes, onions, chili peppers, garlic, orange juice, oil, cilantro, and red pepper; cook and stir over medium-high heat for 5 minutes. Reduce the heat to medium; cook, stirring frequently, for 15 minutes, or until the sauce is thick.

BLACK BEAN SALSA

Makes 2 cups

Per ¼ cup
Calories 44
Total fat 0.2 g.
Saturated fat 0 g.
Cholesterol 0 mg.
Sodium 60 mg.
Fiber 1.4 g.

Cost per serving

12¢

Black beans are traditionally used in salsas in the Southwest because they are so meaty and flavorful. This colorful concoction tastes great with roast turkey or chicken or on top of enchiladas.

½ green pepper, minced
½ sweet red pepper, minced
1 cup cooked black beans (page 199)
¼ cup chopped scallions
2 tablespoons balsamic vinegar
2 tablespoons minced fresh parsley
1 tablespoon minced jalapeño peppers
    (wear plastic gloves when handling)
2 teaspoons sugar
⅛ teaspoon salt

❊ In a medium bowl, combine the green peppers, red peppers, beans, scallions, vinegar, parsley, jalapeño peppers, sugar, and salt; stir well. Let the salsa stand at room temperature, stirring occasionally, for 20 minutes, or until the flavors blend.

5 Fruit Salsas

❁ *Island Breeze.* Combine 1 can (8 ounces) unsweetened pineapple chunks (with juice), 1 papaya
(seeded and diced), 1 teaspoon minced jalapeño peppers
(wear plastic gloves when handling), and the juice of 1 lime;
mix well. Add chopped fresh cilantro and salt to taste.
Makes 3 cups.

❁ *Melon Cooler.* Combine 3 cups cubed cantaloupe, 1 cup
cubed honeydew melon, ¼ cup minced red onions, and the
juice of 1 small lemon; mix well. Add chopped fresh cilantro
and salt to taste. Makes 3 cups.

❁ *Orange Crush.* Combine 1 navel orange (peeled and
chopped), 1 mango (seeded and diced), 2 tablespoons honey
or sugar, 1 teaspoon minced jalapeño peppers (wear plastic
gloves when handling), and the juice of 1 lime; mix well.
Add chopped fresh cilantro and salt to taste. Makes 3 cups.

❁ *Mediterranean Mélange.* Combine 2 cups chopped tomatoes,
1 cup diced sweet red peppers, 1 tablespoon cider vinegar,
2 teaspoons minced garlic, 1 teaspoon chopped fresh basil,
and ½ teaspoon reduced-sodium Worcestershire sauce; mix
well. Add salt to taste. Makes 3 cups.

❁ *Tomato Time.* Combine 2 cups chopped tomatoes,
1 green pepper (seeded and diced), ¼ cup balsamic
vinegar, 1 teaspoon minced jalapeño peppers
(wear plastic gloves when handling), and 2 teaspoons minced garlic; mix well. Add chopped
fresh parsley and salt to taste. Makes 3 cups.

*Sauces, Relishes,
and Dressings*

Per ¼ cup
Calories 14
Total fat 0.2 g.
Saturated fat 0 g.
Cholesterol 0 mg.
Sodium 35 mg.
Fiber 0.2 g.

Cost per serving

8¢

WATERMELON-CUCUMBER RELISH

Red and green color this vivid fruit relish. Its sweet-spicy taste makes it a delicious addition to grilled fish or chicken. Leftovers keep for 2 days refrigerated.

    3 cups diced watermelon
    1 cup diced cucumbers
    2 tablespoons chopped scallions
    2 tablespoons minced fresh parsley or cilantro
    2 teaspoons minced garlic
       Juice of 1 lemon or lime
    1 teaspoon honey
    ¼ teaspoon crushed red-pepper flakes
    ¼ teaspoon salt

✽ In a large bowl, combine the watermelon, cucumbers, scallions, parsley or cilantro, garlic, lemon juice or lime juice, honey, and red-pepper flakes; stir well. Let it stand at room temperature, stirring occasionally, for 20 minutes, or until the flavors blend. Add the salt. Stir to combine.

Per ¼ cup
Calories 19
Total fat 0.4 g.
Saturated fat 0 g.
Cholesterol 0 mg.
Sodium 32 mg.
Fiber 0.6 g.

Cost per serving

6¢

CORN RELISH

Corn and tomato season is a great time to make this delicious relish. Make double or triple the recipe and freeze leftover relish in small containers for up to two months.

    2 ears corn
    1 cup chopped tomatoes
    ½ green pepper, minced
    ½ cup chopped scallions
    3 tablespoons lemon juice
    1 tablespoon minced fresh basil
    2 teaspoons minced jalapeño peppers
         (wear plastic gloves when handling)
    1 teaspoon minced garlic
    ⅛ teaspoon salt

- ✤ Preheat the grill or broiler. Coat the corn with no-stick spray; grill or broil 4″ from the heat for 5 to 8 minutes, turning frequently, or until lightly browned. Cool.

- ✤ Cut the kernels from the cobs and place in a large bowl. Add the tomatoes, green peppers, scallions, lemon juice, basil, jalapeño peppers, garlic, and salt; stir well. Let it stand at room temperature for 15 minutes, or until the flavors blend.

PEACH RELISH

Sweet peaches combine with fiery peppers in this robust relish for beef, pork, or chicken.

Makes 3 cups

Per ¼ cup
Calories 26
Total fat 0.1 g.
Saturated fat 0 g.
Cholesterol 0 mg.
Sodium 28 mg.
Fiber 0.8 g.

Cost per serving

20¢

1 sweet red pepper, diced
1 can (8 ounces) unsweetened crushed pineapple, drained
1 cup peeled and diced peaches
1 small jalapeño pepper, minced
      (wear plastic gloves when handling)
¼ cup lemon juice
2 tablespoons lime juice
2 tablespoons minced fresh cilantro
⅛ teaspoon salt

- ✤ In a medium bowl, combine the red peppers, pineapple, peaches, jalapeño peppers, lemon juice, lime juice, cilantro, and salt; mix well.

FARMERS' MARKET BARGAINS

Save several dollars a peck (8 quarts) on peaches, apples, nectarines, plums, pears, and other fruit at farmers' markets. Farmers' markets are best visited toward the end of the weekend, when vendors want to sell up and go home. You can offer less than the asking price for bulk buys of fruit if you have the time to make extra salsa or relish for freezing.

SAVORY ONION-RAISIN CHUTNEY

Per 2 tablespoons
Calories 36
Total fat 0.5 g.
Saturated fat 0.1 g.
Cholesterol 0 mg.
Sodium 1 mg.
Fiber 0.6 g.

Cost per serving

7¢

If you can find sweet onions such as Vidalia on sale, they make this chutney even more delicious. Freeze leftover chutney for up to six months.

2 teaspoons canola oil
2 cups chopped onions
1 cup peeled and chopped apples
1 cup peeled and chopped pears
¼ cup cider vinegar
¼ cup honey
¼ cup raisins
¼ cup frozen orange juice concentrate, thawed
½ teaspoon ground cinnamon
¼ teaspoon ground cloves

✺ Heat the oil in a Dutch oven over medium-high heat. Add the onions; cook and stir for 10 minutes, or until the onions are golden brown. Add the apples, pears, vinegar, honey, raisins, orange juice concentrate, cinnamon, and cloves; bring to a boil. Reduce the heat to medium; cook, stirring frequently, for 25 minutes, or until the chutney is thick.

GINGER APPLE CHUTNEY

This chutney is wonderful for gifts. It tastes like a spicy version of apple butter but takes only 30 minutes to cook. Freeze leftovers in small containers for up to six months.

- 3   cups peeled and chopped apples
- 3   cups peeled and chopped pears
- ¾ cup cider vinegar
- ¾ cup packed brown sugar
- ½ cup chopped onions
- ½ cup orange juice
- 2   tablespoons minced fresh ginger
- 1   teaspoon minced garlic
- 1   teaspoon ground cinnamon
- 1   teaspoon ground cloves
- ½ teaspoon ground red pepper

✳ In a Dutch oven, combine the apples, pears, vinegar, brown sugar, onions, orange juice, ginger, garlic, cinnamon, cloves, and red pepper; bring to a boil over medium-high heat. Reduce the heat to medium; cook, stirring frequently, for 20 to 30 minutes, or until the chutney is thick.

SAVINGS ON SPICES

Look for small bags of generic spices in your supermarket. They're great for refilling spice jars at home, and since the spices are cheaper and packaged in smaller quantities, they're often fresher. You can also order large amounts of spices (in ¼ to ½ pound bags) from mail-order spice companies. Most ground spices have a shelf life of about six months but keep for several years in the freezer.

Makes 3 cups

Per 2 tablespoons
Calories 53
Total fat 0.2 g.
Saturated fat 0 g.
Cholesterol 0 mg.
Sodium 3 mg.
Fiber 0.9 g.

Cost per serving

11¢

Sauces, Relishes, and Dressings

GREEN TOMATO CHUTNEY

Makes 2 cups

Per 2 tablespoons
Calories 98
Total fat 0.3 g.
Saturated fat 0 g.
Cholesterol 0 mg.
Sodium 53 mg.
Fiber 1.2 g.

Cost per serving

24¢

Green tomatoes are abundant in most gardens in early fall. If you gather them right before the first frost, they make wonderful chutney. Freeze left-over chutney in small containers for up to six months.

½ cup diced onions
½ cup diced celery
8 cups chopped green tomatoes
1 cup peeled and diced apples
1 cup peeled and diced pears
¾ cup golden raisins
2 cloves garlic, minced
¾ cup cider vinegar
¾ cup packed brown sugar
½ teaspoon ground red pepper
¼ teaspoon salt

❋ Coat a Dutch oven with no-stick spray; set it over medium-high heat. Add the onions and celery; cook and stir for 5 minutes, or until the onions are golden brown. Add the tomatoes, apples, pears, raisins, and garlic; cook and stir for 5 minutes. Add the vinegar, brown sugar, and red pepper; bring to a boil. Reduce the heat to medium; cook, stirring occasionally, for 20 minutes, or until the chutney is thick. Add the salt. Stir to combine.

SPICED CRANBERRY-ORANGE COMPOTE

This jewel-colored compote tastes wonderful at holiday dinners. Serve it alongside roast turkey, at a savings of $2 per container over store-bought cranberry sauce. Leftover refrigerated compote keeps for three weeks.

1   large navel orange
3   cups fresh or frozen cranberries
2   cups peeled and chopped apples
½   cup cider vinegar
¾   cup honey
½   cup chopped onions
½   cup orange juice
2   tablespoons minced fresh ginger
1   teaspoon minced garlic
1   teaspoon ground cinnamon
¼   teaspoon ground cloves
½   teaspoon ground red pepper

❉ Grate the orange rind and set aside. Peel the orange and chop the orange pulp.

❉ In a Dutch oven, combine the cranberries, apples, vinegar, honey, onions, orange juice, ginger, garlic, cinnamon, cloves, red pepper, orange rind, and orange pulp; bring to a boil over medium-high heat. Reduce the heat to medium; cook, stirring frequently, for 20 to 30 minutes, or until the compote is thick.

Makes 3 cups

Per 2 tablespoons
Calories 57
Total fat 0.1 g.
Saturated fat 0 g.
Cholesterol 0 mg.
Sodium 1 mg.
Fiber 1.1 g.

Cost per serving

14¢

Vietnamese Dipping Sauce

Vietnamese cooks use a variation on this sauce to season everything from chicken stir-fries to spring rolls. It keeps about two weeks refrigerated.

⅔ cup hot water
¼ cup reduced-sodium soy sauce
¼ cup sugar or honey
 2 tablespoons lime juice or lemon juice
 2 tablespoons shredded carrots
 1 small jalapeño pepper, seeded and minced
      (wear plastic gloves when handling)
 2 teaspoons minced garlic
 1 teaspoon dark sesame oil
¼ teaspoon crushed red-pepper flakes

❋ In a small bowl, combine the hot water, soy sauce, sugar or honey, lime or lemon juice, carrots, jalapeño peppers, garlic, oil, and red-pepper flakes; stir well.

Sesame Soy Marinade

Marinades for meat or fish can cost $2 or more for an eight-ounce bottle; this one rings in for less than $1 for the same amount. It jazzes up fish fillets or boneless chicken breast halves. Marinate them for 30 minutes before grilling or broiling.

¾ cup cider vinegar
 3 tablespoons packed brown sugar
 3 tablespoons reduced-sodium soy sauce
 2 tablespoons minced fresh ginger
 2 tablespoons minced scallions
 2 teaspoons dark sesame oil
 1 teaspoon minced garlic

❋ In a small bowl, combine the vinegar, brown sugar, soy sauce, ginger, scallions, oil, and garlic; mix well.

COUSIN LOU'S SPICY GRILLING SAUCE

Fresh from the bayou country of Louisiana, this spicy barbecue sauce is used to baste meats for grilling. It keeps about 2 weeks refrigerated or 2 months frozen.

1 cup defatted chicken stock
3 cups chopped onions
2 cups diced celery
1 teaspoon canola oil
1 can (6 ounces) tomato paste
½ cup chopped green peppers
⅓ cup reduced-sodium ketchup
6 cloves garlic, minced
1 tablespoon sugar
1 tablespoon stone-ground mustard
1 tablespoon cider vinegar
2 teaspoons ground red pepper
¼ teaspoon salt
¼ teaspoon ground black pepper

✳ In a Dutch oven, combine the stock, onions, celery, and oil; bring to a boil over medium-high heat. Cook and stir for 5 minutes. Add the tomato paste, peppers, ketchup, garlic, sugar, mustard, vinegar, and red pepper; bring to a boil. Reduce the heat to medium; cook, stirring occasionally, for 40 minutes, or until the sauce is thick. Cool. Pour into a blender or food processor and puree. Add the salt and pepper. Puree briefly to blend.

HOT SAVINGS

Store-bought barbecue sauce costs $2.29 for a 12-ounce bottle. Every time you make your own barbecue sauce, you save $1.14—even more if you use home-grown produce or buy seasonal produce on sale.

Makes 5 cups

Per ¼ cup
Calories 32
Total fat 0.5 g.
Saturated fat 0.1 g.
Cholesterol 0 mg.
Sodium 117 mg.
Fiber 1.2 g.

Cost per serving

7¢

FRENCH VINAIGRETTE DRESSING

Vinaigrette is the basic French dressing, versatile enough to be a marinade for fish or to drizzle over salad greens. The sweetness of balsamic vinegar allows us to use much less oil than usual. The dressing keeps for about a week refrigerated.

- ½ cup balsamic vinegar
- 3 tablespoons olive oil
- 2 tablespoons lemon juice
- 2 tablespoons reduced-sodium tomato juice
- 1 tablespoon chopped scallions
- 1 teaspoon stone-ground mustard
- 1 teaspoon minced garlic
- 1 teaspoon sugar
- 1 teaspoon chopped fresh parsley
- ⅛ teaspoon salt
- ⅛ teaspoon ground black pepper

❋ In a small bowl, combine the vinegar, oil, lemon juice, tomato juice, scallions, mustard, garlic, sugar, parsley, salt, and pepper; mix well.

Makes 1 cup

Per 2 tablespoons
Calories 65
Total fat 5 g.
Saturated fat 0.7 g.
Cholesterol 0 mg.
Sodium 45 mg.
Fiber 0.1 g.

Cost per serving

14¢

CREAMY FETA DRESSING

Tangy feta cheese is made from sheep's milk. It's used extensively in the Middle East and Greece. This easy dressing is delicious on lettuce or chopped vegetable salads.

- ½ cup crumbled low-fat feta cheese
- ¼ cup nonfat cottage cheese
- ¼ cup nonfat plain yogurt
- 1 tablespoon cider vinegar
- 1 tablespoon chopped scallions
- 1 tablespoon chopped fresh parsley
- ¼ teaspoon ground black pepper

❋ In a blender or food processor, combine the feta cheese, cottage cheese, yogurt, and vinegar; puree. Stir in the scallions, parsley, and pepper.

Makes ¾ cup

Per 2 tablespoons
Calories 32
Total fat 1.4 g.
Saturated fat 0.9 g.
Cholesterol 4 mg.
Sodium 158 mg.
Fiber 0 g.

Cost per serving

20¢

CREAMY CURRIED MAYONNAISE

An easy sauce for coleslaw, this dressing is also thick enough to stand up as a party dip for raw vegetables.

1 cup low-fat mayonnaise
¾ cup low-fat sour cream
3 tablespoons cider vinegar
1 tablespoon honey
1 teaspoon Dijon mustard
1 teaspoon curry powder

❋ In a small bowl, combine the mayonnaise, sour cream, vinegar, honey, mustard, and curry powder; mix well.

Makes 2 cups

Per 2 tablespoons
Calories 57
Total fat 4.7 g.
Saturated fat 0.5 g.
Cholesterol 9 mg.
Sodium 27 mg.
Fiber 0 g.

Cost per serving

7¢

BUTTERMILK AND BLUE CHEESE DRESSING

A small amount of blue cheese goes a long way—as in this luxurious salad dressing. Leftovers keep about 2 days in the refrigerator.

1 cup low-fat buttermilk
½ cup low-fat cottage cheese
3 tablespoons cider vinegar
3 ounces low-fat blue cheese, crumbled
¼ cup chopped fresh parsley
¼ cup minced scallions

❋ In a blender or food processor, combine the buttermilk, cottage cheese, vinegar, and half of the blue cheese; puree. Stir in the parsley, scallions, and the remaining blue cheese.

Makes 1½ cups

Per 2 tablespoons
Calories 35
Total fat 1.7 g.
Saturated fat 0.2 g.
Cholesterol 5 mg.
Sodium 159 mg.
Fiber 0 g.

Cost per serving

16¢

SAVE ON BLUE— STAY OUT OF THE RED

Blue cheese dressing is a popular choice in most families and the price reflects that—about $2.80 for 12 ounces in the supermarket. Low-fat and fat-free versions can cost even more. Homemade dressing costs $1.92, a savings of 88¢. A bonus: It's made with fresh ingredients and tastes better.

MEXICAN GRILLING SAUCE

Makes 1¼ cups

Per 2 tablespoons
Calories 22
Total fat 1.4 g.
Saturated fat 0.2 g.
Cholesterol 0 mg.
Sodium 11 mg.
Fiber 0.2 g.

Cost per serving

7¢

This smooth salsa can be used as a baste for grilling. It also makes a great marinade for lean meats. It keeps for about two weeks refrigerated.

½ cup canned reduced-sodium tomato sauce
⅓ cup lime juice
¼ cup coarsely chopped fresh cilantro
1 tablespoon canola oil
1 tablespoon chopped garlic
1 teaspoon chopped jalapeño peppers
    (wear plastic gloves when handling)

❋ In a blender or food processor, combine the tomato sauce, lime juice, cilantro, oil, garlic, and peppers; puree.

SPICY INDONESIAN PEANUT DRESSING

Makes ½ cup

Per 1 tablespoon
Calories 37
Total fat 2.6 g.
Saturated fat 0.5 g.
Cholesterol 0 mg.
Sodium 157 mg.
Fiber 0.3 g.

Cost per serving

7¢

Use this as a marinade for chicken, fish, or tofu. Or toss it with pasta and chopped steamed vegetables for a warm salad. It keeps for about a week refrigerated.

¼ cup nonfat plain yogurt
2 tablespoons reduced-sodium soy sauce
2 tablespoons lemon juice
2 tablespoons peanut butter
1 teaspoon canola oil
½ teaspoon crushed red-pepper flakes
¼ teaspoon ground cumin
¼ teaspoon curry powder
¼ teaspoon ground black pepper

❋ In a medium bowl, combine the yogurt, soy sauce, lemon juice, peanut butter, oil, red-pepper flakes, cumin, curry powder, and pepper; mix well.

CREAMY LEMON SALAD DRESSING

This lemony dressing is delicious over lettuce or cabbage salad. It keeps about four days refrigerated.

½ cup low-fat mayonnaise
½ cup low-fat cottage cheese
2 tablespoons low-fat buttermilk
2 tablespoons lemon juice
2 teaspoons sugar
½ teaspoon reduced-sodium soy sauce
1 clove garlic, minced
½ teaspoon ground black pepper

❋ In a blender or food processor, combine the mayonnaise, cottage cheese, buttermilk, lemon juice, sugar, soy sauce, garlic, and pepper; puree.

Makes 1¼ cups

Per 2 tablespoons
Calories 46
Total fat 3.3 g.
Saturated fat 0.5 g.
Cholesterol 5 mg.
Sodium 70 mg.
Fiber 0 g.

Cost per serving

8¢

YOGURT CHEESE

A staple of the low-cost kitchen, yogurt cheese can be pureed into a delicious spread, sweetened for cake frosting, seasoned with garlic and herbs for a baked potato topping, or thinned with buttermilk for salad dressings. Yogurt cheese turns out creamier and thicker when made with low-fat rather than nonfat yogurt. It keeps about four days refrigerated. Save the whey that drains out. Add it to homemade bread for extra flavor and protein. See page 14 for directions on making your own yogurt.

1 quart low-fat plain yogurt

❋ Line a colander with several layers of cheesecloth. Spoon in the yogurt and suspend the colander over a large bowl. Cover and refrigerate overnight, or until all the liquid has drained into the bowl. Transfer the yogurt cheese to a container with a tight-fitting lid and store in the refrigerator.

Makes about 2 cups

Per ¼ cup
Calories 49
Total fat 0.2 g.
Saturated fat 0.1 g.
Cholesterol 2 mg.
Sodium 58 mg.
Fiber 0 g.

Cost per serving

21¢

KITCHEN TIP

Choose a naturally fermented yogurt for this recipe. Yogurts stabilized with gelatin won't drain properly.

Cakes, Pies, and Other Desserts

A dessert does more than satisfy a sweet tooth; it rounds out dinner and adds smiles of value. You'll see happy faces on your family as they dig into homemade Pineapple-Banana-Strawberry Cheesecake, Chocolate-Orange Biscotti, or any of the other luscious recipes in this chapter.

We focus on fruit, a low-cost seasonal choice that makes dessert affordable as well as delicious. Fruit is the basis of Brown-Sugar Baked Apples, Baked Mexican Bananas, and Cinnamon-Cranberry Applesauce. All satisfy the sweet tooth while keeping costs within your budget. Plus, they're naturally low in fat and high in fiber.

We also feature several fancy desserts for special occasions when you want something more elaborate—decadently rich-tasting but ingeniously low in cost.

SWEET POTATO SPICE CAKE

Sweet potatoes are an economical side dish, but they also create a surprisingly moist cake. Leftover cooked sweet potatoes work great in this recipe.

2	large sweet potatoes, halved
3½	cups all-purpose flour
1	cup packed brown sugar
1	tablespoon baking powder
1	teaspoon baking soda
¾	teaspoon salt
¼	cup raisins
¼	cup canola oil
2	egg yolks
¼	cup low-fat buttermilk
2	tablespoons lemon juice
3	egg whites
¼	cup confectioners' sugar
2	tablespoons skim milk

❀ Preheat the oven to 400°F. Place the sweet potatoes on a baking sheet; bake for 40 minutes, or until they are very soft. Check by inserting the tip of a sharp knife in the center of 1 sweet potato. Cool, peel, and mash. Set aside 3½ cups of sweet potato puree; reserve any remaining puree for another recipe.

❀ Reduce the oven temperature to 350°F. Coat a 9" × 5" loaf pan with no-stick spray; lightly flour the pan, shaking off any excess.

❀ In a large bowl, combine the flour, brown sugar, baking powder, baking soda, and salt; stir well. Add the raisins.

❀ In a medium bowl, combine the oil, egg yolks, buttermilk, lemon juice, and sweet potatoes; mix well. Add to the flour mixture.

❀ In another medium bowl, beat the egg whites with electric beaters until soft peaks form; fold them into the batter. Pour into the loaf pan.

❀ Bake for 45 to 55 minutes, or until the cake is lightly browned and a toothpick inserted in the center comes out clean. Cool; unmold onto a plate.

❀ In a small bowl, combine the confectioners' sugar and milk; drizzle over the cake.

Strawberry Angel Food Cake

Serve this elegant cake with a sauce of pureed berries, if you wish. The secret of airy angel food cake is the lightness of the beaten egg whites. Fold the flour into them quickly and carefully so they don't deflate.

- 1 **cup sifted all-purpose flour**
- 1 **cup superfine sugar**
- 10 **egg whites, at room temperature**
- 1¼ **teaspoons cream of tartar**
- 1½ **teaspoons vanilla**
- ½ **cup thinly sliced fresh strawberries**

❉ Preheat the oven to 350°F. Sift the flour and ½ cup of the sugar into a medium bowl; mix well.

❉ In a large bowl, beat the egg whites with electric beaters until foamy. Add the cream of tartar; beat until soft peaks form. Add the remaining ½ cup sugar 2 tablespoons at a time, beating until stiff peaks form. Fold in the flour mixture ½ cup at a time. Fold in the vanilla and strawberries. Pour into a 10″ tube pan, spreading evenly and deflating any large air pockets with a knife.

❉ Bake for 40 minutes, or until the cake is lightly browned and a toothpick inserted in the center comes out clean. Cool upside down for 40 minutes before removing the cake from the pan.

Makes 12 servings

Per serving
Calories 95
Total fat 0.1 g.
Saturated fat 0 g.
Cholesterol 0 mg.
Sodium 46 mg.
Fiber 0.4 g.

Cost per serving

8¢

Kitchen Tip

Instead of paying higher prices for superfine sugar, grind regular sugar in a blender until fine in texture.

Be sure to sift the flour before measuring—a large sieve set over a large bowl works great.

RHUBARB BRUNCH CAKE

Make this cake in the spring when rhubarb is on sale for less than 50¢ a bunch—or free from your own garden.

Makes 12 servings

Per serving
Calories 259
Total fat 5.8 g.
Saturated fat 0.9 g.
Cholesterol 18 mg.
Sodium 302 mg.
Fiber 1.4 g.

Cost per serving

27¢

2 cups chopped rhubarb
½ cup sugar
2 tablespoons cornstarch
2 cups all-purpose flour
2 teaspoons baking powder
2 teaspoons baking soda
¾ cup honey
¾ cup low-fat buttermilk
½ cup mashed bananas
⅓ cup prune puree
¼ cup canola oil
1 egg
3 egg whites
1 tablespoon chopped walnuts
⅓ cup packed brown sugar

❋ Preheat the oven to 350°F. Coat a 13″ × 9″ baking pan with no-stick spray.

❋ In a medium saucepan, combine the rhubarb, sugar, and corn-starch; cook and stir over medium heat for 10 minutes, or until the rhubarb is soft.

❋ Meanwhile, in a large bowl combine the flour, baking powder, and baking soda. Mix well. In a medium bowl, combine the honey, buttermilk, bananas, prune puree, oil, egg, and egg whites; mix well. Add to the flour mixture; stir until just blended.

❋ Pour half of the batter into the baking pan. Smooth the top with a spatula. Add the rhubarb mixture. Top with the remaining batter. Smooth the top with a spatula. Sprinkle with the walnuts and brown sugar.

❋ Bake for 40 to 45 minutes, or until golden brown and a toothpick inserted into the center comes out clean. Cool before cutting.

Pineapple-Banana-Strawberry Cheesecake

This light and creamy cheesecake features three fruit flavors to delight your taste buds. Use homemade yogurt cheese to keep this recipe light on the calories and lean on the budget. The graham-cracker crust uses apple juice instead of melted butter to save fat. Frozen, undiluted apple juice intensifies the filling's fruity flavor.

½ cup graham cracker crumbs
2 tablespoons apple juice
1 large banana, sliced
1 envelope unflavored gelatin
¼ cup water
¼ cup frozen apple juice concentrate, thawed
1 cup nonfat yogurt cheese (page 275)
2 tablespoons sugar
½ teaspoon vanilla
½ teaspoon ground cinnamon
¼ teaspoon ground nutmeg
½ cup drained unsweetened canned crushed pineapple
4 large strawberries, halved

✸ In a small bowl, combine the graham cracker crumbs and apple juice; mix well. Pat into the bottom and up the sides of a 9″ pie pan. Arrange the bananas on the crust.

✸ In a small bowl, combine the gelatin and water; let stand for 1 minute.

✸ In a saucepan over medium-high heat, bring the apple juice concentrate to a boil. Remove from the heat and pour over the gelatin mixture. Stir until the gelatin is completely dissolved. Pour over the bananas.

✸ In a blender or food processor, combine the yogurt cheese, sugar, vanilla, cinnamon, and nutmeg; puree. Transfer to a medium bowl. Stir in the pineapple. Pour over the gelatin mixture. Arrange the strawberries on top.

✸ Refrigerate for 2 hours, or until the cheesecake is firm. Cut into 8 wedges.

Makes 8 servings

Per serving
Calories 94
Total fat 1 g.
Saturated fat 0.1 g.
Cholesterol 0 mg.
Sodium 47 mg.
Fiber 0.7 g.

Cost per serving

25¢

Streusel-Topped Peach and Berry Pie

Makes 8 servings

Per serving
Calories 305
Total fat 5.8 g.
Saturated fat 0.8 g.
Cholesterol 0 mg.
Sodium 9 mg.
Fiber 3.6 g.

Cost per serving

54¢

Perfect for late-summer baking, this pie shows off the sweet flavor of ripe peaches. With only a bottom pastry crust, the servings stay lean.

Oat Crust

1¼ cups all-purpose flour
¼ cup rolled oats
3 tablespoons canola oil
3 tablespoons skim milk

Peach and Berry Filling

4 cups sliced peaches
2 cups fresh or frozen raspberries
⅓ cup maple syrup
⅓ cup sugar
3 tablespoons cornstarch
1 teaspoon lemon juice
¼ teaspoon ground cinnamon
¼ teaspoon ground nutmeg

Streusel Topping

⅓ cup packed brown sugar
¼ cup all-purpose flour
⅛ teaspoon ground cinnamon

To make the oat crust

❋ Preheat the oven to 425°F. Coat a 9″ pie pan with no-stick spray.

❋ In a blender or food processor, combine the flour and oats; grind until the oats are a coarse powder. Transfer to a medium bowl. Add the oil and milk; stir until the mixture resembles coarse cornmeal. Press the mixture into the pie pan. Place the pie pan in the freezer for 5 minutes.

To make the peach and berry filling

❋ In a large bowl, toss together the peaches, raspberries, maple syrup, sugar, cornstarch, lemon juice, cinnamon, and nutmeg; pour into the pie pan.

To make the streusel topping

❋ In a small bowl, combine the brown sugar, flour, and cinnamon. Sprinkle over the filling.

❋ Bake for 40 minutes, or until the topping is brown and the filling bubbles. Cool before slicing.

CUTTING CRUST COSTS

On rushed evenings, you might be tempted to purchase one of the ready-made frozen pie crusts. But you wouldn't if you had a homemade crust waiting in the freezer. Stock up on metal pie pans at yard sales. Each time you make a pie, prepare three times the crust. Roll and shape the crusts in the pie pans. Wrap them in plastic bags; freeze unbaked. You'll save $1.90 each time you use homemade!

Per cookie
Calories 70
Total fat 0.8 g.
Saturated fat 0.1 g.
Cholesterol 9 mg.
Sodium 80 mg.
Fiber 0.3 g.

Cost per serving

3¢

CHOCOLATE-SPICE CHIPPERS

Applesauce takes the place of butter in these extraordinary cookies. Kids love them in lunch boxes.

3½ cups all-purpose flour
⅔ cup sugar
⅔ cup packed brown sugar
2 teaspoons baking soda
½ teaspoon salt
¼ teaspoon ground allspice
⅔ cup semisweet chocolate chips
½ cup unsweetened applesauce
2 eggs

❋ Preheat the oven to 350°F. Coat a no-stick baking sheet with no-stick spray.

❋ In a large bowl, combine the flour, sugar, brown sugar, baking soda, salt, and allspice; mix well. Stir in the chocolate chips.

❋ In a medium bowl, combine the applesauce and eggs; stir into the flour mixture. Drop the dough by tablespoonfuls onto the baking sheet.

❋ Bake for 12 to 15 minutes, or until the cookies are lightly browned. Transfer to a wire rack to cool. Continue until all the cookies are baked.

COOKIE HINTS

❋ Use a baking sheet without edges to prevent over-browning. If you don't have one, turn your regular baking sheet over and use the bottom.

❋ To save time, make double batches of your favorite cookies and freeze the cookies unbaked on a baking sheet. When frozen, stack the cookies in plastic bags. Bake without thawing.

CHOCOLATE-ORANGE BISCOTTI

Biscotti cookies began as a thrifty notion—they were bread dough that was baked twice (a kissing cousin to zwieback). These are tasty, inexpensive treats for dessert potlucks or tea parties.

¾ cup sugar
¼ cup canola oil
2 tablespoons nonfat plain yogurt
3 eggs
2 teaspoons grated orange rind
1 teaspoon vanilla
1 teaspoon baking powder
⅛ teaspoon salt
3 cups all-purpose flour
1 cup semisweet chocolate chips

❀ Preheat the oven to 375°F. Coat a large no-stick baking sheet with no-stick spray.

❀ In a large bowl, combine the sugar, oil, and yogurt; mix well. Add the eggs one at a time, beating well after each addition. Add the orange rind, vanilla, baking powder, and salt; mix well. Add the flour 1 cup at a time, mixing well after each addition. Add the chocolate chips.

❀ Divide the dough into three balls; form each into a 10″ log. Place the logs on the baking sheet.

❀ Bake for 25 minutes, or until the logs are lightly browned. Cool for 30 minutes.

❀ Reduce the oven temperature to 300°F. Using a serrated knife, gently slice the logs into ½″ slices; place on the baking sheet cut sides down. Bake for 20 minutes, or until the biscotti are golden brown and crunchy.

Makes 60

Per cookie
Calories 58
Total fat 1.8 g.
Saturated fat 0.2 g.
Cholesterol 11 mg.
Sodium 16 mg.
Fiber 0.2 g.

Cost per serving

3¢

Per bar
Calories 184
Total fat 3.2 g.
Saturated fat 0.3 g.
Cholesterol 36 mg.
Sodium 86 mg.
Fiber 2.3 g.

Cost per serving

37¢

DATE-APPLE BARS

Fruit bar cookies are a favorite with kids, and these homemade treats save you 15¢ each over packaged varieties.

¾ cup all-purpose flour
⅓ cup sugar
1 teaspoon ground cinnamon
½ teaspoon baking powder
¼ teaspoon salt
1½ cups chopped dried apples
¾ cup chopped pitted dates
2 tablespoons chopped walnuts
⅓ cup packed brown sugar
2 eggs
½ cup semisweet chocolate chips

❋ Preheat the oven to 350°F. Coat an 8″ × 8″ no-stick baking pan with no-stick spray.

❋ In a large bowl, combine the flour, sugar, cinnamon, baking powder, and salt. Stir in the apples, dates, and walnuts. In a small bowl, combine the brown sugar and eggs; beat until frothy. Add to the flour mixture; mix well. Pour into the baking pan.

❋ Bake for 30 to 35 minutes, or until a toothpick inserted in the center comes out clean.

❋ In a small saucepan, melt the chocolate chips over low heat. Drizzle over the bars.

HOMEMADE DRIED FRUIT SAVINGS

Dried apples contribute so much intense flavor to desserts that you can use much less sweetener, but they are expensive to buy. Jonni McCoy, author of *Miserly Moms*, recommends making your own at home. Chop unpeeled apples into small pieces and lay them in a single layer on a baking sheet lined with wax paper. Place in the oven; turn the oven to 250°F and leave it on for 20 minutes. Turn off the oven and keep the oven door closed. Leave the oven light on. The fruit will dry in the warm oven overnight. You'll save over $3 a pound this way!

Brown-Sugar Baked Apples

Tart cooking apples like Stayman Winesap or Granny Smith taste best in this recipe—buy them in bulk at your local farmers' market or farmstand in late autumn. They keep for several months in a cool place, so you can enjoy these baked apples all winter.

 6 large tart apples, cored
½ cup packed brown sugar
½ cup raisins
½ teaspoon ground cinnamon
 1 cup apple juice
 1 cup low-fat sour cream
 1 tablespoon honey

❋ Preheat the oven to 350°F. Place the apples in a 13" × 9" baking pan. In a small bowl, combine the brown sugar, raisins, and cinnamon; stuff into the apple cavities. Pour the apple juice into the baking dish around the apples.

❋ Bake for 45 minutes, or until the apples are very soft. Check by inserting the tip of a sharp knife in 1 apple.

❋ In a small bowl, combine the sour cream and honey; drizzle over the hot apples.

Makes 6

Per apple
Calories 261
Total fat 3.1 g.
Saturated fat 0.1 g.
Cholesterol 13 mg.
Sodium 36 mg.
Fiber 3.6 g.

Cost per serving

38¢

Cinnamon-Cranberry Applesauce

When apples go on sale at the start of the school year, make extra batches of this rosy sauce. It keeps for 3 months in the freezer.

 2 cups fresh or frozen cranberries
 2 cups peeled and chopped tart apples
¾ cup apple juice
¾ cup packed brown sugar
 1 tablespoon ground cinnamon

❋ In a large saucepan, combine the cranberries, apples, and apple juice; bring to a boil over medium-high heat. Reduce the heat to medium; cook, stirring occasionally, for 30 minutes, or until the fruit is soft. Cool slightly; spoon into a blender or food processor. Add the brown sugar and cinnamon; puree.

Makes 3 cups

Per ½ cup
Calories 163
Total fat 0.3 g.
Saturated fat 0.0 g.
Cholesterol 0 mg.
Sodium 12 mg.
Fiber 2.2 g.

Cost per serving

48¢

Per serving
Calories 322
Total fat 3 g.
Saturated fat 1.7 g.
Cholesterol 45 mg.
Sodium 61 mg.
Fiber 2 g.

Cost per serving

41¢

BAKED BANANAS WITH FROZEN YOGURT

This simple dessert tastes great after a Mexican dinner. It's a bargain to make in September, when bananas go on sale for school lunch boxes. Any leftover servings can be refrigerated for five days and reheated.

8 bananas, peeled
½ cup packed brown sugar
1 large orange
4 cups low-fat vanilla frozen yogurt

❋ Preheat the oven to 350°F. Place the bananas in a large baking dish. Sprinkle with ¼ cup of the brown sugar; bake for 10 minutes.

❋ Grate the orange rind and juice the orange. In a small bowl, combine the orange juice, orange rind, and the remaining ¼ cup brown sugar; pour over the bananas. Bake for 15 minutes more, or until the bananas are soft and the sauce is syrupy. Spoon the bananas and sauce over the frozen yogurt.

THEY'LL SCREAM FOR THIS ICE CREAM

Buy over-the-hill bananas for pennies from your supermarket produce department; they're often bagged separately for as little as 5¢ a pound. Peel, mash, and freeze in 1-cup plastic containers. Cut or break the frozen puree into chunks and puree in a blender or food processor. Add berries, tofu, vanilla, or sweeteners if desired. The bananas' creamy texture makes a super-smooth frozen dessert.

SPICED PUMPKIN CUSTARDS

These sweet and spicy custards will remind you of the best pumpkin pie—at half the calories and fat because there's no crust. This recipe is also delicious with cooked pureed winter squash instead of pumpkin. Serve the custards at Thanksgiving and other festive occasions.

2¼ cups skim milk
 2 tablespoons cornstarch
¾ cup canned pumpkin
⅔ cup maple syrup
 2 tablespoons molasses
 1 tablespoon ground cinnamon
 1 teaspoon ground ginger
 1 teaspoon ground nutmeg
½ teaspoon ground cloves
 4 eggs, lightly beaten
 1 cup nonfat vanilla yogurt

❋ Preheat the oven to 350°F. Coat eight (4-ounce) custard cups with no-stick spray; set them on a baking sheet.

❋ In a medium saucepan, combine the milk and cornstarch; stir well to dissolve the cornstarch. Add the pumpkin, maple syrup, molasses, cinnamon, ginger, nutmeg, and cloves. Bring to a boil over medium-high heat; cook and stir for 5 minutes, or until the sauce thickens slightly. Remove from the heat; cool for 5 minutes. Add the eggs; stir well. Pour into the custard cups.

❋ Bake for 30 minutes, or until the custards are firm and a toothpick inserted in the center comes out clean. Cool slightly; top with the yogurt.

Makes 8 servings

Per serving
Calories 180
Total fat 2.9 g.
Saturated fat 1 g.
Cholesterol 108 mg.
Sodium 94 mg.
Fiber 0.7 g.

Cost per serving

39¢

Per serving
Calories 241
Total fat 2.1 g.
Saturated fat 0.8 g.
Cholesterol 29 mg.
Sodium 149 mg.
Fiber 1 g.

Cost per serving

31¢

BREAD PUDDING IN HONEY SAUCE

This traditional New Orleans dessert is usually made with a dozen eggs and plenty of heavy cream. We've cut at least 15 grams of fat per serving and halved the cost by using skim milk and egg whites, plus crushed pineapple for flavor.

Bread Pudding

3 cups skim milk
¾ cup apple juice
½ cup rolled oats
¼ cup packed brown sugar
4 egg whites, lightly beaten
1 tablespoon ground cinnamon
2 teaspoons vanilla
3 cups cubed fresh whole-wheat bread (with crusts)
½ cup raisins
¼ cup drained unsweetened canned crushed pineapple

Honey Sauce

½ cup honey
1 teaspoon butter
1 teaspoon cornstarch
1 egg, lightly beaten

To make the bread pudding

❀ Preheat the oven to 350°F. Coat a 9″ × 5″ loaf pan with no-stick spray.

❀ In a blender or food processor, combine the milk, apple juice, oats, brown sugar, egg whites, cinnamon, and vanilla; puree.

❀ In a large bowl, combine the bread cubes, raisins, and pineapple. Add the oat mixture; mix well. Pour into the pan.

❀ Cover with foil and bake for 30 minutes. Uncover and bake for 20 minutes more, or until the pudding is golden brown and firm.

To make the honey sauce

❀ In a small saucepan, combine the honey, butter, cornstarch, and egg; mix well. Cook and stir over medium heat for 8 to 10 minutes, or until the sauce thickens. Serve over the warm bread pudding.

BERRY CUSTARDS

These elegant custards taste as rich as crème brulée—without the high fat of cream and butter. They're flavored with fresh berries and broiled before serving.

Makes 6 servings

Per serving
Calories 174
Total fat 4.5 g.
Saturated fat 2.3 g.
Cholesterol 43 mg.
Sodium 142 mg.
Fiber 1.9 g.

Cost per serving

31¢

⅓ cup sugar
1 egg
1 tablespoon all-purpose flour
2 teaspoons cornstarch
1 cup skim milk
½ teaspoon vanilla
4 ounces low-fat cream cheese, cut into small pieces
2 cups raspberries or blackberries
¼ cup packed brown sugar

❈ In a medium saucepan, combine the sugar, egg, flour, and corn-starch; mix well. Add the milk and vanilla; stir well with a wire whisk. Bring to a boil over medium heat, whisking constantly. Cook and stir for 5 to 7 minutes, or until the custard thickens. Pour into a bowl.

❈ Add the cream cheese; stir for 2 minutes, or until the cheese melts. Cover and refrigerate for 30 minutes, or until the custard cools.

❈ Preheat the broiler. Pour the custard into six (4-ounce) custard cups set on a baking sheet. Top with the berries; press into the custard. Broil 4″ from heat for 2 minutes, or until the custard is golden brown. Sprinkle with the brown sugar. Set aside for 1 to 2 minutes, or until the sugar melts.

291

Banana-Pineapple Sherbet

Instead of cream, this simple sherbet gets its velvety smoothness—and its delicious tang—from yogurt.

1 cup sliced bananas
1 can (8 ounces) unsweetened crushed pineapple, drained
1 cup low-fat banana yogurt

❋ In a blender or food processor, combine the bananas, pineapple, and yogurt; puree. Pour into a shallow pan; freeze for 2 hours, or until frozen.

❋ Cut the sherbet into chunks; place in a blender or food processor. Puree until creamy. Spoon into freezerproof dessert dishes; freeze for 4 hours, or until solid.

❋ Let the sherbet stand at room temperature for 15 minutes, or until it is slightly softened, before serving.

English Summer Pudding

Summer pudding was born when a thrifty Brit decided to use up stale bread and an abundance of fresh fruit. The result is a marvelous concoction that's elegant enough for company—and inexpensive enough for every day.

2 cups blueberries
2 cups sliced strawberries
2 cups raspberries
¼ cup packed brown sugar
¼ cup apple juice or sweet white wine
12 slices bread, crusts removed
½ cup low-fat vanilla yogurt

❋ In a medium saucepan, combine the blueberries, strawberries, raspberries, brown sugar, and apple juice or wine. Cook and stir over medium-high heat for 5 minutes.

❋ Line a 2-quart glass bowl or soufflé dish with the bread; fill the center with the berry mixture. Cover and refrigerate for 12 hours, or until the bread is soaked with the berry mixture. Top with the yogurt.

Makes 6 servings

Per serving
Calories 97
Total fat 0.6 g.
Saturated fat 0.3 g.
Cholesterol 2 mg.
Sodium 23 mg.
Fiber 1 g.

Cost per serving
18¢

Makes 8 servings

Per serving
Calories 179
Total fat 2.2 g.
Saturated fat 0.5 g.
Cholesterol 1 mg.
Sodium 202 mg.
Fiber 3 g.

Cost per serving
68¢

Kitchen Tip

Grind the bread crusts in a food processor and store the bread crumbs in a plastic bag in the freezer.

Cakes, Pies, and
Other Desserts

FIRM UP SAVINGS!

Amy Dacyczyn, author of *The Tightwad Gazette* books, recommends making your own fruit gelatin instead of buying packaged gelatin desserts. At a cost of 32¢ to 50¢ for 4 servings, it's an inexpensive way to satisfy the sweet tooth and get the health benefits of fresh fruit into your meals.

Amy recommends buying unflavored gelatin in bulk from the health food store (at $5.33 a pound—you can buy just the amount you need), rather than envelopes of unflavored gelatin (at $15.20 a pound). Here are some great ideas for homemade gelatin desserts:

❀ *Apple Banana Bonanza*. In a medium saucepan, combine 4 cups apple juice and 2 tablespoons unflavored gelatin; let stand for 1 minute to soften the gelatin. Bring to a boil over medium-high heat. Remove from the heat; stir until the gelatin dissolves. Slice 4 bananas and lay them in the bottom of 8 dessert bowls. Pour the apple juice mixture over the bananas. Chill for 2 hours, or until firm. Makes 8 servings.

❀ *Tangy Melon*. In a blender, puree 4 cups cubed cantaloupe. In a medium saucepan, combine the pureed cantaloupe, ⅓ cup sugar, 2 tablespoons unflavored gelatin, and 1 teaspoon lemon juice. Bring to a boil over medium-high heat. Remove from the heat. Stir until the gelatin dissolves. Pour into 8 dessert bowls. Chill for 2 hours, or until firm. Makes 8 servings.

❀ *Berry Bliss*. In a blender, puree 4 cups blackberries. Strain through a fine sieve into a medium saucepan. Add ½ cup honey or sugar, 2 tablespoons unflavored gelatin, and 1 teaspoon lemon juice. Let stand for 1 minute to soften the gelatin. Bring to a boil over medium-high heat. Remove from the heat. Stir until the gelatin dissolves. Pour into 8 dessert bowls. Chill for 2 hours, or until firm. Makes 8 servings.

❀ *Summer Delight*. In a medium saucepan, combine 3 cups apple juice and 1 tablespoon unflavored gelatin. Let stand for 1 minute to soften the gelatin. Bring to a boil over medium-high heat. Remove from the heat; stir until the gelatin dissolves. Pour into a 13" × 9" baking dish. Add 3 cups mixed frozen berries, such as raspberries, strawberries, and blackberries. Chill for 2 hours, or until firm. Makes 8 servings.

Per serving
Calories 174
Total fat 1.7 g.
Saturated fat 0 g.
Cholesterol 8 mg.
Sodium 160 mg.
Fiber 0.6 g.

Cost per serving

46¢

KITCHEN TIP

When you juice oranges, first grate the orange rind and store in a plastic bag in the freezer to have on hand for baking.

Makes 8 servings

Per serving
Calories 88
Total fat 0.5 g.
Saturated fat 0 g.
Cholesterol 0 mg.
Sodium 1 mg.
Fiber 2.4 g.

Cost per serving

40¢

ITALIAN RICOTTA CREAM

Italian cooks use ricotta cheese in all manner of creamy desserts because it's light and less expensive than cream cheese or heavy cream.

- 1½ cups low-fat ricotta cheese
- 4 ounces nonfat cream cheese
- ¼ cup honey
- 3 tablespoons frozen orange juice concentrate
- 1 teaspoon grated orange rind
- 1 cup mashed strawberries
- ⅓ cup sugar
- ¼ teaspoon vanilla

❋ In a blender or food processor, combine the ricotta, cream cheese, honey, orange juice concentrate, and orange rind; puree. Spoon into a shallow serving bowl.

❋ In a medium bowl, combine the strawberries, sugar, and vanilla; spread over the ricotta mixture. Cover and refrigerate for 2 hours.

FRESH BERRY SORBET

You don't need a fancy sorbet maker—just a shallow pan—for this frozen dessert. Be sure to use perfectly ripe strawberries in season.

- 6 cups sliced strawberries
- ½ cup raspberries
- ½ cup sugar
- ¼ cup lemon juice

❋ In a blender or food processor, combine the strawberries, raspberries, sugar, and lemon juice; puree. Pour the mixture into a large shallow pan; freeze for 4 hours, or until solid. Cut the sorbet into chunks and place in a blender or food processor; puree. Spoon into serving bowls. Freeze for 20 minutes, or until solid but soft enough to eat with a spoon.

CITRUS ICE POPS

Grapefruit juice makes these pops tangy and delicious—and much less expensive than store-bought frozen treats. You can also use orange juice or apple juice when they're on sale. Frozen-pop sticks are available at craft stores, or scout out reusable plastic frozen-treat molds at a yard sale.

1½ cups unsweetened grapefruit juice
  1 cup sliced strawberries
 ¼ cup honey or sugar
  1 tablespoon lemon juice

✽ In a blender or food processor, combine the grapefruit juice, strawberries, honey, and lemon juice; puree. Pour into 8 frozen-treat molds or 2-ounce paper cups; freeze for 1 hour, or until pops are beginning to set. (If using paper cups, insert a frozen-pop stick into each.)

✽ Freeze for 4 hours, or until solid. Dip the molds or paper cups into hot water before unmolding.

Makes 8

Per pop
Calories 75
Total fat 0.2 g.
Saturated fat 0 g.
Cholesterol 0 mg.
Sodium 2 mg.
Fiber 0.6 g.

Cost per serving

26¢

INDEX

· · · · · · · · · · · · · · · · · · · ·

Note: Underscored page references indicate boxed text.

G

H

I

K